Quelch's Gold

Quelch's Gold

Piracy, Greed, and Betrayal in Colonial New England

Clifford Beal

Potomac Books, Inc.
Washington, D.C.

Library of Congress Cataloging-in-Publication Data

Beal, Clifford.
Quelch's gold : piracy, greed, and betrayal in colonial New England / Clifford Beal.
p. cm.
Includes bibliographical references and index.
ISBN 978-1-59797-233-8 (pbk. : alk. paper)
1. Quelch, John, ca. 1665-1704. 2. Pirate—Biography. 3. Trials (Piracy)—Massachusetts—Boston. 4. New England—History—Colonial period, ca. 1600-1775. 5. Massachusetts—History—Colonial period, ca. 1600-1775—Sources. I. Title.
G537.Q43B43 2008
910.4'5—dc22
[B]
2008030984

Printed in the United States of America on acid-free paper that meets the American National Standards Institute Z39-48 Standard.

Potomac Books, Inc
22841 Quicksilver Drive
Dulles, Virginia 20166

10 9 8 7 6 5 4 3 2 1

To my Mother, for all the trips to the Olneyville Library

and

To my Father, for all the overtime

Contents

Illustrations follow page 120.

Acknowledgments

R esearching and writing a work of historical nonfiction is a lot like detective work or forensic science—it's laborious, frustrating, and leads that at first look promising, turn out more often than not to be dead-ends. But nearly as often, finding that crucial missing piece of evidence is an exhilarating and rewarding experience. For this, I cannot claim credit alone.

My "ship" would never have made a successful voyage were it not for the many people who toiled on my behalf below decks. Without their help and insight, I would have had a far more difficult course to sail. My thanks go to Kimberly Nusco at the Massachusetts Historical Society who was there from the start of the project; to Meredith Paine Sorozan of the Rhode Island Historical Society; to Ellen Berkland, City Archaeologist of Boston; and to John Hannigan at the Massachusetts State Archives for helping me unearth critical documents. I am also grateful for advice and direction from the staff of the Marblehead Museum and Historical Society; Lauren Mandel of The Bostonian Society; Diane Shephard of Lynn Historical Society; Malcolm Mercer and Sarah Abbott of the U.K. National Archives at Kew; and to Jenny Ulph and Richard Brigenshaw at The Bank of England. Sinclair Cramsie, barrister at King's Bench Chambers, Temple, London, shared some useful perspectives on criminal law and J. Dennis Robinson at sea coastnh.com helped me with background on the Isles of Shoals and their rich pirate folklore. Tom Johnson at Maine's Old York

Historical Society supplied invaluable details on prison conditions during Quelch's time. My sister Roxanne was a tremendous help to me in tracking sources in Boston and Marblehead. Thanks also to my old friend in Brighton, Henry Hyde, for his cartographical flair. My editor at Praeger, Elizabeth Demers, and my agent Robert Tabian, were not only encouraging of my efforts, but they also provided wise counsel when it was most needed. Finally, I must not fail to acknowledge the support of my dear wife, Anke, whose critical eye and unfailing belief in my project gave me the confidence to see it through.

C.F.B.
Lille, France

Prologue: Splendidum Furtum

Although it was early afternoon, on a hot day in late May, the main taproom of the Noah's Ark in Boston's North End was dim and cool despite the sun shining through the wavy, paned windows at the front of the rambling clapboard inn.

Captain John Quelch, tanned leathery brown after nearly a year at sea in the tropical Atlantic, had his hands curled around a pewter tankard of steaming flip. Strong beer mixed with sugar and a dash of nutmeg and rum, scalded with a hot poker to heat and froth it, flip was a Yankee drink he had gone long without.

He had been in the colony little more than a week, landing where he had embarked, at Marblehead, Massachusetts. Now, his main business in Boston town accomplished, he was sitting comfortably in this old haunt of his down near the wharves, contemplating his future prospects.

A weak fire flickered in the hearth, some of the smoke drifting back into the taproom where other patrons, rough sea folk, or teamsters all, laughed, whispered, puffed on their clay pipes, and drained their mugs of rum and beer. Quelch could afford as much burnt flip as he could stomach. His recent cruise had returned him home a very wealthy man indeed. The look on the innkeeper's face as he pushed a solid gold coin across the counter was a moment to savor.

At thirty-eight, he knew that he was not a young man, but now he could afford a vessel of his own to send out again in search of profit. No longer just a shipmaster, he would be a shipowner too. Fortune was a long time coming; he had taken many risks, but he had finally made it. He had upheld his end of the bargain. It was his moment now.

He heard the heavy wooden door to the taproom swing open noisily as it had been doing every few minutes for the past hour. At first, he did not bother to look at who had just entered. But as heads cranked up and all conversation in the room began to cease like a rippling wave of silence, he slowly turned on his bench to see who had come in.

Standing there, the door behind him still ajar, stood a gentleman in a fine russet brown suit and black riding boots. He was young, no more than thirty, of average height, and wearing a huge periwig of brown curls that cascaded around his head making his somewhat pudgy face look ridiculously small. Unusual as it might have been for a man of such obvious station to enter the Ark (when there were coffee houses down the street better suited to men of business) it was the presence of the two red-coated dragoons that flanked him that set the room on edge. More militiamen carrying short firelock muskets were glimpsed just outside on the street.

Unknown to Quelch or any of the other patrons, the man was Paul Dudley, Attorney General of the Massachusetts Bay province and eldest son of the Governor and Captain General of the colony, Joseph Dudley.

The Attorney General raised his voice and demanded the whereabouts of John Quelch of Marblehead. Captain Quelch slowly rose to his feet, dumbstruck that he had been singled out. In the instant that it took him to step away from his seat, he calculated whether to stand or run for it. To his mind he had done right by his commission. What had he to fear from the law?

He faced Dudley and identified himself, asking what business Boston had with him.

With a nod from Dudley, the two soldiers approached and seized Quelch by each arm. Dudley said aloud for all in the room to hear that Quelch was accused of piratical acts on the high seas and of illegally importing gold and goods into the colony. And before John Quelch could barely stutter a protest of innocence, he was hauled out of the tavern and put into irons. Passersby on the busy waterfront street stopped and gawked as the cursing man was roughly shoved up into the saddle of a spare mount. He knew, even before they set off for the town prison, that he had been betrayed.

His troubles were only beginning to unfold and "his moment" was actually yet to come.

Piracy was not a new phenomenon at the dawn of the eighteenth century. Sea robbers had been a scourge for as long as people had taken to building boats and setting out in them to cross the waters.

In the sixteenth century, as the maritime empires of Spain and Portugal spread out to grasp Africa, Asia, and South America, gold, silver, and spices rapidly flowed back into the Iberian Peninsula. Jealous newcomers, such as the English, French, and the Dutch, were militarily weaker than these juggernauts to be sure, but like hyenas at the lion's kill, they could circle and steal a piece of the feast. Piracy became a major weapon in this struggle for empire and an important adjunct to traditional naval power.

Under Elizabeth I and later James I, pirates gained new prestige and standing. Whereas Henry VII and Henry VIII had made war against Cornish and Devonian freebooters, Elizabeth and her Stuart successors showered them with royal patronage. England's great captains and explorers of the era such as Drake, Raleigh, and Frobisher, did more than "singe the beard" of the Spanish king, they were serving an instrumental role in extending English influence abroad. King James, whose personal and state extravagances led to a proliferation of racketeering and various dirty deals among courtiers and merchants, once characterized privateering as "the committing of a splendidum furtum"—magnificent theft. Privateering, and its alter ego, piracy, was for many an aristocrat a lucrative investment opportunity, and one ruthlessly exploited.

By the time of Charles II, everyone was a "pirate"—it was just that some had official cover and others did not. Henry Morgan, a buccaneer who had ravished Spanish Panama, was later knighted and appointed governor of Jamaica (itself pried away from Spain in 1655). By the 1690s, the collusion of captains and crews, colonial officials, wealthy merchants, and noblemen had forged a vibrant black economy on both sides of the Atlantic.

But times were changing, and rapidly so. Incessant European wars were spawning new institutions—such as the Bank of England, to finance the affairs of state. An explosion of global trade meant that centralization and regulation were necessary to creating and sustaining wealth. An insurance industry and a permanent, powerful navy to protect the merchant fleet were also beginning to take root.

The monopolies of powerful trading companies now swung the balance in favor of legal commerce and controlled risks. Trade agreements were the key to success, not "smash and grab" raids by rogue captains.

What Captain John Quelch had not recognized was that the old ways of doing business were over. It was now 1704, and piracy had entered a new phase, one where the crown was no longer its friend. The unfortunate privateer and former master of the Massachusetts brigantine *Charles* was about to find out this harsh truth for himself.

I stumbled upon the career of John Quelch during a sojourn from my regular line of work. Needing a respite from the world of modern naval affairs where my usual fare might include the replacement options for the Navy's Nimitz-class aircraft carrier, the comparative "kill rate" of cruise missiles, or the look of the country's next-generation Zumwalt-class destroyer, I picked up an eighty-three-year-old book entitled *The Pirates of the New England Coast*.

Written by regional historians George Dow and John Edmonds, this little gem entertainingly and intelligently told the stories of over a dozen freebooters of the seventeenth and eighteenth centuries. The adventures, or rather, misadventures of John Quelch captured my imagination more than any of the others, including the fabled Captain Kidd. Although he is all but forgotten today, Quelch was one of the most successful pirates (or privateers) of the so-called Golden Age, having captured far more treasure than most of his contemporaries, even more than the notorious Blackbeard.

What made his story more compelling was the way in which his society—and the hand of fate—treated him and men like him. Then, as now, pirates were popular. And in Quelch's time, piracy was a cozy business from sailor to merchant and everyone in-between. Hard currency was always in short supply and seaport communities were reluctant to testify against mariners not for fear of retribution but rather for fear of losing their best benefactors. Quelch was just an average seaman caught up in the economics of his time, a "trickle-down" system where the whole community benefited from theft at sea.

The bribery and corruption, secret deals and betrayals, as well as the hypocrisy of the governing class, still strike a familiar chord. More than this, the events of that long-ago stifling summer of 1704 are a prologue to colonial rebellion against English rule. Bostonians resented how their royal governor dispensed justice to local boys "made good." The circumstances of John Quelch's expedition, and what followed, were considered by many as nothing less than an attack on the personal liberty of freeborn men. Colonists were becoming Americans, no longer just Englishmen in America. The lid would finally come off in 1775.

Pirate or privateer, criminal or entrepreneur, Quelch's story, at its most elemental, is about a man adrift and rudderless in a political sea that he does not understand, a world every bit as unforgiving and cruel as the open Atlantic.

CRIME

Chapter One

Ill Tidings

A s John Colman, William Clarke, and the seaman who guided them reached the crest of the hill and looked down from the saddle upon the ramshackle town of Marblehead, its houses sprinkled about upon a rock-strewn bulge of land into the Atlantic; it was most probably with some misgivings. Although the two Boston merchants, in their early thirties and already successful, were undoubtedly glad to give their aching backsides relief from the long morning's ride up from Charlestown, they had come to the hardscrabble fishing village to check on a business enterprise gone awry.

It is likely that the three had stopped somewhere halfway to their destination, perhaps at an inn on the highway at the village of Lynn, to take a draught and a light lunch, and to water the horses. Apart from the worrying reports that had brought them north, Colman, Clarke, and the seaman would have had much to talk about during their hours in the saddle.

In August 1703, the province of Massachusetts was, once again, at war. It was neither a war of its own making nor one that it stood any chance of influencing the outcome, but, nonetheless, it was a continuation of a struggle that had already shaken the colony to its foundations.

For a generation, New Englanders had been suffering tribulations of nothing less than biblical dimensions, and with what seemed relentless frequency. By the end of the seventeenth century,

English settlement in the region was staring at nothing short of ru-
ination.

The troubles had begun in earnest in 1675 with a genocidal
war against a confederation of Indian tribes in southern New
England, sending shock waves throughout the region. King
Phillip's War, which ignited suddenly after repeated bloody incidents between colonists and natives, focused around a rebellion by
one Metacomet, a *sachem* (chief) of the Wampanoag tribe who had
taken the name of "Phillip" in his dealings with the English. The
rebellion ended catastrophically for the cause of native independence, not to mention for Phillip, whose head ended up on a pike
on the gates of Plymouth, Massachusetts. This short but brutal conflagration shattered forever the power and cohesion of native tribes
in Rhode Island, Connecticut, and southeastern Massachusetts. But
the English colonists paid a steep price for their victory: the destruction of some seventy towns and villages, and a civilian death
toll that, per capita, exceeds that of all subsequent American wars
combined.

A decade of uneasy peace ensued between the colonists and
the natives, but political chaos descended upon the region in the
middle of the 1680s with rising tensions over regulation of trade
and civil administrative control. When news of the "Glorious Revolution" and the overthrow of King James II in England reached
Boston, it led to spontaneous rioting that resulted in the roughing-
up of the royal Governor-General, Lord Andros—long a lightning
rod for local puritan anger and resistance to the Stuart monarchy—
and to his imprisonment by the mob in the stone jail at the center
of town.

Having spat out its unpopular governor, who was sent pack-
ing back to Whitehall after his ordeal, Massachusetts ruled itself
without royal charter for the next several years, riven by internal
political squabbling among royalists, ambitious merchants, and the
weakening theocracy of the old Bay Colony and its austere men in
black and white.

The 1690s brought worse still. The Nine Years' War between
France and England led Massachusetts into direct conflict with
French Canada, generating a savage border war fought primarily
by the Abenaki tribes of northern New England. A bold plan to
take the war to the French partially succeeded when a colonial-led
seaborne expedition launched from Boston in 1690 managed to

take the settlement of Port Royal in Acadia (present-day Nova Scotia). However, by year's end, the more ambitious, but unrealistic, scheme to besiege and storm Quebec stumbled and failed miserably.

Cotton Mather, pastor of Boston's North Church and scion of the puritan theocracy, noted the cost at "forty thousand pounds, more or less, now to be paid, and not a Penny in the Treasury to pay it withal." Not surprisingly, this repulse of the English force emboldened the French to pursue the war even harder, taking the fight back to the principal areas of English settlement chiefly with the aid of their native allies, the Abenaki.

By the close of 1691, all English settlement north of the Kennebec River in Maine had been wiped out. The real shock came for Boston when on Candlemas Sunday, January 25, 1691/2, the prosperous border town of York, Maine, was attacked and burned with the loss of a hundred lives and some seventy women and children taken hostage and forced-marched to Canada. News of the raid, only fifty miles from Boston, must have sent a chill through the governor's council chamber more brisk than the winter wind outside.

Fast on the heels of village massacres by Abenakis, the witch hysteria of 1692 severely shook societal cohesion in Massachusetts. With the colony under its greatest external threat ever, the focus of attention in Boston turned to the harrowing self-destruction in the coastal communities of Salem, Andover, and Marblehead and the hanging of innocents. A shocking "own goal" that the colony could ill afford, the affair claimed the lives of at least twenty four men, women, and children before proceedings were called off by the authorities.

While the bizarre terrors of the witch trials came to an end, Abenaki raids continued, leading to the destruction of more villages and outposts in Massachusetts. In 1697, Boston itself narrowly missed fiery destruction by a French armada, thanks mainly to French logistical failures, and the timely arrival of the Treaty of Ryswick that ended the war for New England in December. Even this was a bitter pill because the treaty compelled the colonists to cede Port Royal and Acadia to the French, their only significant conquest in nine years of fighting (even though it had been left ungarrisoned by colonial troops for several years and retaken without a fight).

Ill fortune continued to rain upon New England. Massachusetts was an economic disaster for most of the decade with the treasury nearly broke after the ill-fated Acadian campaign of 1691. But another enemy also stalked the colony. Smallpox struck Boston in the late 1690s in a virulent series of outbreaks that killed at least 300. It is no wonder that the colony's pastors harangued their congregations for sinfulness, sinfulness that had brought down upon Massachusetts the wrath of an angry God.

Based on this recent past and on future prospects, Massachusetts's farmers and merchants had good reason to be anxious. When the wheel of dynastic fortune once again turned in Europe, New Englanders found themselves along for the ride.

The desire of France's Louis XIV to expand and fortify his borders plunged Europe into a series of protracted conflicts, lasting over two decades. The Nine Years' War led to a cold peace of the exhausted. By 1701, when a succession crisis in Spain brought the Bourbon and Hapsburg dynasties into diplomatic turmoil, both sides had recovered sufficiently to renew the fight with shot and steel. The War of the Spanish Succession would last thirteen years and inflict some 384,000 casualties (killed and wounded) among combatants alone.

For those in England, the war made its impact felt more in economic terms than anything else. The triumphs of the Duke of Marlborough may have been celebrated in the cobbled streets and coffee houses of London, but for most, the war was a world away.

It was literally a continent away for New Englanders. However, as subjects of the crown and Englishmen, it was by no means a forgotten war. For the inhabitants of Massachusetts and its poor, usurped, satellite colony of Maine, the war was a personal one. It is revealing that in America these struggles are called "King William's" and "Queen Anne's" wars. To the farmers, fishermen, artisans, merchants, and preachers of the colony, these were wars that were begun by kings but borne as the regrettable burdens of loyal Englishmen and Protestants.

In August 1703, as Colman and Clarke made their way to Marblehead, the northern borders were relatively quiet: the Abenaki tribes were for the moment adhering to the general truce of 1697. But from a merchant's perspective, what pinched was the deplorable state of trade.

The passage of the Trade and Navigation Acts beginning in 1651 and continuing to 1673, renewed and extended many times since, made sea commerce a tightly regulated business for both Yankees and their cousins in England. While some of the provisions aided Massachusetts's merchants through protectionism, others, such as the stipulation that all manufactured goods, as well as tobacco, had to pass through ports in England before going to other destinations, added to costs and depressed profits.

Now, with war once again declared, shipping merchants had to contend with the very real potential of increased losses of cargo and vessels through capture by French privateers. This was in addition to the usual dangers of pirates both English and French who cruised just off the coast. Indeed, New England ships had to run a veritable gauntlet when venturing out on journeys to England, the Caribbean, or even other colonies along the eastern seaboard.

Only the previous summer, in 1702, a Boston privateer had captured the notorious "Captain Baptiste," a Frenchman who had taken a heavy toll on Massachusetts's merchantmen for a decade. Born Pierre Maisonnat, he had plundered English shipping with the full backing of Quebec's royal governor while also serving as a spy on coastal New England. His capture brought a sigh of relief in Boston. Dudley, only just appointed royal governor, fully intended to hang Baptiste as a common pirate. However, both the French and English colonial governments privately knew Baptiste was no common corsair. Pirate though he may have been in practice, Baptiste was also an eighteenth century equivalent of a twentieth century Cold War master spy. He was far too valuable to be hanged. The dynamic privateer languished in Boston's jail as a political pawn, finally gaining his freedom in 1706 as part of a prisoner swap with Montreal.

According to a petition sent to London in 1703 by a group of New England merchants requesting convoy protection, some two-thirds of all ships bound for England had been lost during King William's War. Even with Baptiste safely behind bars, the prospects in this latest war looked no better.

The combined threats of piracy and war had two main effects on the conduct of commerce. The first was the added expense of insurance, normally underwritten in London, to safeguard cargoes and assets in the event of catastrophe. The second was the limited availability and increasing cost of labor in the merchant navy.

Risk had always been a fact of life in the shipping trade. But for many merchants in Massachusetts, on the brink of collapse from years of economic travails, this new war would do no good in keeping them afloat. While some merchants might have forgone the security of having their voyages underwritten during the lull in the fighting against the French, renewed conflict meant that risks were heightened. Insurance was no longer a luxury and it came at a price.

War also meant that those sailors who might otherwise have been employed in the merchant fleet were now in the Royal Navy, either voluntarily or through "the press" in which merchant seamen, vagrants, drunks, and kidnapped fisherman were forcibly enlisted on warships. Those who were able to, or chose to, remain in the merchant fleets of the colonies, could now afford to sell their services to the highest bidder. Equally, they could—and did—desert from one vessel to another, creating havoc for a captain and his first officer. Labor shortages could force captains to set sail with less than optimum crew levels, increasing risks of ship loss even further. A hard occupation even for the calloused eighteenth century, "those who would go to sea for pleasure" as one maxim put it, "would go to hell for pastime." It was not easy or cheap to find and keep good sailors.

Rates of pay for seamen increased by roughly 10 percent once the war was declared. Between 1700 and 1703 the average monthly wage for a seaman in the colonies went from £1.32 to £2.60. Pay rates of over £3 per month were not unheard of in some ports. This compares favorably when one considers that a house servant might earn no more than four or five pounds sterling an entire year at this time. That noted, there was a big difference between scrubbing a wealthy man's floor and scrubbing the deck of a heaving merchant ship.

However, for shipowners and transatlantic entrepreneurs, there was a bright side to consider. War always breeds new business opportunities. For many merchants, this meant price gouging on war contracts with the Navy or colonial governments, particularly in the provision of critical commodities such as pitch and tar, rope and lumber. Smuggling, which had grown enormously since the institution of the Trade and Navigation Acts, also proved a lucrative enterprise. Large sums could be saved through falsely declared cargoes and by trading directly with non-English ports, bypassing London.

A third moneymaking option was the sponsoring of a "licensed" pirate expedition against merchant vessels of the enemy: privateering. It was this type of venture that had these two merchants up from the relative comfort of Boston to down-at-heel Marblehead.

The two were partners in a five-man "syndicate" that had purchased a new Boston-built ship, christened the *Charles*, and were equipping and crewing it for a voyage against the French in the North Atlantic. The *Charles* had departed Boston Harbor a few weeks before and sailed to Marblehead to complete its preparations. It is unsure as to why this was. Perhaps it was to round out the crew list because recruitment had been problematic in Boston. It is also possible that the captain, Daniel Plowman, might have had arrangements with chandlers and victualers in Marblehead. Either way, it was the captain's responsibility to finish fitting out his vessel for the voyage. And it was in response to an urgent letter from Plowman to the sponsors of the *Charles* that had brought them north, in person.

The owners were some of the Bay Colony's most influential businessmen. All were acquaintances of Governor General Dudley, and as such were at the center of political power in Massachusetts. The chief partner, Charles Hobby, a colonel of the province's militia and dragoons and hero of the capture of Port Royal, had political aspirations himself and would be knighted in 1705. The others were also leading lights of the Bay Colony. Nicholas Paige (then nearing sixty) was a colonel in the Massachusetts militia, having fought in King Phillip's War, and was active in both business and civil affairs. His wife was a niece of Governor Dudley. Benjamin Gallop, who was thirty-nine, had some experience of the sea himself having served in 1689 as a lieutenant on a sloop that was ordered by the governor's council to pursue local pirate Thomas Hawkins. In the ensuing encounter off Martha's Vineyard, Gallop took command of the sloop after his captain was killed, defeated Hawkins and his men, and brought them back to Boston to face justice.

Of all the owners, Colman and Clarke were probably the worst suited to deal with last-minute wrinkles in preparing the *Charles* for sea. William Clarke was a proprietor of varied businesses, a land speculator, and future member of the Massachusetts Assembly. John Colman, brother-in-law of Colonel Hobby, was a trader and speculator who would later lead efforts to introduce a uniform system of paper currency in the colony. He would soon have the dubious distinction of placing the first ever newspaper advertisement in America for a slave sale. He was also a local agent— a "receiver"—for the royal consort of Queen Anne, Prince George of Denmark. In his role as Lord High Admiral, the prince was automatically entitled to a percentage from the sale of goods on all captured ships during wartime. Not only was Colman speculating by bankrolling privateers, he was also responsible for collecting the prince's due on every prize ship brought into Boston. This delicate position, and its potential for conflict of interest, would later come to cause much grief for him and for the governor.

However, as to overseeing the practical side of a privateering expedition, neither Colman nor Clarke had any militia or seafaring experience that might have prepared them to handle roughcast maritime folk. Hobby most probably would have gone himself, but at that time he was engrossed in the rebuilding of Boston's fortifications and in organizing "search and destroy" missions against the French and the Indians.

Captain Plowman's letter of August 1, which they had received at Boston, must have caused consternation if not outright alarm.

The letter was short:

> I find every Day I grow worse and worse, and it is impossible for me to think to proceed. I hope to see you down to Morrow by Nine or Ten a Clock, that we may take some speedy care in saving what we can; the Lieutenant the Bearer can give you a full Account, whom I desire you to return withal.

The "Bearer" of these ill tidings, and the man who had no doubt spent much time enlightening Colman and Clarke as to the situation in Marblehead as they rode north, was a London-born mariner and the second-in-command of the *Charles*, one John Quelch.

Chapter Two

"It Will Not Do with These People . . ."

A s Lieutenant Quelch led Colman and Clarke down the hill into the town of Marblehead, they would have had a clear view of the *Charles* lying at anchor in a cove at the lower end of the settlement. Referred to by locals as the "Little Harbour," it was set off from the main bay of Marblehead and was more convenient for captains since it was directly in front of the main part of the town.

Since Marblehead did not have a wharf of sufficient length or breadth to support larger vessels, the *Charles*, a brigantine of around eighty tons, would have sat some distance from the shore. Ships loading and unloading cargo and crew would have had to use lighters such as longboats to shuttle cargo and supplies back and forth between the dock and the ships some distance out in the cove. Inshore of the larger merchant vessels and even run up on the shore would sit the many single-masted fishing shallops and dories of the town. The shallop was the mainstay of the local fishing fleet, typically a wide-beamed open boat some twenty to thirty feet long. Its single mast usually was rigged with a triangular lateen sail but oars were also used for maneuvering and when the wind was still. Although Marblehead could look to a prosperous future as a great commercial shipping port later in the century, in 1703 its main business was catching fish.

Marblehead was typical of coastal New England towns in that it shared a singular disregard for puritan authority or social conventions and as such, was disdained by the likes of most inland inhabitants of the larger, more established settlements such as Boston. Working the sea defined the people of the coast, shaping their dialect, habits, manners, appearance, and interests. While Boston too was a port, it was also the spiritual center of New England Puritanism—and control—and therefore was far more rigid and structured in character. One young Bostonian, Josiah Cotton, nephew of Cotton Mather, came to Marblehead in 1700 to begin the town's first school. His description of the place is a good indicator on how those of a higher social order looked upon the fishing community.

> The whole township is not much bigger than a large farm, and very rocky.... When I came to this place I was raw and young, not 19 years old, and therefore it is not to be wondered at, if I gave way too much to that extravagance, Intemperance, Negligence in Religion, and Disorderliness, that is too rife in that place.

Cotton never did take to life in Marblehead, limiting his social interactions to the few people of standing that lived there, chiefly the town's minister and two or three militia officers and their families. Even this was not enough to keep him content and he left at the end of 1703.

John Barnard, who arrived from Boston in 1714 to take up a position as the new minister, held similar opinions.

> There was not so much as one proper carpenter, nor mason, nor tailor, nor butcher in the town, nor any market worth naming; but they had their houses built by country workmen, and their clothes made out of town, and supplied themselves with beef and pork from Boston, which drained the town of its money...nor could I find twenty families in it that, upon the best examination, could stand upon their own legs, and they were generally as rude, swearing, drunken, and fighting a crew as they were poor.

The strong smell of landed fish would have assailed the nostrils of the two Boston merchants as they made their way down into the town. Marblehead's houses were built of graying timber shingle, higgledy-piggledy, and close together in the narrow twisting warren that was the center of the place. It was small as it was compact, with only some thirty-seven landowners in 1700 and not much over a hundred households.

Lieutenant Quelch may have taken the owners to the Fountain Inn, the biggest tavern in the town, where they could quench their thirst and wait for Captain Plowman to join them. Quelch, no doubt, would have informed them that the full complement of crew had been signed on and that the *Charles* was fully provisioned. The only impediment to weighing anchor now was the health of the ship's captain.

For their part, the owners knew that all paperwork was in order. The previous month, on July 13, Governor Dudley had signed a commission for Daniel Plowman authorizing him "to War, Fight, Take, Kill, Suppress and Destroy, any Pirates, Privateers, or other the Subjects and Vassals of France, or Spain, the Declared Enemies of the Crown of England, in what Place soever you shall happen to meet them; their Ships, Vessels, and Goods, to take and make Prize of." This had followed quickly upon deliberations made by the Council of Massachusetts about the nature of the threat. According to the minutes of the council meeting of July 24, 1703:

> Upon intelligence just now received of a French privateer lying in or about Tarpolin Cove or Martha's Vineyard, that had surpris'd and taken several coasting or provision vessels, Capt. Daniel Plowman, commander of the briganteen *Charles*, a private man of war, and his owners were sent for, and proposals made and agreed to for the enforcement of her with an addition of men, and sending of her forth on a cruise in quest of the enemy.

Plowman's warrant, which had a life of six months from signing, went on to admonish the commander that he "observe and follow the Orders and Instructions" given and that the said brigantine's company be ordered to "Obey you as their Captain." This scrap of paper (with copies held by the Governor) was the only thing that protected Plowman and his crew themselves from being prosecuted as pirates once out to sea. It would have to be produced on demand and shown to naval vessels or port authorities.

Without it, Plowman and the *Charles* would be naked to accusation. To further this distinction of piracy legalized against the Queen's enemies, Dudley also issued a set of instructions to Captain Plowman. These comprised a detailed list of ten points covering how he was to conduct both the mission and his men while under arms.

The first of these instructions ordered Plowman to ensure that all "Swearing, Drunkeness and Prophaneness be avoided or duly Punished" and that the worship of God be conducted aboard ship. The second warned him not to "hurt or injure" the queen's subjects or those of her friends and allies. The instructions were also explicit in defining how he was to deal with any ships he managed to capture—the "prizes," and their cargo, as well as enemy combatants. Prize vessels were to be taken with their cargos intact to the nearest friendly port (preferably Boston, his "commission port") to be "adjudged" that is, legally declared a possession of war. Plowman was warned to take care that any cargoes—or "bulk" not be "Imbezzelled, Purloyned, Concealed, or Conveyed away." So too, he was to preserve all papers relating to the vessel to ensure he could prove to whom it had belonged, and to keep a journal of all of his own actions and orders to complete the record of the voyage.

And, to put more clear blue water between his venture and those of the unlicensed variety, Plowman was told to enforce the laws of war: enemies not to be "in cold Blood killed or maimed, or by Torture or Cruelty inhumanely treated."

The owners of the *Charles*, as well as Plowman and Quelch, would have had a recent salutary lesson of just how badly things could go wrong for privateers. Still swinging in chains at Tilbury Point on the lower Thames was the tarred and rotting body of Captain William Kidd, executed in May of 1701.

Over just a matter of months, the capture and trial of Captain Kidd had enthralled the transatlantic world, setting tongues wagging in taverns, coffee houses, market stalls, and on Exchange floors from Jamaica to London and everywhere in-between. While no angel, Kidd had steadfastly maintained his innocence, claiming that the critical "passes," the papers of ownership from his captured prizes, had been lost by the Admiralty. He stood accused of piracies against merchant ships and Muslim pilgrim vessels of the Grand Moghul (a trading ally), specifically against the great treasure ship, the *Quedah Merchant*.

Unfortunately for Kidd, many of the acts of piracy had occurred after he had lost control of his vessel, the *Adventure Galley*, to mutineers and he himself had been set ashore. His critical papers, taken from him when he was apprehended, never materialized, and he was judged guilty of committing piracy. In any event, he was also found guilty on a second charge for the murder of a crewman, which also carried the death penalty. With so many political careers riding on the verdict, it is likely that the passes would have made little difference to the outcome. The infamous "French passes" of Kidd *were* eventually tracked down among documents of the Board of Trade—in 1910. Too late for Kidd, who was now dust, his life experiences the stuff of notorious legend.

The message to all English privateers from the Admiralty was unambiguous: stick to the instructions of your commission and obey all Admiralty rules. Kidd, among others, had become an embarrassment to both the East India Company and to the crown, upsetting the careful web spinning of trade officials and diplomats in the ports of the Caribbean and the princely states of India and the Arabian Sea. Privateering was an important "auxiliary" arm to the relatively small and hard-worked navy, but not at any political cost.

As Colman and Clarke awaited Plowman's arrival on shore, they were eventually met not by the Captain, as they had expected, but by Quelch or another sailor bearing yet another letter from Plowman. This missive, worse than the first, put the current situation starkly:

> I have heard you are come down, but am afraid I shall not see you, being taken very weak; now my humble Request to you both, to let the Vessel be sent to Boston, and there all the things be landed, in order to prevent all manner of Imbezzlements; and do not let any second Thoughts of a Voyage tempt you, *for it will not do with these People*; the sooner your things are landed on Shoar, the better. I doubt not but we shall be great Sufferers in getting things a Shoar: The main scope in writing this is, *That you may not be drawn in to take a New Commander*, and in Three Months all totally lost: I can see nothing else but that to be the whole end of it. (Author's italics)

The reaction of Colman and Clarke to Captain Plowman's plea is not known. Nor is known what Quelch said to either confirm or deny his captain's assessment. The wording of Plowman's letter intimates that he had some inkling that the owners were considering sending out the *Charles* under new command. The letter makes clear warning about the dubious nature of the crew he had shipped. For Colman and Clarke, Quelch's view, as second-in-command, would have been crucial. Both men had been denied authority to board the ship; Quelch was their only link to the situation in the captain's cabin and below decks. His interpretation of what was happening was the key. But Quelch, and the crew of the *Charles*, had good reason to water down Plowman's dire assessment.

Whether the owners followed all of Plowman's advice and abandoned the project completely, or ordered the ship back to Boston to wait for a new commander to come aboard, the chances of Quelch and a large part of the crew remaining under contract were slim. Because a berth on a privateer paid a tar more than service in the merchant navy, competition was greater for the available places. If the *Charles* went back to Boston, many of the crew would find themselves booted off for good. As far as Quelch's interests were concerned, if the voyage was abandoned, he was out of a job and the chance of a hefty cut of the prize monies. If Plowman was replaced as commander, the outcome was probably the same. A new commander would no doubt bring his own "number two" aboard.

It was in Quelch's interests to play for a little time and to convince the owners to let the *Charles* get under way once the captain had mended. To attain this outcome, he would have not only cast doubt upon Plowman's current state of mind, but probably would also have mentioned to Colman and Clarke that the summer's end was fast approaching in sailing terms. A cruise off Newfoundland in autumn storms would hardly be conducive for the ship or for the chances of capturing treasure-laden French merchantmen. With several hundreds of pounds sterling already expended on equipping the voyage, postponement would mean that they would not recoup their investment for another year at best. And what if hostilities should end? For businessmen with a mind to reap big profits, it was now or never.

Only Quelch knew the true extent of Captain Plowman's condition. He may have been hoping that the Captain would recover after a few more days rest. Alternatively, he may have wished for— and possibly advocated—his own promotion as Captain.

Who was John Quelch? He had always claimed he was a Londoner. If he had been born there, it would have been in 1666, the year of the Great Fire that in four days devoured 436 acres and over 13,000 houses in the heart of the city, erasing the last of medieval London. Despite the disaster (which spared the dockyards further east down the Thames), London was still the busiest port in the world. London was commerce and commerce needed the sea. For a teenager in the new, brick-built, postconflagration London, the streets and wharves around and east of Tower Hill would have provided adventure, distraction, and if he was so minded, employment. Overseas trade fuelled the prosperity of the city. By 1700, London had thirty-three active shipyards engaged in constructing virtually every class of ship: brigantine, "pink," "snow," shallop, yacht, and frigates of war. Incoming vessels would queue for days waiting to clear customs and to offload cargo at the many warehouses along the Thames. The commodities from the Atlantic colonies such as tobacco, sugar, timber, and dried and salted cod would be hauled onto docks even as exotic spices, coffee, tea, silks, and calicoes from the East Indies arrived from the opposite side of the world. London alone handled three-quarters of all England's trade. It was the supreme entrepot, drawing laborer and lord alike.

Yet no record of a birth or baptism for a John Quelch in London in 1666 has turned up, a situation little surprising given the haphazard nature of parish record-keeping at the time and the unfortunate loss of eighty-seven churches to the Great Fire.

Of the records that do survive from the time, a John Quelch, was born to one William Quelch and his wife Elizabeth at St. Botolph's at Aldersgate in London. But this was in 1654, leaving only the chance that this particular John died in childhood and that a second child was later christened with the same name. This was not an uncommon practice in seventeenth-century England when infant and childhood mortality rates were high.

However, records do exist of the baptism of a John Quelch in 1666—but in Hurley, Berkshire, near Maidenhead. The village of Hurley lies on the upper Thames and the Quelch surname appears frequently in Berkshire records in the seventeenth and eighteenth centuries, a higher concentration than in any other county in England. It is certainly possible that the John Quelch who turns up in Boston in 1703 could have been born and raised in Berkshire, later making his way to London in the early 1680s to find his fortune. The lure of the city brought people from far and wide, and for a denizen of the Thames Valley, it was not far even by seventeenth-century concepts of distance.

For the unruly on-the-run tradesman's apprentice, for the poor looking to find money, and certainly for the son of a maritime man, the merchant fleet and its quayside industries offered the chance to glimpse a world beyond and possibly to escape the drudgery of urban existence. John Quelch, whether a London tradesman's son or a Berkshire country lad, could either have been born to the sea or driven to it. There is no surviving record as to how he became a mariner.

A search through Admiralty records, also unfortunately patchy in this era, shows no one of this name having passed out as a Captain or a Lieutenant in naval service. Nor does a John Quelch appear in navy files of warrant or sailing officers for the period. Similar records of examinations and warrants for the merchant navy would not be instituted until the 1740s. We do know that movement between the maritime and naval fleets was common, either by choice or coercion, so Quelch could have served as a common tar in the 1680s or 1690s before obtaining a berth on a merchant ship. Equally, he may have begun his career as a sailor in the merchant fleet, never having served on a naval vessel.

To become a Lieutenant in the merchant service he would have to possess the skills of navigation such as reading charts, understanding the night sky, and using the instruments of the day. The latter would have been few: the compass to determine direction, the backstaff to give approximate latitude using the sun's position relative to the horizon, and "the log" where a stick tied to a rope with knots at regular intervals indicated a ship's speed (which is why to this day a ship's speed is indicated in "knots"). He was also most likely literate or semiliterate.

Perhaps he had worked his way up the ranks in the barely regulated merchant navy, from rating to master's mate, having demonstrated an aptitude for piloting a vessel. Aged thirty-seven in 1703, he had probably been a mariner for many years, living where his voyages took him. He may well have met Captain Plowman in New York where Plowman had been active as a privateer for a few years prior to coming to Boston.

The Anglo-American maritime community was a transient one. Sailors (as well as merchants, officials, soldiers, and clergy) would move from one side of the Atlantic to the other, sometimes more than once. For a journey that would have lasted eight to twelve weeks, and been perilous even at the best of times, it is difficult today to conceive of such a far-flung community. In 1703, vessels in Boston, London, Bristol, Newport, Charlestown, or New York would have had crews comprising English and colonial-born men both, but all would have been considered *English.*

Just how Quelch and the owners parted that day, and what was said amongst them, can only be conjectured. None of the parties ever put to paper what was agreed. Even subsequent events did not bring the "arrangements" to public light. Whatever transpired, Colman and Clarke left Marblehead after a day having concluded that the ship probably ought to stay put for the moment so they could make further deliberation on replacing Plowman—or the crew—once Colonel Hobby and the others had been apprised.

Quelch must have been filled with doubts as he was rowed back to the *Charles.* His golden opportunity to become a wealthy man was hanging by a slender thread. If Plowman was sacked then so was he. Perhaps he had already failed in trying to convince Colman that he could handle the captain's job. He knew the crew was restless and argumentative about Plowman's condition. Would the crew make their own decisions before the owners could?

One day later, on August 4, without notice and without new orders, the *Charles* raised anchor, hoisted canvas, and sailed out of Marblehead. Down on the docks, in the taverns and ordinaries, the fishermen and chandlers of the town muttered dark suggestions about what had transpired on board the brigantine. It was not a happy ship that at least was known well enough. But who was calling the tune? Had the crew turned or had Plowman miraculously recovered?

The *Charles* was bound for neither Canada nor Boston. Whether or not those on board realized it, they had just crossed the line into unknown and dangerous waters.

Chapter Three

A Change of Plans

W hile Lieutenant Quelch had worked to smooth the feathers of Colman and Clarke over a tankard or two at the Fountain Inn, the situation for Captain Daniel Plowman had gone from bad to worse.

A number of the seventy-man crew of the *Charles* had already formed a conspiracy to mutiny. Just how many had rebelled is not known. Discontent in the age of sail usually ran high and rebellion could be petty or serious. Mutineers might be a minority of the crew with an even smaller minority in vocal opposition to the plan and the majority sitting quiet to see which way events would go. Somehow, the crew had obviously gotten wind of what Plowman was intimating to the owners and quickly surmised that they had little to lose by taking a gamble.

One William Whiting, a twenty-two-year-old Londoner who had worked previously as a clerk and could therefore read and write, had scribbled out the letters to the owners as dictated by the captain as he lay ill in his cramped cabin at the stern. It is highly probable that Whiting was afterwards interrogated by the would-be mutineers in order to learn what Captain Plowman intended to do and whether or not the voyage would go ahead.

The fateful decision was then taken to seize the *Charles*. Acting before the return of Lieutenant Quelch in the longboat, Anthony Holding, the principal ringleader, jammed a marlinspike—a metal awl for separating rope strands—into the door of the captain's cabin, thus preventing Plowman from getting out. Holding then set on watch Peter Roach, a thirty-year-old Irish-born sailor, to make sure that no one came in or out.

When Lieutenant Quelch climbed back aboard the vessel late that afternoon or early evening, he would have immediately been placed in the position of making his choice—join the mutineers or be placed in irons. If we are to take at face value his later recollections of what happened, he claimed that he was unaware of the captain's predicament until *after* he had returned to the ship. Whatever transpired in those first few minutes after his return, Lieutenant Quelch did, at least, assume command of the *Charles*. What is less certain is the level of complicity he chose to be aware of. If Captain Plowman was incapacitated, either physically or mentally, Quelch had the right to assume command anyway. Did Quelch choose to interpret Holding's actions as "securing" the captain rather than imprisoning him?

Shortly after his return, Quelch gave the order to make sail. He was walking a very fine line, hoping to make his actions appear legitimate while awaiting his captain's demise. As luck would have it, the awkwardness of his situation did not last long. Within forty-eight hours, Captain Plowman was dead. It was never proven, nor even alleged, that Plowman had been murdered in cold blood. Indeed, none of the crew ever owned up to such a deed even among themselves. Plowman *was* gravely ill. However, while it may be that no blade or pistol ball ended his life, neglect and deprivation certainly must have hastened his end.

If the crew of the *Charles* had indeed "gone on the account" and turned pirate, then an informal but strict code of operating principles would now be in effect. The most important of these would have been that the new captain serves at the behest of the majority of the crew. Under the widely accepted pirate "code of conduct," a captain could be deselected at any time by vote of the men underneath him. Normally, this would occur when there was a question over his leadership, particularly in deciding when to attack prey. Cowardice was never a quality esteemed in commanders, not the least of which pirate captains.

Unfortunately, "cowardice" is a subjective thing and what might seem a sound tactical decision in avoiding engagement could be interpreted by others as a lack of fortitude. A pirate captain relieved of his command would quickly find himself set adrift in a dory or marooned on the nearest rock of land, along with any who disagreed with the sentence. This is precisely what befell Captain Kidd off Madagascar when his men took exception to his strategic decision-making. In Kidd's case, his crew abandoned him on a sinking ship with eleven loyal men and four cabin boys while they absconded on a captured prize vessel.

The second element that faced the test of this protodemocracy at sea was destination. It had been Plowman's intention to cruise the North Atlantic in search of French ships, chiefly French privateers that had been taking such a heavy toll of New England merchantmen. This obviously held little appeal to the crew of the *Charles*, who knew where the real treasure lay. That was hundreds of miles to the southward and the warm waters of the Caribbean. Quelch knew this too. But his sights were set on a cruising ground potentially just as lucrative but without the level of dangerous competition from other men of similar enterprise or from pirate-hunting warships.

The question remains, though, whether Quelch and his crew were consciously conducting themselves as pirates, or rather, as the crew of a licensed privateer. With Plowman dead of his illness, to all intents and purposes, Quelch was legally in command. So too, he could set the destination, even to the Caribbean, since his commission and orders clearly identified the Spanish as permissible quarry.

Moreover, pirate crews normally would sign a covenant, the so-called "articles" of their voyage, clearly laying out the rules and customs by which they agreed to govern themselves. No such articles for the *Charles* ever came to light, nor did any of the crew ever make mention of them. Authority was carefully delineated on a pirate vessel. The captain's word was law only in active battle: "in fighting, chasing, or being chased" but in all other matters he was to be "governed by a Majority." He would also have complete say over the fate of prisoners and whether they should be put to the sword or spared.

In fact, the entire command structure on a pirate vessel differed considerably from that in the merchant service or navy. A quartermaster was elected as second in command to serve as the trustee of the crew's interests and a counterbalance to the captain. In the punishment for small offences, the quartermaster would have authority. He would also normally be the first to board any prize ship and would take charge of the division of any captured cargoes or treasure. Next, the ship's carpenter or cooper, the equivalent of a modern ship's chief engineer in the wooden world, would be elevated to "officer" status. So too would the ship's gunner be promoted. In such a way, the pirate crew elevated noncommissioned positions, eliminating first officers, lieutenants, or midshipmen.

This is made clear when one sees the division of spoils among pirate crews. It was usual that the captain would receive one-and-a-half to two shares of the booty; the quartermaster the same; the boatswain, gunner, and carpenter would receive between one-and-a-quarter to one-and-a-half shares. All other crew members would gain one share each. Compared to privateering or merchant marine service, this was a remarkably egalitarian distribution of shared fortune.

The articles also dealt with discipline and proscribed behavior. Corporal punishment was normally only carried out after a majority decision, if at all. Again, this was a radical departure in an age when sea captains were known to have beaten their sailors to death while the others had to watch. For an occupation that so routinely suffered under the arbitrary lash, it is not surprising that pirates kept "the cat" in the bag and seldom inflicted it on their fellows. Fighting or dueling on ship was often forbidden. Those who chose to quarrel had to do it on land with knife, cutlass, or pistol in an officiated bout that might end with just the drawing of first blood. Gambling, which often led to bloody frays, was also sometimes proscribed above or below decks. Drinking, on the other hand, was not usually regulated.

Ironically, in addition to cowardice, what was a great transgression for pirates was stealing—from each other. This was usually punishable by marooning, referred to in pirate argot as making someone "governor of the island." For extreme transgressions, such as desertion or bringing a woman (or boy) secretly aboard, the penalty was death.

Everything about the articles was designed to promote harmony in an extraordinary situation: men working together to break the law and answerable to no one but themselves.

There is one clue that Quelch and the crew of the *Charles* had confederated as pirates and had not maintained their commission as a privateer. It is known that they had elected a quartermaster who stood by Quelch as a second-in-command. Had Quelch been operating according to the norms of a naval ship, this would not have been the case. Although he would not have authority to name a lieutenant to replace himself, it certainly would have been permissible for Quelch to appoint a first mate to conform to naval conventions. He did not do so.

That said, the clue is not certain proof. The protonaturalist and buccaneer, William Dampier, a skilful navigator who circumnavigated the world three times, tells of a *privateer* vessel whose quartermaster was second-in-command. Recalling his first voyage around the world in 1679, he speaks of a privateer vessel that accompanied his own vessel to the Isle of Tortugas: "After our parting, this Mr. Cook, being Quarter-Master under Captain Yanky, the second Place in the Ship according to the Law of Privateers, laid Claim to a Ship they took from the Spaniards."

Perhaps conventions had not changed in the ensuing twenty-four years leading up to Quelch's voyage. Yet Quelch's own rank under Plowman had been as Lieutenant, not quartermaster. For whatever reason, it would appear that the convention aboard the *Charles* was not followed.

With Captain Plowman's death, Quelch was in command, but a command with strict caveats. No doubt Quelch felt he could have the best of both worlds: the legitimate cover of a privateer's commission *and* an unlimited choice of whom he could attack and seize.

Before the *Charles* had rounded the tip of Cape Cod, headed south, the body of Captain Plowman would have been sewn up in a tarpaulin, weighted with a cannonball, and heaved over the side. Whether this task was treated with ceremony or respect it is not recorded. Still, sailors were deeply superstitious if not always religious, and it would have been bad form not to pause in silence while Quelch said a few words as their former captain was laid to rest in the deep. There would be enough risk to contend with without worry of a restless spirit stalking them.

Just what sort of vessel did Quelch now hold sway over as he stood upon the quarterdeck of the *Charles*, the dunes, and rocky shoals of the Cape off his starboard beam? The vessel was a *brigantine*, a type of ship whose definition evolved over the

succeeding years of the eighteenth century. In 1704, a brigantine was generally two-masted and rigged with square-set sails
on its foremast and a triangular fore-and-aft or lateen rig on
its mainmast. Such a configuration afforded maximum flexibil-
ity in managing variable wind conditions and brigantines were
renowned as fast sailors. That made them the vessel of choice
for privateers—and pirates. Brigantines were probably the most
widely built of all types of merchant ships in the American colonies
during the latter part of the seventeenth and the early eighteenth
centuries.

The *Charles* was not a large vessel, nor was it technically a
"ship." The term *ship* was reserved for a three-masted vessel that
was square-rigged all around. Weighing in at eighty tons, the
Charles was probably not much more than ninety feet long including its bowsprit, possessing a beam (width) of roughly twenty feet.
She probably had only one deck for living space below the main
deck. Beneath this would have been the cargo hold. At the stern and
level with the main deck would have been the main cabin shared
by the captain and his lieutenant. The roof of this would have comprised the quarterdeck where the brigantine was steered by means
of a tiller. This would mean that a large pole would protrude below
the quarterdeck through the main cabin and down into the deck
beneath where the mechanism would exit at the stern to connect to
the ship's rudder.

There are a few mentions in period documents of Quelch's vessel being referred to as the *Charles Galley*. If this were accurate,
then the ship would have had another design element in its favor compared with its prey. The *Charles* would have had nine or
ten "tholes"—or sets of double pegs—mounted on the gunwales
on each side of the vessel, through which, oars (referred to as
"sweeps") would be manned by the crew standing on the weather
deck. If becalmed, the ship could then be transformed into a rowed
galley, able to close with an enemy—or outrun one. This was a fea-
ture that several privateers and pirates of the era found to their
advantage: Captain Martel in 1716 in the *John and Martha*, Captain England in 1719 in the *Victory*, and Captain Gow in 1724 in
the *George Galley* to name but a few.

The brigantine's guns would have been mounted on the main
deck, exposed to the weather. Most likely "four-pounders" this

nomenclature refers to the weight of iron shot that they fired. Set upon wheeled wooden carriages, the cannon would normally be lashed down to the deck and gunwales of the vessel to prevent them from rolling and toppling with the motion of the ship. To keep them relatively dry, tarpaulins would be used as shrouds. When in firing position, the guns would be rolled out in cutouts or gaps in the ship's railing, larboard (port) and starboard.

These ten to twelve main guns would sometimes be supplemented by smaller swivel guns mounted on the railing near the bow and at the stern and capable of being trained in an arc of nearly 180 degrees. These would normally be two-pounders, used for firing when chasing another vessel or being chased. Some captains preferred heavy firepower, and might supplement their armament by placing four- or six-pounders up on the quarterdeck, protruding out over the stern. Nor was it out of the ordinary for a gun carriage to be placed in the great cabin so that it could also be fired out of the stern through the casement windows.

Gunpowder, the most hazardous substance carried on the *Charles* (other than rum), was stored in small wooden kegs below decks, and only brought up when action was imminent.

While Captain Quelch would not have had to worry about his ship having rotten timbers, it being newly built in a Boston yard, he would have had to worry that it had been caulked and planked properly. Captain Kidd too had sailed in a virgin warship, his *Adventure Galley*, only a few years before. By the time he had gotten around Africa on his way to Madagascar, the *Adventure Galley* had sprung so many leaks from poor workmanship and attack by burrowing sea worms that he had to have crew members manning the pumps nearly continuously to keep her afloat. She eventually was run aground on St. Mary's Island off Madagascar, scavenged, and burned.

That the *Charles* was not a large vessel and that she held a crew of seventy men, would also have been a concern to Quelch. Had she been in merchant service, the *Charles* would likely have needed only twelve to fifteen hands to handle her reasonably well. However, fitted out as a privateer, the *Charles* needed muscle power. Men were needed not just to sail her but to serve her ten guns, to grapple, board, and, if necessary, to fight with the enemy in hand-to-hand combat.

A large crew on a small warship presented several problems. First, would be the challenge of boredom, combined with the fractiousness that life in close quarters would engender. With roughly four times the number of hands actually needed to handle the sails and rigging, what was there for the majority of the crew to do while waiting for action? This was an open invitation to gambling, drinking, and brawling below deck and one can only imagine the stench of seventy unwashed souls living on salt beef, salt pork, and hard biscuit for months on end. Without the diversion of battle, discipline could easily and quickly unravel.

Below deck, a man of medium or tall height would not be able to stand erect. He would have to navigate the relative gloom while bent over, taking care not to knock his head upon the great oak beams that traversed the low ceiling. All living, cooking, mending of kit, weapons, and clothing, relaxing, and sleeping would be done on this deck by the light of tallow candles. Hammocks had already come into fashion, adopted by European sailors that had journeyed to the coast of South America and the Caribbean islands and seen their use by the natives. These would be slung at night and taken down and stowed during the day, a most practical solution for sleeping at sea in cramped conditions.

Second, there would be the problem of logistics. Seventy men had to be fed and watered, with room only for so many supplies. What could not be carried in the hold would have to be obtained during the voyage. That would mean taking it from another ship or else stopping somewhere along the way and foraging for provisions. This was no small consideration in voyages across the expanse of the Atlantic. Indeed, some crews perished of thirst in the infamous "doldrums" of the South Atlantic while waiting in vain for a breeze to fill their sails.

It was not unusual, therefore, for vessels sailing south to the Caribbean to make stops along the coast of America, or among the dozens of islands offshore. It is worth keeping in mind that in the age of sail, the shortest distance between two points was not always a straight line. A ship's master would have to work with the prevailing winds and currents—changeable at different times of the year—in order to make best progress.

A sailor pushing forty years of age, John Quelch would have been aware of the challenges. As lieutenant of the *Charles*, it would have been partly his charge to anticipate and plan for them. He had now accepted responsibility collectively for his crew. They placed their qualified trust in his seamanship, his navigation skills, and his artfulness as a naval tactician. But this was always a *mutual* arrangement and one that he and the crew knew was subject to change if fortune did not smile upon them.

The conventions governing those who turned pirate were widely known in the maritime world of the time. Writing in 1709, the suspiciously fictitious sounding "Barnaby Slush," a sea-cook aboard the HMS *Lyme*, made this clear:

> If the Chief have a Supreme Share beyond his comrades, 'tis be-cause he's always the Leading Man in e'ry daring Enterprize; and yet as Bold as he is in all other Attempts, he dares not offer to in-fringe the common Laws of Equity; but every Associate has his due Quota.... As great Robbers as they are to all Besides, are precisely Just among themselves, without which they could no more subsist than a Structure without a Foundation.

Slush's little book on the Royal Navy, essentially a screed against the mistreatment of sailors and the subsequent corrosive effect on the defense of the realm, is either the work of the most literary ship's cook in history or else a thinly disguised polemic by someone in high authority. Regardless of the true identity of its author, it shines a light on the reality of life at sea at the beginning of the eighteenth century. Slush knew very well that sailors and mer-chant seamen were often driven to mutiny.

> Their Daily and repeated Desertions, whereby some loose one, two, nay Three Years Pay due; with the Hazard of a Swing at the Yard Arm, is a convincing proof, that it's not Money so much as fair Us-age, that has the strongest Influence over them.

Quelch would have to walk a delicate line indeed in governing his ship. We know the ages of only twenty-five of the seventy or so crewmembers of the *Charles*. The youngest was fifteen, the oldest fifty-four. The average age was twenty-nine, a figure that comes close to the norm for seamen in the first part of the eighteenth century—twenty-seven years (this according to research based on surviving records). As a privateer crew, most would have possessed many years of labor upon the sea. Privateer billets were sought after, being more lucrative than the merchant service, meaning that a captain would often have a good pool of experienced seamen from which to select his crew. Sailing, as a profession, was beginning to become more regularized, if not yet codified, and specialties had now arisen even if formal qualifications for these lagged behind.

By the middle to late eighteenth century, skill sets would become highly defined and regulated on both military and merchant ships, institutionalized by a system of "ratings" based on experience and demonstrated ability. In 1700, most crews would have been divided into master and first-mate on one side, a nascent warrant officer grouping of boatswain, quartermaster, carpenter, and gunner, and ordinary seamen to serve as general toilers at deck, line, and canvas.

Although uniforms had now become the fashion in European armies, with colored coats and facings to denote regiments, the idea of a naval uniform had yet to surface. Unlike on land, clothing for mariners was more utilitarian: wide-cut breeches that reached to mid-shin—a kind of early trousers—were worn rather than tight breeches and stockings secured at the knee. Baggy linen shirts were worn but rather than the long-sleeved, knee-length woolen coat worn by landsmen, the sailor often wore a waist-length canvas or woolen jacket called a *fearnought*. Both breeches and jacket could be coated with tar to provide a measure of waterproofing, the practice that gave rise to the term "tars" or "Jack Tar" for English or colonial seamen. Aboard ship, most mariners would go barefoot. Captains or masters would normally wear buckle shoes or boots. As there was no regulation regarding dress, individuals could improvise with whatever came their way. Civilian waistcoats with pewter buttons, either sleeved or sleeveless, or a three-cornered hat might be seen, most mariners would also have worn a neck scarf, a headscarf, or a knitted woolen cap.

Pirates would have had even more scope in dress. As sea robbers, they could take from their victims what they pleased: a gentleman's brocade waistcoat, rings and pendants, waist sash, fine lace and linen, or cloth or brightly colored silk and taffeta from the East from which to fashion their own clothes. Indeed, many pirate or privateer captains were as immaculately turned-out as the wealthiest merchants of London.

Even if dashingly attired, the work itself was exhausting and dangerous. If not swept away by a heavy sea or killed by a fall to the deck from the rigging, a sailor might find himself permanently disabled after an accident, ruining his livelihood. Far more a danger though, was sickness. Disease came quickly to men confined on a ship, brought aboard by those already infected at departure, or else picked up during ports of call in the tropics. Bad diet, tainted drink, and constant exposure to weather further reduced immunities against illness. Scurvy, malarial fevers, cholera, dysentery, and tuberculosis killed far more seamen in this age than any enemy's shot or blade. According to the opinion of a contemporary naval surgeon, William Cockburn, at sea there were four deaths by illness or accident for every one killed in action.

The chosen cruising grounds may have been Quelch's idea or it could have come from some of the crew such as Holding. Far from following their original orders to pursue the French in the North Atlantic, a dangerous enterprise with little prospect of reward, the new destination selected was far more promising.

Beyond the blue waters of the Caribbean and past the equator was where the *Charles* set her course. In 1703 it was no secret in the maritime world that, less then ten years before, gold had been discovered in the Portuguese colony of Brazil. Now, mines were pouring forth the precious metal, which, in turn, was being transported to the coast, minted into coins, and sent back to Lisbon. Here was a treasure worth risking one's life for. Not French pewter plate, tarnished silver, or a few barrels of rum and salted fish. Gold.

Chapter Four

"Such Desperate Men"

W hile dozens of merchant ships lay tied up along the two great wooden piers of Boston harbor in the heat of early August, the brigantine *Charles* was not among them. The harbor, a sheltered inlet of the Atlantic dotted with numerous islands, some no more than grass-topped rocks, could hold some 500 sailing ships comfortably, according to travelers of the time. The two piers, jutting out from opposite sides of the town's shoreline and running parallel with it, were each nearly 700 feet long. These created an artificial breakwater for ships loading and unloading, all under the watchful eyes of the stone and log fort on Castle Island, hunkered in the middle of the harbor.

"The Bay of Boston," wrote visitor Daniel Neal in 1719, "is spacious enough to contain in a manner the Navy of England. The Masts of Ships here, and at proper Seasons of the Year, make a kind of Wood of Trees like that we see upon the River of Thames about Wapping and Limehouse.... Upon the whole, Boston is the most flourishing Town for Trade and Commerce in the English America..." Though these lines were written some fifteen years after 1704, even at this time Boston was the premier English port on the eastern seaboard, clearing thousands of tons of cargo in a year. Regionally, only Newport, in the tiny colony of Rhode Island, and New York, came close.

When the *Charles* had not arrived at Boston after nearly two weeks, her owners, not surprisingly, feared the worst. That she had unexpectedly weighed anchor on August 4, caused worry enough, but her only permitted destination could have been Boston and that she should have reached from Marblehead in less than a day's sail.

For the owners, particularly Colman and Clark, the missing vessel was a personal and commercial embarrassment. Governor Dudley was also placed in an awkward position having just signed a commission for the *Charles* only a few weeks before. Moreover, it meant that the security of sea trade in Boston was doubly under threat. Under threat by the continuing presence of the French privateer who was cruising off Martha's Vineyard and now, perhaps, by the very vessel sent out to take *him*. Dudley was furious at this turn of affairs.

The only surviving portrait of Dudley, painted in 1701 when he was fifty-four and just a year before he was named governor, shows the very public face of a man who appears both intelligent and successful. While he has the air of privilege about him, his expression is neither imperious nor austere. Rather, he appears almost a gregarious sort, ready to welcome a friend or associate with a smile and compliment. He wears an expensive full French-style periwig with a middle parting, and a flowing cravat of fine silk.

What the portrait cannot show is how Joseph Dudley was already by this time a great political survivor on both sides of the Atlantic. Born into the Puritan aristocracy of Massachusetts at Roxbury, his father was an early governor of the colony. Family connections and a good marriage assured his early career prospects. At the age of twenty-six he was elected to the Massachusetts legislature, known then as the "General Court." In just a few years, he proved himself an able administrator and negotiator, serving as a commissioner with the militia in King Philip's War. Dudley's attainment in 1682 of a position as a royal agent for the colony sent him to England for a year where his social skills assured him renewed political patronage.

On his return, he was elevated to the upper house of the Massachusetts legislature and also received a commission as a militia officer, becoming intimately involved in the defense of the colony. But not all was smooth sailing. As he developed politically and socially he began to favor the Crown's interests in colonial affairs, forsaking the old Puritan theocracy he had been born into along with its foundation beliefs in local independence from England.

He found himself on the wrong side of the Glorious Revolution in 1688 and, being seen as closely tied to the Stuart-appointed governor Lord Andros, was thrown into jail and then placed under house-arrest where he languished for ten months before the new Protestant king, William III, ordered his release and transportation to London. The new regime recognized that Dudley's loyalty was to the crown and not to James II personally and rewarded him with a posting to New York as Chief of the Council; the political climate in Boston remaining too hot for Dudley to return there. The Privy Council in London, through the Lords of Trade, needed intelligent and talented administrators who understood the workings of New England rule. Dudley was diligent, crafty, and youthful. He was worth investing in. His own ambition was a secret to no one. Even a political ally, the courtier Edward Randolph, while recognizing that Dudley had no truck with the "country" faction around the old Puritans, knew that Dudley would say what people wanted to hear if it would further his own interest.

> Major Dudley is a great opposer of the faction heere.... who, if he finds things resolutely manniged, will cringe and bow to anything; he hath his fortune to make in the world, and if his Majesty, upon alteration of the government, make him captain of the castle of Boston and the forts in the colloney, his Majesty will gaine a popular man and obleidge the better party.

And London is again where Dudley went in 1693, to further cement his own alliances. Moving in the rarefied air of Whitehall, he climbed higher by leveraging his connections with those who had an interest in fomenting change in colonial affairs and commerce. Although he was passed over for the governorship of Massachusetts due to the machinations of his enemies back home in 1696, he did manage to obtain the deputy governorship of the Isle of Wight and was also elected to the Parliament. When the incumbent governor of New England, Lord Bellomont, died in harness in 1701 it was finally Dudley's moment.

By 1703 he was in the thick of it. War with France and her Indian allies, little money in the treasury, his own legislature refusing him a salary, and the intrigues of his numerous enemies in Boston all tested him fully. When Colonel Hobby, representing the members of the *Charles* syndicate, met with the governor at the Town House, it could not have been a happy meeting.

Filled with mutual recriminations and blame for what had been allowed to happen and dire forecasts of what the consequences could be, Dudley knew something had to be done. It was decided that, until further intelligence might find its way to them, that letters be drafted for the governors of those places likely to be destinations for the pirated ship. Two separate letters were written and signed on August 18, one by Colonel Hobby collectively for the owners and the other by the governor. Copies were made and prepared for posting on the next available merchantmen headed for the West Indies. The letters provide interesting detail about the *Charles* and her crew, but they also provide a clue: namely, that at this point, the owners assumed Quelch was loyal and probably overwhelmed along with Plowman by the mutineers.

Boston August 18th 1703

SIR

We lately fitted out a New Briganteen, Capt. *Daniel Plowman*, to go into *Canada* River, &c. A Private Man of War; the Commander we fear is Dead, and the Men we are advised are in Rebellion against their Officers; and went away the 4th Currant with the Vessel, without notifying to any of us what their Intention was, which makes us fear their Design is not to do justly by us. If therefore the said Briganteen should come into any of your Ports, or bring or send any Prize within the same, we pray you to appear for us: Inclosed is a letter from Col. *Dudley*, our Governor, to your Governor, about this Affair: Please to deliver the same, and inform him, we have wrote to your self to take care for us. You will find by the Articles Aboard, we are to have one Third of all Purchase for our Vessel and Provision. After the Vessel was fitted, we found the Men are not able to fit themselves out, so we supplied about Three Hundred Pounds in Small Arms and Ammunition for them, for which we are to have *50 per Cent* Advance (and they to keep the Arms) out of their Shares of the First Purchase. We pray you also in time to secure the Briganteen's Stores from Imbezelments; also Two Negroe Men belonging to Col. *Hobbey*, Namely *Charles* and *Caesar*, One Negro Boy belonging to Captain *Plowman*, named *Mingo*, and their Shares. The Briganteen send us for this Place, put some honest Man in Command of her, and lade in her our Parts of her Earnings, as also what you receive for our Arms, also the above Negroes and their Shares, in any Goods proper for this Market, and be as Expeditious as may be. Any Civility your Governor shews us in this Affair, please to Retaliate. We have wrote to all the *Indies* to this Effect, not knowing where to meet her: Else had not given your Governor the Trouble of our Lines; so please to excuse us to him, and give him our best Respects: We kiss your Hand, and remain,

SIR
Your very Humble Servants
Charles Hobbey for himself, and
Col. Nicholas Paige,
William Clarke, Benjamin Gallop, John Colman

Hobby was optimistic enough, or thorough enough, to assume that the crew would make a successful voyage, taking prizes as they went and that the shares coming to him and his partners had to be assured. He also specifically mentions that his property be physically secured, chiefly the two slaves and their share of any spoils. It was not unusual, for both privateers and pirates that slaves or free black men be given equal shares with the crew they served alongside. Hobby's phrase "against their *Officers*" seems to indicate that Lieutenant Quelch was, thus far, being given the benefit of the doubt as to his complicity in the affair.

Governor Dudley's letter, shorter but in similar vein, exhorted his colleagues in the Caribbean "to secure the said Briganteen and any Prize she may have with her, and Examine their Papers, and you will see what is above alleged." In concluding, he asked that the vessel be put into some merchant's hands for security and that "on Her Majesty's Behalf I desire they may be prevented from any Piracy that such desperate Men may easily fall into." Strangely, no mention is made in either letter about the fate of the crew or that they should be returned to Boston. Dudley and the owners seemed to be implying that they expected the crew of the *Charles* to meet with local justice should they be apprehended.

Under the circumstances, the shipowners and the governor had done all that was possible, and although stung, turned to other pressing business while awaiting any news, news that they must have realized would take many months to arrive, if at all. So many outbound ships were being taken by French privateers that mail delivery to England and the sister colonies had become a lottery. For the moment, there was nothing more to be done.

Unfortunately for Dudley and the members of the syndicate, they had roundly misjudged Quelch's destination. More than that, it is unlikely that the *Charles* even ventured near the West Indies, at least not upon its outward journey. In the words of William Dampier: "Experience often shows us that the farthest way about is the nearest way home..."

Given the time of year, early August, the best way to Brazil was an indirect course, catching the northeast trades and sailing due east with the wind on the starboard side. This would take them to the Azores, or "Western Isles" that lay in the mid-Atlantic some 1,100 miles from Cape Cod. For two centuries, these lush green Portuguese-settled volcanic islands had been a stopover for transatlantic voyages. Here, Quelch could take on fresh water and food, and let the crew ashore to indulge in drinking wine, whoring, and eating fresh meat. Even with favorable winds, their cruise would have taken some four to six weeks sailing in the vastness of the North Atlantic. The opportunity to get on land once again would have been a welcome change, knowing that the next leg of the voyage to the Brazilian coast would be equally arduous as their first.

From the Azores, their course would be south to south-by-southwest, wind upon the larboard quarter. This would speed them past Africa and take them to the Cape Verde Islands, some 800 miles distant. Reaching these, they could again anchor and replenish, make any repairs to canvas, spars, or rigging, and enjoy the hospitality of the islanders, renowned for their friendliness and easygoing sexual mores.

The ten tiny volcanic islands (and eight islets) that make up Cape Verde archipelago sit in a semicircle some 200 miles off the coast of Senegal. Lush and green when discovered by the Portuguese in the mid-fifteenth century, the islands were uninhabited and pristine. Two hundred and fifty years on, when Quelch arrived, the islands were the home to thousands of African slaves, Portuguese plantation owners and traders, and mulatto laborers. Intensely farmed and populated, the islands were much more scrub-like than in former times. Denuded by thousands of foraging goats and pigs that ranged freely, periodic (and worsening) droughts further sapped the land, hastening its evolution to rocky escarpments more like the Aegean than equatorial Africa. Cotton was the chief commodity, grown, picked, cleaned, and woven into cloth in the towns before being shipped to Lisbon or Brazil.

In 1700, the governor of the colony had complained to a newly arrived bishop from Portugal that marriages had been celebrated between local women and foreign pirates on both Sao Nicolau and Santo Antao, despite the fact that "His Majesty does not want foreigners, much less pirates" in the islands. Indeed, so poor were its inhabitants that English or Dutch seafarers could purchase sweet wine and meat on the hoof—or a woman—for practically nothing. Despite the wariness toward foreign visitors by the authorities, the fate of geography, wind, and current meant that Cape Verde was a natural stopping point for Atlantic voyagers.

Quelch and his crew did not linger there; they were intent upon reaching their chosen cruising grounds. In Cape Verde waters they were likely only to find slave ships and not much gold. Quelch also knew that the last leg would again be roughly 800 miles long, taking them over the equator and into the South Atlantic in what would be a demanding run.

Navigating was altogether trickier as they approached the imaginary line that separates the earth's hemispheres, the midpoint of the world. The trade winds begin to shift: sailing too far eastward one can get pulled into the African currents or be calmed. Before they reached the area of the southeast trade winds, they faced a band of sea called the doldrums. This region of low pressure, situated between the trade wind zones of the northern and southern hemispheres, is fickle and was deadly in the age of sail. The zone can stretch anywhere from 15 to 150 miles in width: a harsh gauntlet that cannot be run quickly. Even with a galley, pulling sweeps on an eighty-ton vessel in an equatorial furnace demands great muscle power—and drinking water. One moment the atmosphere is oppressively hot and muggy, the next, with little warning, a vicious squall or thunderstorm bursts upon the sea. French sailors nicknamed the doldrums *Le pot au noir*—"the black hole."

At the beginning of the eighteenth century, calculating one's position on the surface of the Earth and finding it on a chart or a map required knowledge of the imaginary grid, vertical and horizontal, which covers the globe. Latitude, the north-south measurement, was straightforward enough and could be measured by the sun's position or even by the position of Polaris, the "polestar," by night. Judging longitude, one's position east or west, was a difficult and imprecise art until the late eighteenth century, but measuring latitude was far easier, calculated using a backstaff or quadrant. These devices measured the angle between the sun at its highest point, and the horizon as viewed from deck. Consulting the navigation tables and plugging in the measurement between zero and ninety degrees would then give a reasonable approximation of the ship's current latitude, its position, in degrees, north or south of the imaginary zero line, the equator.

Longitude was a different story altogether. Measuring the east-west position was a function of time as the earth revolved around its axis. By knowing how much time had elapsed since the sun had reached its zenith or meridian at one point, say in London, and when it reached its zenith where one's ship lay, one could calculate longitude. Every hour of sun transit time equals fifteen degrees of longitude.

If Captain Quelch, sitting to the west of the Cape Verde Islands at noon could have known that exactly two hours previously it had been noon in London, then he could easily calculate that his position was at thirty degrees west longitude. But that simply was not possible in 1703. No timepiece was then accurate enough to keep proper time for days on end without it being reset. Without such a timepiece, longitude could not be determined with any sense of accuracy. Instead, navigators would have to rely on piloting skills—recognizing landmarks, and "dead reckoning." The latter method required a navigator to plot his last known position, say one of the Cape Verde islands, measure his set and drift, that is, the deviation due to wind, current, and helm error. By knowing the deviation, the relative speed of the vessel in knots, and the time elapsed, one could—with skill—calculate how many miles one had traveled from the "fix" or known point. It was complicated business, and still imprecise.

More often than not, sailors would set a course for the desired latitude and then just sail east or west until they literally ran into what they were looking for. Such practice sometimes ended in disaster, with ships blissfully unaware of the dangers ahead. In

October 1707, a helmsman's mistake in calculating longitude on Admiral Cloudesley Shovell's flagship, the *Association,* sent the vessel straight onto the rocks of the Scilly Islands, in darkness, on a return voyage from Gibraltar, drowning all aboard including the admiral. Several other vessels of the squadron, obediently following the flagship, shared her fate. Over 1,000 sailors lost their lives. For a ship as small as the *Charles,* burdened with so many hands, overshooting an island in mid-ocean through poor navigation could spell death by scurvy and thirst.

When the *Charles* had reached about three degrees south latitude, and the equator behind her, the ship would have then swung toward the west, sailing as straight as possible for its intended destination.

Sometime around the end of October 1703, the *Charles* sighted land. It was Fernando Island, or more properly, Fernando de Noronha, a small volcanic archipelago 215 miles off the coast of Brazil. These rocky but green tropical islands would have been well known to Quelch. They had served as waypoints for the lands of South America for more than 200 years, guiding first the Portuguese, then the Spanish, followed by the Dutch. Not much bigger than seven square miles and uninhabited in 1703, Fernando de Noronha had been a geopolitical football for most of the seventeenth century.

By the time Quelch surveyed the cliffs and outcrops of Fernando de Noronha, the Dutch had long gone, their stone fort at Nossa Senhora dos Remedios already crumbling. Having abandoned their toeholds on the Brazilian mainland in the colony of Nieuw Holland, the Dutch no longer needed the islands as a base. They now were a maritime "squat" for whoever happened by and a convenient resting place for pirates.

The *Charles* had arrived during the dry season and the normally verdant vegetation that blanketed Fernando would have appeared as brown and reddish colored scrub. However, the islands were blessed with numerous coves and inlets that offered shelter, fresh water, and abundant numbers of fish and fowl, ready for the eating. The south side of the main island, facing the mainland, is a natural shield from the high surf that pummels the northern shore during the dry "winter" months. It is possible that given an early

November arrival, the *Charles* may have anchored on the south side in the large cove protected at its mouth by the tiny island of Chapeu do Sueste.

The wide sandy beaches were ideal for grounding a ship to inspect the condition of the hull. After the crossing of the open sea and the entry into equatorial waters, Quelch may have ordered the ship careened whereby the crew would have heeled over the beached vessel using block and tackle, exposing the planks of the hull. If encrusted with barnacles and kelp, the crew would scrape or burn these off until the bottom was smooth once again. Any accretions could bleed off precious knots of speed during a chase, allowing prey to escape, or even allowing a warship to catch them up. After some two months at sea, the *Charles* would have likely been in need of some level of restoration to either wood or canvas and the seclusion of the island would allow this in relative safety.

The crew was now in desert island luxury, dining on freshly caught green sea turtle, crabs, and fish as well as exotic birds such as the long-tailed *viuvinha* that roosted in rocks and bushes throughout the islands in great numbers. As they spent the time working and foraging by day, and drinking, singing, gambling, and brawling by campfire on the beach at night, the talk would have been of taking prizes.

For nearly three months the crew had endured cramped and foul conditions at sea, with only brief respite at the Azores and Cape Verde. Now that they had reached the Promised Land, Quelch would have to deliver—and soon. Under the rules of "no prey, no pay" the crew would now be desperate for plunder, having spent or lost what money they had. With seventy men itching to attack the first ship that hove into view, Quelch would have had to exert strong leadership to keep his men under control. Up until this point, they had been cajoled with the promise of gold. Now, it was time to take it.

What John Quelch may not have known, however, was that events at a much higher level were conspiring against his endeavor. On June 16, 1703, at Lisbon, John Methuen, the English ambassador to the court of Dom Pedro II, had signed a treaty of alliance with Portugal. The treaty brought Portugal into the Grand Alliance against the French, a primary aim of the negotiations, but it is chiefly known for leading to a second treaty in December that year granting preferential trade rights for Portuguese wines, namely Port, in exchange for Portugal granting similar low duties on English textiles.

Whitehall put the Great Seal upon the treaty documents on July 13, whereby the articles contained entered into force. Although mention of the treaty was carried in the *London Gazette* at the end of May and again in the middle of July, such news would have only reached Boston some eight weeks later, at best. Copies of the *London Gazette* theoretically might have been found on the sticky trestles of Boston's coffee houses but it is unlikely John Quelch or any of his crew ever glimpsed them.

Article Eighteen of the treaty had particular resonance for many in Boston:

> Piratical ships, of whatever nation, shall not be permitted or received into the ports which their Portuguese and Britannic Majesties, and the States General of the United Provinces, possess in the East Indies, but shall be deemed the common enemies of the Portuguese, the English and the Dutch.

Although the *Charles* was far from the East Indies, she was still cruising in Portuguese waters. And with the treaty's ink barely dry, she was now about to precipitate a diplomatic crisis through ignorance, self-interest, and avarice.

Chapter Five

"We Are Frenchmen"

"**A** Hell for Blacks, a purgatory for Whites, and a paradise for Mulattoes." That was how one Portuguese
wit of the time uncharitably described seventeenth
century Brazil.

This huge expanse of the creaking Portuguese empire, although productive and lucrative, was by the 1690s, in social
turmoil. Tragically, this was a condition that would persist in Brazil
for the whole of the eighteenth century as well. Thousands of West
Africans had been enslaved by the Portuguese and sent to work the
plantations of the coastal settlements. By 1700, a complicated caste
system was already in existence, a roiling, thriving, community
of whites, blacks, indigenous peoples, and after several decades
of colonization, those of mixed race. Sons of noble Portuguese
houses, freemen, indentured servants, and slaves created a vibrant
but cruel economy that ran on sweat and blood and produced
sugar and tobacco. As settlement expanded over the years, new
immigrants began to pioneer the scrub-covered hinterland beyond
the coastal rainforest.

To this volatile mix of peoples and cultures, gold was added.
Within just a few years of its discovery in the province of Minas
Gerais in the mid-1690s, thousands were flocking to the region to
stake their claims. It was a situation that neither the crown nor the
colonial rulers of Bahia and Rio de Janeiro could contain or control.
Since most of the region's gold was alluvial—washed out of rivers

and streams—it was literally there for the picking. Prospecting camps—and the villages that sprouted to support these—were lawless places that cared little for officialdom. At times they were godless and guideless too; accounts frequently mention the involvement of local priests in gold smuggling. One friar's scheme involved placing nuggets in terracotta religious statues for transport to the coast. Gold fever spread fast, touching everyone. By 1700, there was a shortage of plantation hands as those who could, whether white, mulatto, freeman, or slave, escaped to head south and west for fortune. More slaves were imported to fill the worsening shortage of labor both in towns and on farms. Prices soared for nearly every commodity. In parts of Minas Gerais, famine conditions prevailed. In 1700, a dog or cat cost thirty-two drams of gold dust, the equivalent of two days' toil in the mines.

Despite the institution of draconian law to control smuggling, it was nonetheless rampant. Tax collectors, always few in number, were never able to effectively gather the "royal fifths" that the crown was legally entitled to from every parcel of gold brought in. It is reckoned that by 1704, some 30,000 people were in Minas Gerais. But in 1701, local records show that only thirty-six individuals (including two priests) bothered to pay the royal fifths. Gold dust was sifting through the hands of the crown like so many grains of beach sand.

Unlicensed smelting houses sprang up in the mining region itself as well as all along the coast. Gold bar could be obtained easily and gold dust became everyday currency for most people. Contraband gold was everywhere and colonial authorities came to recognize the futility of trying to orchestrate the chaos. Eventually, a reluctant Lisbon gave in to the logic that what benefited all in thriving Brazil would somehow, at the end of the day, benefit the crown as well.

For John Quelch and the crew of the *Charles*, cruising off the coast in November of 1703, little, if anything, about Brazil's troubles was known. Nor would it have mattered.

However, what was well known to English sailors was the appalling state of the Brazil colony's defenses. Despite the gold rush, the authorities had done little to beef up their coastal forts and towns. Local militia forces, where they did exist, were small, badly equipped, and had dubious training. Portugal had few standing military forces in the colony, mainly at larger towns such as Rio or Bahia. The Portuguese navy, anemic as it was by this time, only sent a flotilla to the colony once a year to accompany the merchant fleet back to Lisbon. This departed Portugal normally in December or January and so not reaching Brazil until February or March. Quelch's timing was perfect. The cat could be among the pigeons with scarcely a man-of-war in sight.

After leaving Noronha, Quelch sailed due west until he sighted the mainland of South America. Then, he changed course southward, the land off his starboard. They would make for Pernambuco province, the former Dutch colonial outpost that had been abandoned to the Portuguese. It is likely that he called into one or two ports soon after he made landfall in order to replenish. It is also likely that during one of these port calls that Quelch gained something else to give him the edge on his privateering cruise: a local pilot and translator.

Almost nothing is known about John Twist, the man that Quelch found. He apparently knew the Brazilian coast well and is called "pilot" by at least one of the crew. He could also speak Portuguese and English and at times is referred to as the ship's "linguister." Twist may have been an English sailor who had jumped ship years earlier in Brazil or a Portuguese who spoke English whose name the crew later anglicized. Less likely is the possibility that he had been signed on in Boston by Plowman or Quelch. Plowman had never planned to sail for Brazil and though the Brazilian cruise *may* have been Quelch's idea, the chances of finding a man in Marblehead with Twist's skills were remote.

Unfortunately for Quelch and his crew, Twist did not survive the Brazilian voyage. We do not know at what point he died or how, but his loss could have influenced the timing of the *Charles's* trip home.

However, Twist was present during the *Charles's* first capture on November 15, a small fishing shallop that was sailing a few miles off the coast at about seven degrees south latitude.

One can only imagine the apprehension of the five Portuguese men aboard her as the English brigantine hove into view. Flying English colors, the *Charles* swung alongside and hailed the little craft, making plain that they intended to board her. Several tars went over the side and clambered into the single-masted shallop.

One was Twist. Perhaps the fishermen hoped that the foreigners were merely looking to make a transaction at sea. Their fears were proved only too real when they were ordered to get aboard the *Charles* as involuntary guests. Their boat, containing only fish and salt to the value of just a few pounds, was taken in tow or else crewed by a few English sailors. Quelch's first prize was hardly worth bragging about, yet he had a sound reason for confiscating the vessel. The *Charles* now had a tender capable of reconnoitering inlets and shallow coves. It was the first vessel of what would become a small squadron for Quelch.

It is not known what the unfortunate Portuguese fishermen were told—if anything—about the reasons for their capture. Bewildered and frightened, they would have been confined below deck, awaiting their fate. Whether he felt justified in his course of action because he was taking his rightful prerogative as a privateer or because he considered it a misdemeanor of little consequence, Captain Quelch had just committed his first act of piracy.

Three days later, he found a second opportunity to make a capture. Some seventy-five miles south of where he took his first victim, the *Charles* sighted a small brigantine of about fifteen tons, and well within view of the shore. Although the capture began in the same manner as the last, this time an element of collusion came into play. Quelch, Twist, and several others boarded the brigantine from the captured shallop while the *Charles's* guns were run out and fixed on the little brigantine.

Quelch found aboard only five men, three Portuguese whites, and two blacks. This time, Twist told the Portuguese that they were English bound for the River Plate to plunder the Spaniards. This seemed to rouse the detainees who, with the exception of one of the black men, volunteered to join the crew to find their fortune. The fate of this lone dissenter was not recorded. He was either given the opportunity to swim for the shore or else joined those kept below. Indeed, there is no mention in surviving sources as to the fate of most of these victims. If they were dispatched and thrown over the side, it never came to light. More likely is the possibility that they were released at an opportune time. This was not unusual in cases of piracy during this era and often those at the lower end of the social spectrum would have fared reasonably well. There are numerous examples of pirates throughout the Golden

Age only taking what they wanted and giving the boat back to its occupants. It was more often the situation that prisoners would be murdered when they had resisted capture or had tried to hide valuables.

However, one of the sailors aboard the *Charles,* John Clifford, later recalled that the little brigantine was immediately taken up by Quelch as their third vessel. Conditions aboard the *Charles* were already becoming less cramped. Another sailor, Matthew Pimer, observed that the Portuguese apparently came to regret their decision: "Afterwards as we took Prizes, the two White Men hid themselves, that their Country-men might not see them."

Besides gaining another vessel, Quelch and his crew also acquired five chests of sugar valued at £150 and six barrels of molasses worth about £6. Certainly, it was a more lucrative haul than their first prize.

Sometime either just before or after Quelch made his second capture, it is likely that he sailed, proudly flying the flag of St. George, straight into the coastal settlements of Olinda and Recife lying on opposite banks of the Rio Capabaribe. English vessels were welcome in Brazil, even before the new treaty between England and Portugal came into existence. Quelch's commission and the ship's papers could have been presented to local officials with no qualms: they clearly indicated that the *Charles* was on the hunt for French and Spanish prey. Long suffering from the predations of French buccaneers and Spanish warships, the governor of Olinda would no doubt have welcomed the presence of the English privateer.

Although Olinda was a small town, it was the regional capital, but one held under the sway of the wealthy sugar oligarchs of the area. It, therefore, had the trappings of importance: large white-washed churches with ornate bell towers, convents, and great villas for the plantation owners that dotted the hilly and lush settlement. Neighboring Recife was the ugly relative that did all the work. The seaport was the principal loading and embarkation point for the area's sugar loaves: an overbuilt but thriving shantytown of laborers, fishermen, and small merchants. Largely built on swampy ground, Recife was situated on a spit of land that projected into the sea, flanked by the river which helped to form a natural harbor.

Quelch's chief preoccupation in visiting, other than replenishment, would have been gaining intelligence of comings and goings in the region. According to the testimony of some of the crew, Quelch did put into a few ports along the Brazilian coast, putting it about that he was privateering against the Spanish. However, in light of subsequent events, it is clear that Quelch and his crew were not particular about the nationality of their victims.

With his "cover" established, Quelch could scout out Recife and the surrounding area for fat merchant ships, preferably those carrying contraband gold.

By November 24, Quelch had sailed another seventy-five to a hundred miles down the coast but without apparent success in finding more prey. But on that day, he ran down his third victim, the largest thus far. It was again a vessel with a brigantine rig, this time weighing about forty tons. According to later testimony, it was Quelch who once again led the boarding party. No resistance was offered but this time Twist told the unfortunates that Quelch's crew were Frenchmen. This turned out to be a poor ruse when one of the Portuguese sailors recognized English being spoken and enquired as to why the English would be involved with seizing Portuguese ships. One of the *Charles's* tars, a "Dutchman" named Isaac Johnson, let slip that they were indeed Englishmen. The Portuguese were relieved of their cargo: five more chests of sugar were hauled over to the English brigantine along with a few barrels of farina and rice.

But Johnson's indiscretion had angered Quelch. Interestingly, he and the ship's anonymous quartermaster *jointly* ordered the sailor to be whipped at the mast. This is a further clue that Quelch was captain by consent and that he was following the strict pirate's code concerning the meting out of punishment. The man who actually performed the whipping was none other than Anthony Holding, alleged ringleader and the man who had ordered Captain Plowman to be locked up.

The identity of the ship's quartermaster remains problematic. However, there is good reason to suspect that the quartermaster and William Holding were one and the same man. Either mutinous ship's bully or older authority figure, or both, he would have been a logical contender for the post. As the crew member who had chief responsibility for discipline and goods held in common (including prize booty) he would have had to command the respect and fear of the entire crew and serve as a counterweight to the ship's captain.

Quelch held on to the Portuguese brigantine only a few days before giving it back to its crew. He may have also turned loose the other prisoners at this time.

Quelch's first three prizes were modest at best. But their capture and the manner in which they were taken, conforms closely to what we know about how both privateers and pirates went about their business. The truth about their tactics and methods was more often than not a far cry from popular literature and cinema.

It remains an enduring myth that most pirate victims were treasure ships. Of the thousands of vessels that fell foul of pirates and privateers between 1700 and 1725, the vast majority were small boats and merchant vessels carrying household goods, fish, grain, sugar, and rum. While it is certainly true that silver and gold were highly sought by pirates, most crews "on the account" would have to wait long and hard before snatching a prize that held such a cargo. It was far more usual that a pirate crew would squabble, disintegrate, and disband, or else be captured or killed, before they struck it rich. We associate vast hordes of gold and gems with pirates primarily because of the few celebrated instances where such treasure was seized. But few pirates had the success and good fortune of Henry "Long Ben" Avery who captured treasure worth £600,000 and then disappeared into history. And even the notorious Bartholomew "Black Bart" Roberts and Edward "Blackbeard" Teach, while making great captures in their time, both suffered the same fate: death at the hands of the authorities.

Pirates were, on the whole, opportunistic in their selection of victims. They may have sought treasure but what they needed was food, sails, rope, tar, candles, rum, and fresh water. There was no point in buying these commodities if they were there for the taking. And "taking" was all too often easily accomplished.

Most merchant crews did not resist attack by pirates. For those that did so, it was usually a bad gamble. Both pirates and privateers normally would be heavily crewed and heavily gunned, outnumbering the normal ship's complement of between six and fifteen men. Merchant sailors had no personal stake in cargoes and rightly believed that risking their life for them was a poor trade-off.

Merchant crews did not fight because they had little motivation to do so and every motivation not to. It was certainly customary by the turn of the century that those crews that resisted boarding, or who killed or wounded their attackers, would receive no mercy upon surrender. This operating principle of applied terror would grow rapidly during the first two decades of the eighteenth century. Every gruesome tale of a ship's crew tortured or slaughtered would make the rounds at seaport taverns and wharves, providing reinforcement to the belief that discretion was the better part of valor.

Quelch's use of a small boat to board one and possibly two of his first three prizes was also typical. Indeed, some pirates only ever used small open boats for their attacks. These were swift and of shallow draft, ideal for fast dashes or making an escape.

Some of Quelch's victims freely opted to join with him. Again, this was not an unusual occurrence. Many fishermen and merchant sailors felt they had little to lose in turning pirate. Apart from the freedom from ill-paid servitude, there was at least the chance of finding fortune and escaping drudgery. The wisdom of Barnaby Slush and his warning about the abuse of the hardworking tar was not hard to see, even at that time.

What *is* interesting about Quelch's tactics is what appears to be his use of English colors throughout his attacks. It was common practice for ships to carry and fly flags from many countries, as a *ruse de guerre,* and this might even explain why Quelch thought that telling his victims he was a Frenchman might be believed. Certainly, flying English colors off the coast of Brazil would have been a means of approaching his victims with less suspicion but if that were the case, why not fly the ensign of Portugal?

Some sources indicate that Quelch flew one of the earliest versions of the infamous "skull and crossbones" or "Jolly Roger," the classic black flag of pirates. There is no documentary evidence to support this and no claim of flying the black flag was ever made at the subsequent trial. Had Quelch flown the Jolly Roger, the prosecuting authorities would have been keen to make this known, even by a perjured witness. This never happened. The alleged Quelch flag, "an anatomy [skeleton] with an hourglass in one hand and a dart in the heart with three drops of blood proceeding from it in the other," although used by later pirates, appears to have been an embellishment by an Edwardian-era historian.

It is certainly true that by this time pirates were using the black flag to intimidate their intended victims. Initially, this was a flag of solid black, symbolic of fatalism—death freely dealt, and accepted, by the pirate crew. Into the first and second decades of the eighteenth century the use of the infamous Death's Head and bones became prevalent.

Red flags were also sometimes used. Referred to as the "Bloody" flag or ensign, this became a universal signal that no quarter would be given to those who resisted the attack. As such, it would be used as an additional weapon of psychological warfare to intimidate the crews of merchant ships into fast surrender. However, the red flag had an older meaning going back to the second half of the seventeenth century. It was the traditional ensign of a privateer and by the mid-1690s the English Admiralty had directed all privateers to fly the "Red Jack" in addition to the flag of St. George. To cause further confusion, there were cases of privateers flying a black flag as well, to signal that no quarter would be given to a resisting vessel.

Quelch flew neither, the only surviving references being to "English colours" being shown. This lends further credence to the theory that he was conducting himself as a privateer, albeit a sloppy one. By not using such overt symbols of piracy, was Quelch building a case of "plausible deniability" to safeguard himself?

After cruising for nearly two weeks off Pernambuco and having taken three prizes, Quelch and his little flotilla continued southward staying just in view of the Brazilian mainland. The probable destination was no doubt the waters off the principal coastal settlement in Espiritu Santo province: Rio de Janeiro. But first, they would try their luck by prowling the Bay of All Saints off Bahia, or modern-day Salvador.

As the colonial capital of Brazil, Bahia was, like Lisbon, situated on steep, hilly ground overlooking the sea. It was also wealthy and prosperous, the center of the African slave trade, South Atlantic whaling, shipbuilding, and commodities exports. It would be a promising hunting ground if they could maintain the semifiction of their anti-Spanish crusade.

But for Quelch, keeping the crew from grumbling meant making more captures and taking more booty. As November turned to December in the heat and haze of tropical blue waters, John Quelch knew that his captaincy, and possibly his life, depended upon him not being too selective about his victims. As always, this was going to require a delicate balance between prudence and risk.

Chapter Six

Patience and Plunder

O n December 5, 1703, the *Charles* was about nine miles off
the coast of Brazil at thirteen degrees south latitude. For
John Quelch, it was "lucky" thirteen.

Ten days had passed since their last capture. Now, cruising
south off Bahia, they were about to take two prizes on the same
day. The first, a shallop that had just left Bahia, fell to Quelch without a fight. He boarded her from the previously captured tender,
crewed by twenty-four hand-picked men from the *Charles*. Aboard,
he found not only three Portuguese crew but also some women passengers. However, after a quick scavenge of the open boat, all that
could be found were earthenware pots bound for some village, a
few bolts of linen cloth, and two jars of rum.

Despite the meager haul, Quelch allowed the crew and passengers to take their boat and head back to Bahia, though it is not
recorded if any suffered abuse at the hands of the pirates.

A short time later, a second victim was spotted closer toward
the shore, again, making her way out of Bahia. It was another small
shallop and Quelch in the tender steered a course to intercept her.
The Portuguese offered no resistance as Quelch overhauled the little vessel and then boarded. The story unfolds much the same as
with his previous capture. All that he found was cloth, including
some fine silk worth about £20 sterling, destined for some local
town market. But booty is booty and the quartermaster oversaw its

distribution to the crew. James Parrot later recalled that he gained a share of the silk "so much as would make a pair of breeches."

One of the pirates ripped the white heraldic ensign of Portugal from a mast stay as a souvenir while the others made the shallop ready to be towed back to the Charles to join the squadron. But in the process, something went awry and the boat's rudder was pulled off and lost. Useless to Quelch now, he gave orders for the vessel to be staved in with axes and sunk, much to the consternation of the crew and the captives alike.

Quelch had managed to snare a few prizes but he was yet to find cargo valuable enough to placate an impatient and sunburned crew. He decided to drop some canvas and wait for more ships to show themselves leaving port. He knew that the area would be profitable and so bided his time. Three days later his patience was rewarded.

This time it was a twenty-ton brigantine rig out of Bahia, crewed by just three, including one slave. The small vessel also towed along an open boat, which slowed their progress. Quelch, close-hauled in his little brigantine tender, was again personally in pursuit. And again, it was no contest.

The English sailors leapt onto the deck of the Portuguese ship, short single-edged swords and pistols drawn, and were bemused to find only a skeleton crew aboard the ship. The questioning then began, either with Twist's linguistic help or by intimidation. Quelch quickly found that the ship only carried a few barrels of rice and farina; however, the petrified crew also handed over a small canvas bag to Captain Quelch, playing the only card they had left: total compliance.

After so much fish and farina, the bag contained what he had been hoping for. It was filled with newly minted Portuguese gold coins worth around £50 sterling. This, though the equivalent of twenty times a New England sailor's monthly wage, still had to be shared out over some eighty men. Yet it was gold and it was a start. Quelch's own currency had just risen. The elation at this first taste of real treasure must have contributed to Quelch's generosity—he gave back the brigantine to the Portuguese after hauling out the grain and allowed them to sail away.

However, the black slave, a teenage boy, remained with the pirates. He was judged to be worth about £20, and as a slave, he too was a commodity. A baptized Catholic named Joachim, the boy soon found himself aboard the *Charles* where he was rechristened "Cuffee" or "Coffee" by the crew. Whereas previously he had only one master, one Joseph Galeno of Rio, now he found he had dozens. For the next few days or weeks he was forced to wait upon the entire crew.

Apart from making his captivity a life of misery, this arrangement must have eventually led to fighting amongst the crew. Quelch or the quartermaster undoubtedly intervened because within days Joachim was "sold at the mast" to one of the pirates, Benjamin Perkins. It is interesting to speculate what the other West African men on board, namely Mingo, Charles, and Caesar-Pompey, would have made of this reluctant new arrival. Indeed, we are not ever clear as to what their own status was. The story of the black crew members flows silently, and largely untold, underneath that of Quelch's. Hostages to the voyage and serving as ship's cooks and "trumpeters," Colonel Hobby's two slaves would not necessarily have been segregated from the "brotherhood" aboard ship. They were even granted shares. Plowman's cabin boy, Mingo, had witnessed his master's demise but was still a member of the ship's complement. But their station as slaves and not free men presented problems for both them and the crew. If Quelch was running as a privateer, they were still slaves. If he had turned pirate, then it was possible that they might be offered freedom *and* part of any booty in return for "signing the articles."

While there are numerous examples of mixed-race crews during piracy's Golden Age, it is still not fully understood under what circumstances black pirates fared. Confusingly, there are several scraps of evidence portraying black pirates of the period as variously free men, lower caste crew, or as outright maritime slaves. It is known that at least fifteen pirate captains during the Golden Age had black sailors under their command. The most dramatic example of this is Blackbeard's last crew in 1718, more than half of whom were black men.

Fundamentally, however, in the eighteenth century African people were a commodity to be bought and sold; slaves, while not specifically sought after by most pirates, were nonetheless taken when the situation suited. The question remains: how did white crews and captains treat blacks as living "goods" one minute and as brethren-in-arms the next? More to the point, as former slaves, how did West African pirates feel about the "theft" of other black men and women? When it came to race, the world of pirates mirrored that of European (and emerging American) society as a whole. Specific and varied circumstances often determined the treatment of blacks, sometimes for better and sometimes for worse. Many undoubtedly earned freedom and friendship in action, some were escaped slaves seeking to maintain their liberty, others remained as slaves to pirates either performing menial "landsmen" chores on ship or being sold off at the first commercial opportunity.

Quelch's attitude to the West Africans in his charge was, at best, contradictory. While one black Brazilian (who was possibly a free man) was offered a place, another was kept in bondage and auctioned off to the crew. Whatever their status was during the cruise, the slaves on the *Charles* would later play a brief but significant role in the fate of Quelch and his crew. So too, the ruling of the authorities on the status of the African men on the *Charles* would also dictate their own fate as well.

After the capture of December 9, the *Charles* resumed her southerly course along the coast. Perhaps some of the new crew members with local knowledge advocated the change of hunting grounds. It is also possible that Quelch felt uncomfortable staying overlong on any particular stretch of coast for fear of attracting retribution. All probably were aware that they still lay some distance north of the chief gold-mining district.

After a week's sailing, the *Charles* found herself in the waters near the Isle of Grande, just south of Rio. This region was well known to sailors for its verdant, steeply sloped rain forest that spilled down practically to the sea, only shallow slivers of bone-white sandy beaches separating it from the surf. More importantly, the green craggy island of Grandee itself, a short distance from the mainland and separated by a narrow channel, offered a host of sheltered inlets, fresh water, fruit, fish, and fowl. It was also a favored waypoint for French and Dutch pirates.

Strangely, despite its natural perfection, Grandee was uninhabited. This particular stretch of coast had been known to the English for some time and its geography, flora, and fauna were described with a seaman's eye for detail in the journals of William Dampier, Woodes Rogers, and Edward Cooke during their privateering expedition around the world in the same decade as Quelch's visit. In November of 1708 they stopped off on their way to the "South Sea" or Pacific Ocean, anchoring in the bay and visiting the island and the village of Angre de Reys that lay on the mainland a few miles down the coast.

Cooke described Angres de Reys as "very small, consisting of 50 or 60 houses, low built, very indifferent, with Mud Walls, and cover'd with Palmito Leaves." He remarked that it had a Franciscan monastery and two churches "decent, but not so richly adorn'd as in other Places." He also noted that the town had a guardhouse down near the landing, which housed about twenty men-at-arms under the command of a lieutenant and ensign.

Indeed, the bay must have had attraction to many. Two of Rogers's crewmen deserted while on a foraging mission on the mainland. He noted the episode in his journal, not without a little humor.

> Last night one Michael Jones and James Brown, two Irish Lands-men, run into the Woods, thinking to get away from us; the two such Sparks run away the 25th from the *Duchess,* and in the night were so frighted with Tygers, as they thought, but really by Monkeys and Baboons, that they ran into the water, hollowing to the Ship till they were fetch'd aboard again.

Moreover, this tropical paradise, lying only a ten-day march from the gold fields, made Angres a regular target for attack by brigands. Rogers wrote that: "They told us the French often sur-prise their Boats, and that at one time when the French staid to water, which could not exceed a month, they took Gold above 1200 *l.* in weight (in Boats from the Mines bound to Rio Janero, be-cause the Way is not good by Land)." In hindsight, it is tempting to consider that perhaps at least one of these raids by French pirates was a case of mistaken identity.

Quelch was off the far side of the Isle of Grandee on Decem-ber 20, 1703. Taking his command to the smaller brigantine tender, he sailed into the narrows on the mainland side and toward Angres de Reys. Just off the beach from the village, he spotted a brigantine of twenty-five tons lying at anchor. Piloting his vessel straight for it, Quelch pulled alongside while a few of his men jammed their boat hooks between the tender and the Portuguese vessel. The English shouted, cursed, and waved their cutlasses as they blooded themselves up for the fight. The Portuguese crew, in a state of complete panic, abandoned the ship even before Quelch's men could board, diving over the side and swimming for the shore. However, one man remained behind to face the pirates.

Fearlessly, he stood his ground on deck and saluted Quelch as he approached. Yet he was not defending his ship, but rather, handing it over to the attackers. He was a North European who the English first believed to be a Dutchman. Later, it transpired that he was actually a Dane, from Jutland. More than handing over the ship, he made it clear that he wanted to join the English on their voyage. There was little time for debate so close to the town and the Jutlander helped Quelch to raise anchor and set sail while the rest of the crew returned to the tender. Before the alarm could be raised in the village, Quelch fled the narrows with his prize in his wake, sailing out and around the island to rejoin the *Charles*.

Quelch's takings were reasonable: the vessel contained five chests of sugar worth about £150 and a small parcel of gold and silver worth about £50. Back on the *Charles*, the quartermaster took possession of the gold and silver, and Quelch pondered what to do with his new recruit. This took a complicated turn when the Jutlander, made of sterner stuff than most, argued his case when Quelch refused to grant him a share equal to that of the original crew members. The Jutlander threatened to inform on Quelch if he was not given his due. This proved too much for Quelch who put the man's fate to a general vote.

The Danish sailor was fortunate. The crew decided he was to be marooned rather than executed. Somewhere further down the coast, he was transferred to either the tender or the shallop along with a few of Quelch's men, and was set on shore with only the clothes on his back, a gun, powder, and some shot.

The episode is yet another indicator that Quelch's command was not that of a typical Royal Navy officer or merchant navy privateer, but instead that of a captain and crew "on the account." Pirate crews frequently put most choices to a vote where they would normally be decided solely by the captain. This covered questions such as destinations, changes of course, the fate of prisoners, or the transgressions of the captain himself. Quelch's actions in this situation (assuming that the testimony upon which they were based was true) clearly demonstrated that he had ceded much of his authority to a "cooperative" aboard the *Charles*. The presence of William Holding and his comrades loomed large in the background.

With the booty transferred to the *Charles*, the "squadron" went on the prowl once more. Quelch lingered at this latitude for some two weeks, but no further prizes were taken. Impatient, the crew probably agitated for a resumption of the journey southward. On January 15, 1704—notated in the "Old Style" as 1703/4—a new victim was sighted at about twenty-four degrees south latitude, not far from the Isle of Sao Sebastiao. It was a small brigantine making its way northward about two miles off the shoreline. Quelch's ships gave chase.

As the Portuguese vessel was overhauled, ten pirates were detailed for the shallop to serve as boarders. This time, Quelch remained on the deck of the *Charles*, following events through his glass. The little brigantine was seized without a fight, despite being crewed by fourteen men. The pirates also discovered two women aboard "of good fashion."

By the time Quelch boarded the prize, some minutes later, there was mayhem on the deck as the English capered and danced, laughing and shouting. The tiny ship's cargo was found and the tars had ripped open the small canvas bags to learn straight away that it was a fortune. It was the treasure that they had been dreaming of for six months. It was gold dust—lots of it.

Quelch and the quartermaster restored order and then quickly took personal charge of the treasure. After Quelch's arrival, even more was found. According to later recollections in Boston, when weighed aboard the *Charles*, it proves to be "one hundred weight" or nearly 112 pounds (fifty-one kilos) of gold dust. In addition, there are 900 pieces of gold coin, all minted in the last year or two. Together, the haul is worth between £7,000 and £10,000. It is a staggering amount of money by the standards of the time. Even in London, a family of the lower middle-class could exist comfortably for a year on £25. Successful merchants in England typically earned anything between £200 and £400 per year. Life in the colonies, more austere than that of the London metropolis, was even cheaper. Every member of the crew of the *Charles* was now a wealthy man by any standard of measurement and none more so than Captain Quelch.

Exactly how much gold was taken from this ship will probably never be known. Once back in Boston, the person or persons who knew the true amount of the treasure, beginning with Quelch himself, would be at a distinct advantage in determining the accounts payable—including rightful shares. The devil was in the details, or more accurately, in the numbers. From the point this treasure was captured, it was in constant danger of being "siphoned" by those with access to it. Moreover, the whole issue would be moot in the event that Quelch truly turned pirate, holding the entire fortune for him and his crew. The mystery of Quelch's gold was only just beginning.

To put this treasure in perspective, it is necessary to compare it with other pirate captures of the era. Although most pirate hauls were of commodities and not treasure, without doubt, the most lucrative pirate cruises were those to the Indian Ocean. In the last few years of the seventeenth century, pirate attacks on the annual Muslim pilgrim fleets yielded some fabulous hauls of gold and precious gems. Pirate captain James Gilliam reportedly took some £2 million off the coast of Madagascar in 1699; Henry Avery stole some £325,000 off from just one Muslim treasure ship in 1695; and Edward England reportedly took diamonds worth a few million on the same route in 1720.

Such vast plunder is indeed the stuff of pirate legend but these examples must be treated cautiously. There are virtually no records of these stupendous cargoes and, not surprisingly, pirates kept no accounts of their illicit transactions and disposals. Oft-mentioned figures for pirate hauls are based on contemporary reports that were themselves rumor and conjecture. Pirates, when successful, usually squandered their wealth or lost it to the elements.

We are on more certain ground with the more modest hauls attributed to other well-known pirates such as Thomas Tew who captured £60,000 in 1695 or Sam Bellamy who made off with £20,000 in 1717. Official reckonings, when available, prove disappointing: Blackbeard's treasure, *including* his vessel, was worth only £2,500 when tallied by the authorities in Virginia.

In terms of wealth, John Quelch was certainly no Avery or Gilliam, nor did he achieve the notoriety of Kidd or Blackbeard.

However, his captures, which *are* documented, position him as one of the more successful, if anonymous, pirates (or privateers), of the Golden Age.

After a night of raucous carousing, and in all likelihood, the drinking dry of the last of the jars of captured rum (one worries about the fate of the two women captives) Quelch was magnanimous in the aftermath of his conquest. He gave back the prize brigantine to its crew and released all the prisoners. He, the quartermaster, and the ship's carpenter then divided up the gold dust and coin among the crew according to the agreed-upon share system. No man wished to leave his fortune in commune for the remainder of the cruise lest it be lost to weather or fate. While one might regard this as prudent, it also left the crew open to violent accusations of thievery against one another. However, given the known punishment for such a transgression, it cannot be considered unusual that no mention of any such act is recorded on the *Charles*.

Having made an astounding capture—and perhaps because of it—Quelch set his course again for the south, leaving behind the Tropic of Capricorn. He had now fully redeemed himself in the eyes of his crew. Such a haul gave him the personal credibility he needed to more freely propose the next moves without argument from the ringleaders. It was time to make for the River Plate, time to find Spanish prey, and clothe the nakedness of the lie they were living.

Chapter Seven

"Kill Him"

A s he peered through the slightly blurred, imperfect lens of the spyglass, Captain Bastian could barely discern the vessel that lay far off astern his own ship. At this distance, at least some three or four leagues—nine to twelve miles in modern terms—he could not even tell for certain whether she was a two-master or three. But whatever she was, she had piled on the canvas and against the lapis blue sky of a February day she stood out bright and white on the horizon.

Off his port side, just out of view due to the curve of the Earth's surface, the *Rio de la Plata* spilled into the sea. A vast river, over 150 miles wide at its mouth, it cuts deep into the South American continent. The western bank lay under Spanish domination while *La Banda Oriental*—the eastern shore—was a hodgepodge of Spanish outposts and those of his own country, Portugal. He was only twenty-four hours out of the port of *Nova Colonia do Sacramento* and though he had managed a decent night's rest in his cabin he was still tired from the previous day's labors at the fort. There, he had shouted himself hoarse directing the stevedores and slaves in the loading of a hundred bales of tanned leather and dozens of barrels of tallow and cured beef. Now his 200-ton ship, fully laden, ploughed the waves of the South Atlantic on a northeasterly course, bound for the colonial capital Bahia.

But she was low in the water and battling against the prevailing warm currents from the north. His journey might last weeks and he would have to play the winds carefully so as not to bleed-off too much speed. He knew well how fickle the breezes were on this stretch of the coast, often contrary and requiring deft seamanship. Far better once he had rounded the coast above Rio de Janeiro where the trade winds would gently push him from behind. And with the coast of the *Plata* barely out of sight, his voyage was only just beginning. It was too early and damned poor luck, to have to contend with an unknown vessel.

He lowered the spyglass and cast his eye about the deck. Emanuel, his black cabin boy (and slave) was dunking a hand-line over the side, trawling for his supper. The odds were good he would be eating fresh white fish. These waters held huge numbers of fish, especially anchovy and hake, encouraged by the great algae blooms at the mouth of the river that attracted the smaller prey of the larger species.

The rest of his crew, numbering thirty-five, were scattered above and below decks, aloft in the rigging and at the tiller and compass at the stern. Thirty-five was a hefty crew for a ship of this size. He could have shipped easily with a third less men, but times were dangerous and profits were tight. He'd rather have a strong crew on hand than risk losing his cargo. Scrimping on crew might mean more money in his own purse, but if things went badly, a storm or a bloody-minded Spaniard for instance, he would have fewer hands to save the situation. He knew the risks.

The helmsman at the tiller kept watch on the sails over his head. Looking like a giant's crossbow, the ship's tiller was connected to the great rudder at the stern and held steady by a rig of ropes and blocks. The helmsman gripped the carved finial of the ten-foot piece of timber with both his gnarled hands. By watching how the canvas held the wind, whether billowing fully or flapping madly, he was able to push or pull the tiller and point the bow so as to fill the sails while still holding course.

Bastian had heard on his last voyage to Bahia that a French merchantman had recently arrived at the port fitted with a remarkable means of steering. The rig resembled a ship's capstan (the turnstile used to raise the anchor) lying on its side and connected to the rudder by means of lines and pulleys. The helmsman would turn the contraption by the handling pegs that studded the circumference of the device, winding the lines and so turning the rudder. It was called the ship's "wheel." Whether or not the invention would catch on with the rest of the world, he did not know.

He ordered a lookout aloft the mainmast to keep the unknown vessel in view and to identify her if and when she drew closer. She might be a Spaniard hauling for the River Plate, in which case she would eventually pass behind them. Equally, she could be a French or Dutch pirate on the prowl even though he was well south of the usual cruising grounds of such brigands.

It was of little use waiting to see what colors she bore from her spritsail topmast. Most vessels carried with them the flags of half a dozen nations to confuse other ships. A pirate might fly an ensign to match its prey and lull the unwary. It was wiser to judge a friend from a foe by the rig of her sails or the design of her prow.

He thought about the value of the cargo he bore in his hold, a large sum that he had given bond for. He also thought about the little extra something that he had secreted in his cabin: A large leather purse of 200 gold Spanish *escudos*. Like many masters on the Brazil coast, Captain Bastian always hedged against a drop in commodities by smuggling gold each voyage. Little did it matter to him whether it was Portuguese or Spanish coin.

Captain Bastian gave orders to put on as much sail as his ship would bear. And he prayed that the distance between him and the stranger would not grow smaller. It was an unfortunate fact of life that the sight of a fellow seafarer on the vast rolling expanse of blue was not a cause for cheer, but rather, a cause for suspicion and dread.

On the contrary, from the view of Captain John Quelch's spyglass, the large merchant ship was a very welcome sight. He had not taken a prize in a month, despite the fact that he was now mainly in Spanish waters (though these were still contested with Portugal). The windfall of gold dust from the last prize had kept the crew both merry and diligent, but with each passing day the restlessness was growing again. Moreover, Quelch must have been beginning to worry about the chances of taking a Spanish vessel as the days went by. He needed a ship's papers or an ensign to help cover his tracks. Without these, his alibi would be a slim one indeed.

The position of the *Charles* gave him cause to be confident. In addition to Spanish settlements in the area, the River Plate was also the "back door" to the Viceroyalty of Peru. The southern route for the export of Peruvian gold, shipped downriver after a mountain trek, was still quicker than any other way back to Spain. For Quelch, cruising off the mouth of the great river, it was just a matter of time until he spotted a ship with Andean treasures aboard.

Now, they had a likely treasure ship within their reach. Quelch's intention was undoubtedly to keep his prey between him and the shoreline. By doing so, he could attempt to maneuver up-wind of the other vessel and gain "the weather gauge." If the wind was blowing toward the shore, then Quelch could bear down with all speed on his prey. The other captain would drastically lose speed when he tacked to change course in order to "break out" for open water. Catching an enemy "on a lee shore" was a classic naval tactic; Captain Bastian had to run fast, then cut out in front of Quelch, or risk being driven onto the beach or the rocks.

Quelch or his sailing master gave the command to lay on all canvas and the smaller brigantine tender did the same, two hounds running for the stag. Captain Bastian was a skilled mariner and for more than a day kept his vessel on course and out of reach of his unknown pursuer. But as the distance narrowed slowly on day two, Bastian would now have clearly seen that *two* vessels were closing on him. He would have also now seen that they were flying English colors. While he could not have known for sure this was a ruse, the clear intention of these vessels was to intercept his own and that could be no good thing under any circumstances.

As the afternoon wore on and the two English vessels drew nearer to their victim, the deck of the Portuguese ship must have been the scene of anxiety, anger, fear, and confusion. With his pursuers practically in hailing distance, Bastian ordered the Portuguese ensign to be raised aloft. It was a last gamble to convince Quelch that he was no Spaniard and, therefore, not fair game to the English. When that failed to dissuade the English from breaking off the pursuit, he gave orders to run out the guns on the starboard side.

Meanwhile, aboard the *Charles*, all hands were preparing for what was likely to be their first real taste of battle. Until then, their quarry had been smaller and weaker. They were now about to engage a larger vessel with some dozen cannon and a crew of unknown size. If they were to take this prize they would have to fight for it. Quelch had his gun crew ready as he bore down on the

Portuguese vessel. Disappointed as he was that it is not a Spaniard, he had come too far to break off now.

Before the ships were even alongside, a shot rang out from the Portuguese ship and passed far out over the bow of the *Charles*. As the *Charles* finally started to overhaul the merchant ship, another gun was fired, barely missing them. The English gunners had readied their pieces some minutes or hours earlier and Quelch gave the order to return fire. Not yet level with the Portuguese, the *Charles* would have fired off one of its smaller bow guns, perhaps a swivel gun on the railing, aiming for the deck of the enemy vessel. The object, at this point, was not to sink or disable the Portuguese (unlikely anyway with such a small piece), but to persuade her captain and crew to stand down and surrender.

The English tars swarmed onto the deck; those not manning the guns stood ready as boarders, armed with grapples, boat hooks, axes, cutlasses, and pistols, eager to join the fray or else filled with trepidation about the prospects of hand-to-hand fighting. Far from the vision of romantic swashbucklers swinging from ratlines and engaging in feats of magnificent and coldly perfect swordsmanship, the reality of combat aboard ship was much more brutal and horrific.

Even a good swordsman would be challenged by the conditions of naval combat. Apart from heaving, slippery decks (first with water, then with blood) the cramped confines of the ship dictated a different manner of fighting—with weapons to match. The cutlass was by this time already the edged weapon of choice of sailors. A derivative of the hunting "hangar" of the early seventeenth-century that found favor among foot soldiers, the cutlass was often single-edged with a blade length of between two and two-and-a-half feet. The hilt and grip could be a simple brass bar and knuckle bow or a more elaborate affair with a scalloped-shell plate or a full basket hilt of iron. Short and stiff, such a weapon was equally adept for thrusting, hacking, or blocking in close quarters. Fights were often a two-handed business, and a sailor might be armed not only with cutlass in one hand but with a pistol, knife, or another sword in the other—or even just a fist.

Swords of this type inflict gaping wounds and broken bones, and given the lack of hygiene or antiseptics of the day, even nonlife-threatening wounds could turn rapidly gangrenous and mortal. Serious cuts could only be treated by cauterization or amputation. Blackbeard's last fight proved a graphic example of the ferociousness of swordplay during the Golden Age. In 1718, an embattled Blackbeard found himself up against several opponents simultaneously. A sword thrust by Lieutenant Maynard of the British sloop *Jane* struck Blackbeard's cartridge box on his belt and bent nearly double. Maynard stepped back and fired the pistol in his other hand, wounding the pirate. At the same time, another Royal Navy man thrust at Blackbeard, cutting his face. Still another, a Scot, came at Blackbeard with a broadsword.

According to a contemporary account, "One of Maynard's men being a Highlander, engaged Teach with his broad sword, who gave Teach a cut on the neck, Teach saying 'well done, lad'; the Highlander replied, 'If it be not well done, I'll do it better.' With that he gave him a second stroke, which cut off his head, laying it flat on his shoulder."

Maynard later said that Blackbeard fell dead with five pistol balls in him and twenty cuts in his body. This was all a far cry from a gentlemen's duel on land with small swords, the whisking metallic "conversation" of the blades sounding with every thrust, parry, and riposte. This was butchery.

It is likely that some of Quelch's crew would have experienced this sort of action in their careers at sea, but equally, many would have not. Gripping their weapons and shouting their bravado, the crew depended upon their camaraderie to see them through as they closed with their enemy. As a third shot whistled over the *Charles*, zipping past the foremast and rigging, Quelch may have now been able to lay one of his main deck three- or four-pounders (known as "minions") on the stern of the enemy vessel.

Loading, sighting, and firing an iron cannon on the heaving deck of a ship at sea was a complicated exercise—and one fraught with danger to the giver as much as to the recipient. Having been pulled in from the gun port using block and tackle, gunpowder filled canvas or paper sacks, called cartridges, would be rammed down the gun's muzzle. The shot, whether a single ball or a canister filled with smaller balls or nails, would be rammed down next, followed by a canvas wad to secure the load.

Next, the crew would haul on the ropes and pulleys, running the four-wheeled gun out the port on its wooden "truck." Finally, a handspike would be shoved into the touchhole, penetrating the powder cartridge in anticipation of the primer: finer-grain gunpowder poured out from a horn down into the touchhole. Sighting or "laying" the gun was accomplished—with some art—by means of "quoins," a simple wedge of wood that could be pulled or pushed to raise or lower the elevation of the cannon on its wooden truck as the gun master looked down its length.

When ready, a lit match cord, impregnated with saltpeter to keep the spark alive, was thrust to the touchhole. With luck, after a half-second pause, the main charge would ignite, firing the gun with a large tongue of flame and a huge cloud of billowing yellowish-white smoke. If accidentally contaminated by water, or if it was too old, the powder might not ignite at all. Equally, if the gun had developed cracks or was overheated, it could blow up, killing its crew.

Quelch managed to loose off one or two rounds of his guns, but caused little or no harm to the Portuguese vessel or its crew. However, the Portuguese ship stopped firing after its third round, some of its sails dropping. The *Charles* pulled alongside and grappled its victim as the vessels slowed, the English ship lowering its own sails while her sailors prepared to jump across the groaning and scraping hulls.

The engagement that followed was swift and decisive, but what exactly occurred in the minutes before the final attack and during the raid itself, remains a partial mystery. There is some evidence that indicates a possible mutiny on the merchantman even before the English boarded her.

According to the later testimony of the Brazilian slave boy, Emanuel, one of the English crew leveled a pistol at Captain Bastian as soon as the pirates had spread out on the deck of the merchant ship. Emanuel recalled that he heard someone shout, "Kill him!" and after a single shot in the chest, Bastian fell to the deck dead. That the skirmish ended as quickly as it had begun is not questioned. No members of Quelch's crew were killed and other than the death of Bastian, only two Portuguese sailors were wounded. It is unlikely that the Portuguese put up a struggle at all.

Even the pirates could not agree on who had actually killed Bastian. Emanuel fingered Christopher Scudamore, the cooper on the *Charles*, as the man who pulled the trigger, but Scudamore later vehemently denied the murder. Moreover, how could someone who knew no English recognize the phrase "kill him" when it was shouted out? Matthew Pimer testified that "there was a Controversie on Board our Briganteen concerning who it was that kill'd the Captain ... Scudamore saying it was he, and another said it was he that did it." Some of the crew thought that Bastian had been wounded before they had boarded—meaning that his own men had attacked him. Had Bastian been caught up in a violent argument with his crew about whether to surrender the ship? Knowing that most victims of pirate attacks did *not* resist, there is a possibility that Bastian led the defense of his vessel single-handed, and paid the final price. Wounded by a terrified compatriot or not, there is no doubt that one of the English tars did shoot Bastian.

Quelch, for whatever reason, was late arriving on the enemy ship, striding across the deck armed with a brace of pistols and a cutlass in his belt. Bastian was already dead and the Portuguese sailors were lying or kneeling on the deck, hands spread wide. Bastian's body was immediately heaved over the side and into the sea. With the prisoners secured, Quelch and his crew searched the prize.

It is a good haul. They carried off barrels, dried beef, beer, a dozen small arms, four cannon and four smaller swivel guns, gunpowder and shot, and a new mainsail, foresail, and foretopsail. All told, the arms and provisions were worth some £90. The victory was made complete when after a search of the great cabin, Bastian's sack of money was found. Quelch finally had his Spanish gold but he neither had a Spanish ship nor, more importantly, Spanish papers to prove it.

Emanuel, who had witnessed the slaying of his master, was subjected to the same fate as the previous captured slave: he was auctioned before the mast and sold to a crew member, one George Norton. It is not recorded what price he was sold for, but later, Emanuel's value was assessed at £40—less than half of what the provisions and stores were worth.

Quelch held onto the captured ship and its prisoners for some time, perhaps as long as a few weeks. With the smaller brigantine and the 200-ton, three-masted ship, he now had three sizeable vessels plus possibly a smaller shallop too. But his crew was now thinly strung-out manning this entire squadron. Still, he could intimidate the Spanish or Portuguese and with eighty men, could at least manage to sail all three vessels even if not lead them into any major engagement.

Unfortunately for the *Charles*, the sea ran dry of victims. The Plata did not reveal any other prizes, whether fair or foul. After some two weeks, Quelch decided to head north again. Somewhere along the route, he decided to turn loose Bastian's ship, handing her back to the prisoners. What had determined his course of action? Although it may have been coincidental, the warrant that he had "inherited" from Captain Plowman had a life of six months. This meant that it had now run out, probably in late January. Any ships he took now—whether Portuguese, French, or Spanish—would not be legal prizes. His last fig leaf had blown away.

With the South American winter slowly coming on, the weather turning wet and squally, and no sails on the horizon, Quelch's options were getting few. Yet, if he retraced his route north, although slow, he would eventually pick up the southerly trade winds above Rio. These would speed up their progress to the Caribbean and North Atlantic.

But John Quelch made a decision, in full concordance with the majority of his crew, which few would have expected him to make after the adventures of the previous seven months.

They were going home—to Massachusetts.

PURSUIT

Chapter Eight

Diaspora

John Campbell, a bookseller and the second official postmaster in Boston history, would not have dreamt that he was creating an institution when he started *The Boston News-Letter* in April 1704. A one-page broadsheet, printed on both sides and combining news both foreign and domestic, it was the first regularly published newspaper in America. Winging its way around town and country each week, copies smudged by the hands of countless readers as it was passed along from toper to toper at coffee or ale house; the newsletter remained in continuous circulation until 1776. Its publication was in that year, sadly, interrupted by the War of Independence, the blockade of Boston, and the subsequent collapse of the Boston economy.

Campbell, as postmaster, was well placed to be the editor of a newspaper. The New England colonies had only recently set up a regular postal system and this depended upon known drop-off and pickup points for the mail to be distributed—usually at taverns or inns. Dispatch riders would make weekly or biweekly runs between Boston, Providence, New London, and New York, exchanging incoming and outgoing post before continuing the next leg of the journey and picking up spoken "news" as they went along. No one in Boston had a better intelligence service than the postmaster. He knew, practically before anyone else, the coming and goings of ships across the region, official announcements, tall tales, word of accidents or Indian attacks, and the deaths of notable citizens.

And the mail service was rapid by the conventions of the time. News could be passed between Boston, and Providence or Newport, Rhode Island, for example, in not much more than a day. Dispatch riders would often travel evenings as well as by day along the early turnpikes and post roads, and these often muddy and deeply rutted by carts, or so narrow as to make riding abreast difficult. In winter, ramshackle bridges, rotted or covered in ice, presented treacherous going for both the rider and the horse. Larger rivers required crossing by either fording or ferry, weather permitting, with the ever-present hazard of being swept away to a watery death.

Sarah Kemble Knight, a wealthy thirty-eight-year-old widow, plucky, opinionated, but observant, kept a remarkable diary of a journey she made—without a chaperone—from Boston to New Haven in October of 1704. It was a journey of some 200 miles and for most of her trip she traveled with the post riders, from stage to stage, and somehow managing to keep up despite the fact that they "Rode very hard." Her account provides an insight into the extent of the wilderness that was New England at that time: untamed country from the point where a village or town ended. It was an adventure.

> I askt him of the rest of the Rode, foreseeing wee must travail in the night. Hee told mee there was a bad River we were to Ride thro', which was so very firce a hors could sometimes hardly stem it: But it was but narrow, and wee should soon be over. I cannot express The concern of mind this relation sett me in.

Travel by night, necessary to cover the distances in the shortest time, afforded its own peculiar dread in a world without electric light:

> The only Glimering we now had was from the spangled Skies, Whose Imperfect Reflections rendered every Object formidable. Each lifeless Trunk, with its shatter'd Limbs, appear'd an Armed Enymie; and every little stump like a Ravenous devourer. Nor could I so much as discern my Guide, when at any distance, which added to the terror.

Given the arduousness of a trek through the interior, aggravated by continuing Indian raids, it is no surprise that most commerce traveled by coastal sloop and shallop. The post riders, wrapped up in their oilcloth capes, armed with pistol, and slinging a brass horn that they sounded at each stop off, formed a tenuous but determined long-distance link across the colonies.

Fortified by the services of the post riders, *The Boston News-Letter* was the mouthpiece of the governor (when required), gazetteer, shipping log, court register, and town notice board, all in one. Campbell modeled it on the longstanding *London Gazette,* copying wholesale the two-column layout, typeface, and banner, even the "Published by Authority" tagline. The latter meant it had the blessing of the Governor's Council: by practicing self-censorship the *Boston News-Letter* avoided the fate of an even earlier paper that had been ordered to shut down under Governor Andros.

But self-preservation was not the only reason for its lack of criticism of the authorities. Campbell was a supporter of the governor's circle, and, as a member of the "royalist" or Tory Anglican congregation in Boston, also at odds with the Puritans for the soul of Massachusetts. This safe approach to publishing did not make for the most exciting periodical. Cotton Mather, who had an opinion on just about everything, described it using terms such as "paltry" and "filthy and foolish." It was, he said, "a thin sort of diet." Its general dullness notwithstanding, the publication can also claim another "first" in American history: it was the first regular vehicle for advertising, and this included advertisements for the sale of slaves, an inauspicious start for the media industry.

The Boston News-Letter is more than a snapshot in time, it is a glimpse of the *worldview* of New Englanders, and particularly, of what they found threatening to their society, both internally and externally. The fifth issue of the newsletter, for the week of May 15, 1704, was filled with events grand and mundane, glorious and tragic. Campbell's lead article was a copy of a fulsome and loyal address from the House of Lords to Queen Anne, followed by her gracious reply. Unfortunately, this dated from mid-November last, hardly breaking news even by the standards of the day.

Of more relevance, in column two, we learn of enemy attacks, both in New Hampshire and in Massachusetts. From the town of Northampton, some sixty miles due west of Boston, came news, just two days old:

A Company of Indians and French, between day break and Sunrising, about 60 Set upon a Garrison-house of Benj. Jone's, about two

Miles from the body of the Town, and set fire to it ere they were aware of it; Kill'd and carryed Captive about 30 Persons. The Town, being Alarmed, pursued them, the Enemy finding it, scattered themselves into parties; and so did the English into Ten in a Company, pursuing them; Capt. Taylor was kill'd in the pursuit.

The story was similar from New Hampshire, where news came from Wells, Maine, that Indians, a "Sculking Adversary" as Campbell labeled them, set upon several soldiers who were guarding cattle of the settlement. Two Englishmen were killed and one was taken captive but before the rest of the militia could assemble, the enemy had withdrawn. Campbell also announced that the governor's council had declared the upcoming eighteenth of the month to be a day of public fasting with prayer. Most of the Puritan divines in Boston lamented the continuing attacks of French and Indians as God's punishment for the community's own sinfulness. This was an affliction made more vexing by an enemy that did not fight like Englishmen, but rather, struck silently and swiftly in the dead of night or early morning before melting away into the wilderness.

Yet, New Englanders were no safer further afield. Campbell details a lengthy story of the adventures of one Jacob Fowle of Marblehead, recently, and miraculously, returned from the Caribbean. He had been taken prisoner by the Spaniards and sent to the mines of New Spain, more often than not a one-way trip for those unlucky enough to find themselves in such circumstances. However, his trade as a sailmaker saved his life; he was put to work mending canvas and eventually put on a ship again (albeit a Spanish one). After a daring escape and several subsequent hairbreadth scrapes, he had finally returned to Massachusetts to tell his tale.

The rest of the issue was devoted chiefly to shipping notices. These were delivered in perfunctory style, bereft of line breaks or sometimes even of punctuation, a catalogue of the comings and goings from ports up and down the coast. A determined local reader possessed of a good memory would have spied, early down in the column, one entry of particular note: "Arrived at Marble-head, Capt. Quelch in the Brigantine that Capt. Plowman went out in, are said to come from New Spain & have made a good Voyage."

In a strange coincidence, the address by Parliament in this same issue makes a reference to "the late Alliance with the King of

Portugal." These two small and unrelated details of recent and not so recent events one on the front page and one buried at the back, would shortly take on a whole new significance for the people of Boston.

Sometime around May 14, the men of the *Charles* sighted once again the Province of Massachusetts. The little brigantine had covered some 13,500 miles in just under a year at sea. For the last of their journey they were back in familiar waters having sailed through Crab Bank, past the unbroken white sandy beaches of Cape Cod and around its tip off Provincetown before entering Massachusetts Bay. Several hours later, the rocky coastline of the north shore would have appeared on their horizon, and soon, Halfway Rock, where Captain Plowman's bones lay somewhere on the bottom, picked clean after a year in the deep. They were nearly home.

Battered and weatherworn by the Atlantic—like her crew—the vessel pushed on the last few leagues to the port from where she had departed so many months before. The few Marblehead boys in the crew must have been ecstatic at the prospect of seeing family and loved ones again in the old town. The majority, from other ports along the coast, probably were laying plans for where they would next go, and how they would spend their newfound fortunes. But despite the good feelings that a homecoming engendered, there must have been a ripple of doubt among the crew, especially below decks, concerning the nature of their reception. After all, they had not done *exactly* what they had set out to do. And then, worryingly, on the return leg once they had reached the latitude of Bermuda, there had been a lecture by Captain Quelch with all hands assembled on deck.

According to the later testimony of crew members Matthew Pimer and John Clifford, Anthony Holding assembled all the crew topside before Quelch came to them to deliver his address. That Holding gathered the crew is yet another indicator that he was the quartermaster of the vessel or at least the quartermaster's right-hand man. As the ship's enforcer, Holding must have been an intimidating and brutal mariner. To some extent, Quelch owed his captaincy of the vessel to Holding, as well as his longevity in keeping it. Once the mumbling and jibing had been silenced by Holding, Quelch spoke up to tell them of the importance of keeping their stories straight once they landed home again.

Quelch told them to say that "we had met with some Indians who had got great Treasure out of a Wreck, of whom we had our Gold." This concocted tale of chancing upon a recent Spanish shipwreck in the West Indies and being assisted by friendly Carib tribesmen must have amused some of the crew. But others would have read between the lines and started thinking hard about why they needed such an alibi at all. Pimer, who had been shipped personally by Captain Plowman, told how he was upbraided by shipmate Peterson when he appeared late on the deck for the briefing. He had kept a journal of the voyage, probably as a result of Whiting being incapacitated for most of the cruise. Whether he was ordered by Quelch to serve in this capacity or that he had voluntarily begun such a journal already, is not known. At any rate, in front of the assembled crew, Quelch, at the behest of the ship's company, demanded that Pimer tear out the pages "lest I had Writ something that might do them damage" as he later recalled.

When Pimer refused to do so, Quelch seized the journal from him and tore out the offending pages himself: all those covering the taking of the Portuguese vessels. He then demanded that any of the crew who held "Portuguese prints" should throw them overboard. All traces of the Portuguese being the source of their fortune would have to be gotten rid of. This was a dramatic, almost theatrical action by Quelch, one that spoke volumes for the seriousness of their situation. For some of the crew, it must have planted the first seeds of doubt. However, their commander remained optimistic. He knew from previous experience that when it came to bringing in gold and silver to the province, most people would ask few questions, the selfsame metals being a convincing emollient. The return was a risk, but it was a risk he was willing to take.

An "old hand" of New England ports, Quelch's decision to return home may be less bizarre than one might think. He undoubtedly would have been aware of recent celebrated examples of "privateers" that had sailed into New York and Newport to receive a wink and a nudge from the authorities (after handing over a cut of the booty).

Privateersmen, both small and great, had been sailing in and out of New England for some twenty years armed with commissions from colonial governors. The rules of the game were strict but simple. Make friends in high places, bribe a legitimate privateer's commission, sail under pretences, attack whomever you choose, then return home and pay off your backers and the authorities. Captain Kidd is probably the best known of these privateersmen today, having been double-crossed by the Earl of Bellomont, governor of New England and New York, and sent back to London for trial and execution in 1700. Some Yankee mariners, including Quelch, may have considered Kidd's fate an aberration. Perhaps he had broken the rules. The real facts concerning Kidd's case did not come out until many years later. For locals, a more relevant model of an enterprising privateer was Thomas Tew.

Tew came from a respectable and long-established family in Newport, Rhode Island. He went to sea to find his fortune in 1691, eventually gaining a part share in a privateering sloop out of Bermuda. These early days taught him the value of coopting the authorities and one of his business partners in the sloop, the *Amity*, was a member of the governor of Bermuda's council, thereby easing the grant of a privateering commission against the Spanish and the French.

He and his crew were soon off to prowl the Arabian Sea to rob Muslim treasure ships. As luck would have it, his first capture was an Arab merchant vessel that although heavily armed, put up little fight. Suffering no losses on his side, the bold action netted a vast quantity of gold and jewels. As noted by Captain Charles Johnson, in his authoritative 1726 *History of the Pyrates*:

> In rummaging this Prize, the Pyrates threw over a great many rich Bales, to search for Gold, Silver and Jewels; and, having taken what they thought proper, together with the Powder, part of which (as being more than they could handsomely stow) they threw into the Sea; they left her, sharing 3,000 *l*. Sterling a Man.

Tew, as captain, came away from the vessel some £8,000 richer. Far from preying on French privateers and pirates as were his orders, he fell in with them instead. He chanced upon Captain Mission, a well-known pirate commander of the *Victoire*, and joined with him in further attacks upon Arab vessels. Such was their love of liberty (or their need for cheap labor) that they also attacked slave ships off the Guinea coast, unshackling the unfortunate Africans and offering them billets as crew and passage as free men.

The two captains and their crews based themselves in Madagascar, already infamous as a pirate kingdom where bands of Anglo-American, French, and Dutch buccaneers (and freed slaves) coexisted peacefully, living a "counter-culture" lifestyle that included polygamy, open homosexuality, and egalitarian self-rule (which meant few rules). After a year of cruising and carousing in Madagascar's roughhewn settlements and pirate fortresses, Tew and the *Amity* returned to the Atlantic out of a combination of homesickness and a desire to spend their treasure where there were actually things worth buying. His plan was to stock up on ship supplies, clothes, and luxuries and bring them back to Madagascar for sale.

Blown northwards while trying to return to Bermuda, Tew ended up changing course and making for Rhode Island instead. He was heartily welcomed from his successful "privateering" adventure by the Newport community and he immediately sent word to Bermuda to his old business partners to send their agents to Rhode Island to collect their share of the treasure (some of which he buried in his backyard). The agents of the owners, including that of the governor's advisor, duly came to Newport and claimed their prizes.

Not one to stay at home overlong, Tew was soon out trying to get a new commission from colonial governors. Turned down by Governor Bellomont in Boston, he had better luck in his native colony of Rhode Island. Governor John Easton was more than happy to oblige Tew—at a fee of £500. Tew also journeyed to New York to meet with wealthy merchants to entice them into investing in his next expedition. He had little trouble convincing them to do so. The biggest investor was one Frederick Phillips. He was later rumored to have amassed an estate worth £100,000 from his Madagascar trade with the pirates.

Tew had a new ship and was soon back in the Madagascar colony, named "Libertatia." Reunited with Captain Mission, they went on the prowl again and captured new treasure: diamonds, gold bullion, silks, and spices. A few months later, a Malagasy native rampage destroyed the Libertatia settlement and Tew was finally soured on remaining.

Returning to Newport with his men and with most of their treasure intact, Tew's crew went their separate ways and he himself decided it was time for a life of leisure. The authorities showed no interest in probing the source of his wealth, no doubt due to Tew's generosity. But pirates and their wealth are soon parted. After a year or so, some of his old shipmates began calling at his house in Newport. Captain Johnson summed up the result:

> But those of his Men, who lived near him, having squandered their Shares, were continually solliciting him to take another Trip: He withstood their Request a considerable Time; but they having got together (by the Report they made of the vast Riches to be acquired) a number of resolute Fellows, they, in a Body, begg'd him to head them but for one Voyage. They were so earnest in their Desire, that he could not refute complying.

Tew was hooked. Already familiar with the merchant community in New York, and having disposed of his diamond hoard there, he approached Governor Benjamin Fletcher, a man with a reputation for doing business that was less than ethical. In November 1694, Fletcher sold Tew a new privateer's commission for £300, a better deal than even that offered in Rhode Island. Fletcher, later indicted for his shady dealings, defended his decision. "Tew appeared to me," he wrote, "not only a man of courage and activity, but of the greatest sense and remembrance of what he had seen of any seaman that I ever met with. He was also what is called a very pleasant man."

In early 1695, Tew and his crew of forty aboard the *Amity* were again cruising the Red Sea, this time as part of the squadron of the celebrated Long Ben Avery. Tew's story ends shortly thereafter for he is believed to have been killed in action sometime later that year, according to contemporary reports although this was never confirmed. Johnson's later account concluded, "They met with, and attack'd a Ship belonging to the Great Mogul; in the Engagement, a Shot carried away the Rim of Tew's Belly, who held his Bowels with his Hands some small Space; when he dropp'd, it struck such a Terror in his Men, that they suffered themselves to be taken, without making Resistance."

No doubt, Tew's untimely disappearance was greatly mourned by the business community in New England and New York. Gold coins that he imported during his two voyages were in circulation in the colonies for many years after.

Seen from the perspective of John Quelch and his maritime contemporaries, there were far more examples of Thomas Tew's ilk
making a good go of it from illicit trade than there were examples
like Kidd. The fate of William Kidd was the exception in an enterprise that always carried a certain degree of risk, but it was just
that—an exception.

While Quelch had accepted the calculus of risk in his own situation, there is evidence that not all his crew shared in his assessment. According to some reports from Marblehead, about forty-
three crew members disembarked from the *Charles* early in the third
week of May. Quelch had left Marblehead with seventy men and
even taking into account fatalities at sea due to sickness and accidents, this was a much reduced roster. It is likely that some of
the crew disembarked *before* reaching Marblehead, asking to be
put off near Connecticut or Rhode Island, or possibly Nantuck-
et. If these crew members were from these points (or claimed to
be) it would not be strange given the unconventional nature of
the expedition that they would be let off ship rather than parting
company at Marblehead. Whether by chance or foresight, most of
these early leavers, clutching their little rough-fashioned canvas or
leather pouches of gold dust, disappeared into comfortable obscurity. Those that remained aboard the *Charles*, staying long enough
to hear her anchor splash into the Little Harbor, would face a very
different fate.

It is interesting to speculate just what went through the minds
of the chandlers, tavern-keepers, sailmakers, and fishermen of
Marblehead when they recognized the *Charles* sitting at anchor in
the safety of the cove. In 1704, Marblehead was not yet the great
port of commerce that it was to become later in the century. Locals would not have forgotten the little brigantine that had left
them under mysterious circumstances and its sudden reappearance after nearly a year would have set tongues wagging within
hours.

The Fountain Inn, where Quelch had met Colman and Clarke
the year before, lay just a stone's throw from Little Harbor. It sat
high above the water upon a seagrass and wildflower-strewn granite and felsite bluff, affording an excellent view of the cove. Opposite the inn, facing inland, the town burial ground was laid out,
full of lumps and bumps and outcroppings of rock. There was very

little that was flat in Marblehead; even the dead had to deal with the uneven terrain. The Fountain was for the remaining crew members, probably the first stop on land. The Three Cod Inn, which unlike the Fountain still stands today, is a few hundred yards further, on the Marblehead Bay side of the peninsula. Other small taprooms, or ordinaries, were scattered about the town and the returning seamen would have had no shortage of drinking establishments to patronize, nor lack of money to preclude it.

The news of the luck of the *Charles* would also have spread like wildfire through the town and over to the nearby towns of Salem and Beverly. Every Portuguese gold or silver coin proffered in exchange for mugs of rum begged an explanation—and a story. That such a story could remain consistent and credible, across many retellings by drunken men, requires a prodigious leap of faith. In all likelihood, the story of "Spanish" treasure began to unravel within a few days. However, this in itself did not mean the game was up for Quelch. After all, the townspeople of Marblehead, and any other town that Quelch's former shipmates traveled to, stood to gain from the pirates' largesse. And no truly practical Yankee merchant would kill such a golden goose.

How much money did these sailors now possess? A good guide to the division of shares on a privateer mission can be gleaned from Captain Kidd's commission of 1695. In addition to the usual "no purchase, no pay" clause, it also stipulated that the crew would receive no more than one-quarter of the total haul of treasure and goods. Essentially, three-quarters of the wealth would go to the expedition's backers and to the captain.

While there is no surviving record of individual shares for Quelch and his crew, it is possible to extrapolate what the ordinary able seaman would have received. During the subsequent trial, it was alleged that a single sick crew member who was unable to perform his duties for some time, was given a nominal share out of "generosity" amounting to sixteen ounces of gold dust. Although by no means certain, one could assume that an able-bodied seaman would get perhaps double that amount—say, thirty-two ounces. Indeed, crew members Pimer and Austin were relieved of amounts close to this once apprehended. Since one Troy ounce of gold at this time was worth around eighty-seven shillings, this would mean that each man had around £140.

This was eight times an average London worker's annual wages. Yet other variables could have come into play. Some of the gold dust could have been spent or lost shortly after it was gained (not an unusual happening). *Most* of those apprehended had far less than thirty-two ounces on them. There also remains the possibility that the true amount confiscated by the authorities was deliberately falsified (with the difference put into the pockets of those in charge).

Crucially, there is another factor that must be reckoned with. Any division of the spoils based on a privateer's rules would mean far lower amounts for the crew than had the treasure been divided up according to the rules of pirates. Had Quelch played his role as legitimate privateer to the very end? Did the crew consider themselves pirates or just slack privateersmen? The answer was given by Quelch within a few days of his landing.

Most of his crew were now split up and scattered to the four winds, with perhaps a few loyal tars remaining on the *Charles* to stow gear and make fast the ship. Quelch himself had important business to transact in Boston, business that according to the rules he was living by, could not be delayed.

He was going to meet the merchants of the syndicate. It was time to settle accounts.

Chapter Nine

The Devil His Due

T hose who have found themselves carrying nearly $2 million
on their person as they walked the streets of a big city might
well understand how John Quelch felt as he entered Boston
in the third week of May, 1704. The joy of possessing such a won-
drous wealth not withstanding, the anxiety of transporting it in
one's pockets with no means of security, must make for a nail-biting
experience.

We do not know exactly how he transported the treasure from
Marblehead to Boston. It is most likely that he rode there on horse-
back by himself or in the company of just one or two others. Trust
was a commodity in short supply. Perhaps the crew appointed one
of their own to oversee the "delivery" and ensure that Quelch did
not vanish with the fortune. At any rate, Quelch carried with him in
his saddlebags some 960 ounces of gold and silver—over twenty-
seven kilos—as he made his way along the highway from Marblehead, through Beverly, Lynn, and finally to Charlestown across the
river from Boston. Although he had disbursed the shares of the
crew, he still held the majority of the treasure, which was destined
for the syndicate and, of course, his own share of the loot. This
he was unlikely to leave alone in Marblehead and besides, he had
plans for his gold and silver, as shall be seen.

It was typical New England weather for May: sun and showers,
cold mornings and warm afternoons, strong steady winds gust-
ing up from time to time. Several of Quelch's crew were ill in

Marblehead. William Whiting, the ship's clerk and reluctant crew member, lay confined to a bed in a local inn, very ill and not expected to survive. He had taken sick shortly after the voyage began and had never completely recovered. Another crew member, James Austin, had left Marblehead heading north for the colony of New Hampshire. He too would be gravely ill within a few days. It is possible they had contracted tropical diseases such as malaria, robbing them of their strength and sending them into raging fevers. We can never know how many of those crew members that had disappeared as soon as the ship made landfall also sickened. For these men it was a desperate irony. They were now richer than at any times in their lives but all the money in the world would not be able to buy them back their health in an age before antimalarial and antiviral drugs had been invented.

As he stood on the claylike mud bank of the River Charles, waiting for the ferryman's barge to return to his side, Quelch would have had a perfect view of the North End of Boston.

At his back was Charlestown's main square, which contained the original Town House of the settlement, now converted to a large two-story tavern known as The Three Cranes. Charlestown's warehouses and rickety wharves lay just beyond, piled with barrels and trussed bales, the scene of back-breaking labor as mariners, dock workers, and apprentice boys bustled and jostled one another while hefting cargo and stores. A few pottery kilns belched stinking smoke as they fired the local red clay plates, pitchers, and bowls that most townsfolk used. Large and small ships were being loaded and unloaded, while new ones sat on oaken frames in the town's dry dock (the first in the New World), their "ribs" bare as clinker-boards were nailed to their sides by shipwrights. The smell of dried salted fish, stale beer, and pitch tar carried strongly on the air. Charlestown was the site of the first English settlement of Governor John Winthrop's expedition of 1630. But the lack of available freshwater led the new colonists to decamp for the peninsula across the river. Called "Shawmut" by the natives and "Trimountain" by the English due to its three prominent hills, it was soon renamed Boston, in honor of the market town of Lincolnshire (from where many of the Puritans had set out).

But it was Boston town where Quelch's thoughts of the moment lay. The large oar-drawn ferryboat would not have taken long to make the crossing. Here the river channel was narrow, but with a strong current. How he would have disguised the muffled clink of hundreds of coins from prying eyes and curious ears of other passengers and the ferryman we cannot know, but it must have caused him worry.

The ferry made landfall at a wharf near the edge of the peninsula that bordered the Mill Pond and looked up toward Broughton's Hill where the town's windmill was situated. Quelch would see this stretch of shoreline again in the next month but under dramatically different circumstances. Yet these events lay in the future, a future for Quelch that would in the ensuing days descend into an ever-tighter spiral of despair.

His first concern, however, was to reach the house of John Colman, the merchant and shipowner he had escorted from Boston to Marblehead one year ago. It must have been obvious that carrying such a huge amount of gold with him was risky. Either through misadventure (such as the ferry capsizing) or robbery, the treasure could easily be lost, leaving him with nothing except responsibility for the entire fiasco.

The picture that has long survived of Puritan-era Boston and its tight-knit community of law-abiding and pious pioneers, rigid in their beliefs but temperate in character, was always an inflated myth. Bostonians were then as mixed a group of saints and sinners, rogues and wastrels, do-gooders and hard-grafters, as any across the sea in the England they had left behind.

Although Quelch had undoubtedly taken the precaution of traveling by day, Boston, a town of somewhere between 7,500 and 8,500 inhabitants, was far from peaceful. Mirroring future gang "turf wars" of the nineteenth and twentieth centuries, and predating the formation of town wards, young apprentices and bullies had formed themselves into loose-knit groups "North-enders" and "South-enders" who preyed on each other and anyone unfortunate enough to get in their way. Laws and lawbreaking, of which there were copious levels of both, were influenced by the steady rise of local distilleries and the consumption of their chief output: rum. Boston was home to the first distillery in America in 1700 and within just a few years the town and surrounding area was exporting some 600,000 gallons annually. It took practically no time for the beverage, locally made and therefore cheap, to become the drink of choice, surpassing the demand for ale.

Even as early as the 1670s, Boston's reputation for orderliness appears to have existed only in its own collective mind. Two Dutch visitors from New York, Jasper Dankers and Pieter Sluyter, commented: "All their religion consists in observing Sunday by not working or going into the taverns on that day; but the houses are worse than the taverns. . . . There is a penalty for cursing and swearing such as they please to impose, the witnesses thereof being at liberty to insist upon it. Nevertheless, you discover little difference between this and other places. Drinking and fighting occur there not less than elsewhere."

Remarked another visitor, John Dunton, a bookseller from London during his four-month stay in 1686: "For being drunk, they either Whip or impose a Fine of Five shillings: And, yet notwithstanding this Law, there are several of them so addicted to it, that they begin to doubt whether it be a Sin or no; and seldom go to Bed without Muddy Brains." By 1704, with the old ways fast changing and the Puritan elite losing its grip on the society, crime and disorder were on the rise.

Being a city of traders, warehouse burglaries were common. With dozens of taverns, inns, and alehouses—probably more per capita than anywhere else in colonial America—incidents of assaults, theft, and prostitution occurred with regular frequency and are recorded in the provincial and colonial record. Moreover, since this was a time of war, overall uncertainty and public fears grew, feeding the response of the government, which attempted to legislate what it thought would lead to an increase in security.

This included the establishment of a curfew. For years, those citizens walking the streets and lanes of Boston after nine o'clock at night could find themselves challenged by the town's watchmen. But in 1703, after a series of incidents involving black house servants drinking and allegedly accosting whites (most were allowed free time away from the master's house each day), the curfew was made absolute for black slaves and freemen, as well as Christianized Indians who had up until then been permitted to walk the streets freely after their day's work.

Under attack from the outside by the French and their Indian allies and on the inside by those of their own who followed the devil's path of drink and delinquency, the town's elite must have despaired of deliverance. Boston's criminal law at this time was based more on Mosaic Law than English Common Law. Punishment for offenses was draconian and meted out for even minor transgressions of the social order. Public humiliation played a large role in Puritan "corrections." While more serious crimes such as theft, assault, and debt would lead the transgressor straight to the town jail, lesser offenses were also dealt with in a fashion borrowed from Europe. Crimes of blasphemy, idleness, drunkenness, scolding, and nonattendance of Sunday service were usually punished by the use of the whip, the pillory, or the cage. Set just to the north of the main town square in the shadow of the Town House, petty criminals and town drunks would find themselves fastened wrist and ankle in the pillory for hours or a day. Public whippings were also a common sight with the malefactor tied by the arms to the wooden post that stood near the pillory. This was a usual punishment for the crime of adultery or fornication. The cage, about the dimension of a telephone booth, was also sometimes used. Passersby would hurl at these shamed citizens whatever they found at hand: mud, rotten apples, or kitchen slops in a kind of public-participation ritual of ostracism.

Such an experience might mark a townsman for a very long time. In 1671, a man from Braintree was found guilty of plowing his fields on a day formally set aside for public thanksgiving. He was sentenced to sit a spell in the pillory. Five years later, after winning election to the General Court of Massachusetts, he was not allowed to take up his seat due to his past disgrace.

For theft and other serious crimes, apart from jail time, public maiming was also sometimes employed. Convicted forgers, for example, would have their ears cropped or noses slit. Such public punishments were not finally taken off the Boston law books until 1813. In Puritan society—even late-Puritan society—such punishments went beyond the mere purpose of deterring others. They served as a powerful indicator of the importance of conformity and station in the body politic. In the end, such a penal code did little to stop wrongdoing. Human nature and the inability to tackle the causes of unrest meant that crime and punishment were a normal aspect of everyday life, even in the New Jerusalem of Boston.

It was into this tumultuous, stratified, suffocating, and some-what frightened society that John Quelch found himself immersed that May as he made his way from the north end toward the heart of the of town. This short journey would have taken him along Black Horse Lane (later renamed Prince Street) running south parallel to the expansive Mill Pond that a century later was reclaimed to create the Back Bay section. This stretch of road was residential at the time but not heavily built upon. Legend claims that it was the cows that laid out Boston's eccentric streets: the narrow rutted paths of the foraging animals becoming the main thoroughfares. Indeed, there was little rhyme or reason to the early layout of the town. The fur-ther into the peninsula one traveled, the more congested it became, until the nexus was reached where the Old State House and Quincy Market stand today

As Quelch rode on, turning into what became Salem Street but was then called Back Street; houses were more closely set together, the scene appearing more urban. Once he crossed the little wooden bridge over the shallow Mill Creek (where the peninsula narrows) he was in the center of the town. He undoubtedly knew the town well as he had been a resident leading up to his appointment as Lieutenant of the *Charles,* and may have boarded somewhere near the main wharves of the North End.

A sojourn in Boston would have evoked a nostalgic haze in any visiting Londoner in his fifties or older. While central London had been largely rebuilt in brick after the Great Fire in 1666, Boston in 1704 still had an almost medieval feel to it. Despite no less than seven major fires in the town between 1653 and 1702, rebuilding was generally carried out with the same timber-frame architecture. After all, wood was cheap and plentiful. Only after the devastating fire that swept the town center in 1711 did brick construction begin to predominate.

Boston's houses, typically two- and three-stories high, doubled as residences and workplaces or shops. Oak-framed and clapboard covered with slate roofs, these houses were distinctively gabled and adorned with leaded-glass windows. Many, as in England, had upper stories that extended out over the street below. Along the main streets these dwellings were cheek-by-jowl with little or no space between them, presenting a solid frontage. Long, narrow, backyards, containing sheds or outbuildings lay behind. Boston had become increasingly crowded by the end of the seventeenth century; the harbor area stretching from the Town Dock all the way up into the North End was increasingly subdivided to accommodate the growing number of workers. Other sections of the town were already "gentrified" where space and leafy expanses with primly fenced grand residences proclaimed the wealth of their inhabitants.

In another throwback to earlier times, for a population that was largely illiterate, signage using visual cues was vital. All shops, inns, apothecaries, taverns, coffee houses, or official buildings displayed swinging "shingles" adorned with images to identify their wares. Boston records are replete with mentions of its commercial ventures, referenced by "at the sign of." The list of such enterprises at the turn of the eighteenth century is a collection of the fantastic: Blue Dog, Buck's Head, the Magpipe, the Orange Tree, Three Sugar Loaves, the Unicorn, the Golden Ball, the Dolphin, Half Moon, the Dove, the Red Lyon, the White Lamb, the Peacock, and Noah's Ark, to name but a few. For some, such as "The Hand and Pen" where the local public notary lived, the connotation was obvious. Equally, "The Two Palaverers" seems a perfect name for a welcoming tavern. Others, such as "The Three Nuns" are more cryptic: that establishment being a handkerchief and glove shop.

Quelch may have been quickly seduced by the lures of the marketplace after so long at sea but it is far more likely that he did not pause before he reached the house of John Colman.

Colman lived near the heart of the town, indeed just north of the town dock, which had been the site of the original settlement on the peninsula. We know that he was a founding member of the Brattle Street Church that was built in 1699 and lay just a block away from the Town House on the Marketplace. This district, bordered by "Houchins Lane," the future Hanover Street, the Town Dock (near present-day Faneuil Hall), and the government center at the head of King Street (the future State Street), was in 1704 a well-established part of Boston and a mix of wealthy merchants, tradesfolk, and town officials. Just to the west of the Town House lay the prison, recently refurbished in stone.

We have a clue to where Colman stood in the political and social tussle that Boston was going through at the turn of the century. The clue is his involvement with the new Brattle Street Church. Broadly a Congregationalist gathering hatched from orthodox Puritanism, the Brattle Street parish had been created by like-minded up-and-coming merchants of a more liberal mindset. Their statement of faith rejected the orthodox Puritan view that only the church's ordained minister could determine who had been "received" into the church, was eligible for baptism, and, therefore, entitled to full membership and decision-making privileges.

Colman even convinced the congregation's leaders, William Brattle and John Leverett, to invite his brother Benjamin to come and serve as their new minister. This expansion of liberal thinking, adding to the religious pluralism that was taking root in Boston (Anglicans and Quakers were already delicately established), was viewed by the old theocracy, run by the Mathers in the North End, as nothing less than a mortal threat to the soul of the city.

At a time when religion could not be separated from politics and social standing, one's faith automatically placed one firmly in a specific political camp. While the Mathers personified the old order, the governor was part of the newly established and growing Church of England community in Boston, considered little more than crypto-Catholics by the Puritans. In essence, Dudley was the Anglican cuckoo in the Puritan nest. By 1704, even Quakers were finally able to meet openly in Boston (thought still discriminated against). Only forty years previously a vicious campaign to wipe out their "heresy" resulted in several of them being hanged on Boston Neck. Now the Liberal faction of American Protestantism had sprung up to further complicate life for the old guard.

But these fissures would also create tensions for business and political deal making in Boston. With the new liberal thinking came a more untamed view of mercantilism. Puritanism had been geared for the common wealth of those in Massachusetts (though decided by a select few). As Protestantism splintered over the last few decades of the seventeenth century in New England (and as population grew), people began to focus more upon the wealth and success of the individual. The ability to make money, unfettered by the interference of king or governor, was increasingly viewed as a natural right of those who lived in the province.

John Colman was but one example of the new breed of Boston merchant. He had come from relatively humble beginnings, but through enterprise had built himself up. He had married Colonel

Charles Hobby's sister Judith in 1694, further cementing his social standing. Hobby was a major political rival to Governor Dudley and openly touted as his imminent successor. And it was Hobby's connections that had probably gotten Colman involved in the privateering enterprise in the first place. With the theft of the *Charles* by Quelch's crew, Colman and Hobby were already in the governor's black book. While this episode was an acute embarrassment to Dudley, who after all had signed the privateer's commission, it did give him certain leverage over these shipowners who were his political rivals. John Colman, only thirty-four years old and just coming into prosperity as a successful merchant and citizen, could not afford to set a foot wrong with the ruling Council. With Quelch now walking the streets of Boston, the situation was about to become even more complicated.

It is not difficult to imagine the astonishment that must have struck Colman like a musket ball when his house servant informed him who was at his door. Ushered into the main downstairs room of Colman's house, Quelch too must have felt somewhat nervous although he would have had his words well rehearsed. The meeting must have been as awkward as it was extraordinary. Colman would never have expected to see John Quelch ever again in this life, never mind in his own parlor and greeted by the tip of a battered three-corner hat. He would have naturally been suspicious, but it cannot be assumed he would have considered Quelch a pirate, at least not yet. But the real shock would have come as Quelch hefted the great sacks of gold and silver onto the gate-leg table at the center of the room, making it wobble under the load.

And thus, would John Quelch have spun out his tale of the last eleven months at sea, beginning with the relation of the unfortunate (but entirely natural) death of Captain Plowman. While some of his story must have been plausible, an equal or greater part of it must have sounded highly suspect to Colman, even if he was no seaman himself. How did Quelch justify the decision to sail from the North Atlantic to the South Atlantic given that the mission had been to engage French privateers? Had he not managed to find a single French or Spanish prize during the entire cruise? And most amazing of all would have been Quelch's explanation of the chance find of a recent Spanish shipwreck near present-day Venezuela. Embellished by the added mental imagery of friendly

Carib Indians helping the crew salvage the vessel, this part of the story must have posed as many questions as it answered.

And the state of the ship? *Safe, with some captured cargo.* What of the fate of the crew? *Discharged upon reaching Marblehead harbor.* Why were their shares paid out before adjudication of the treasure? *They were becoming unruly.* And so the conversation must have progressed, the one probing the other. But the whole time Colman would have had difficulty taking his eyes off the treasure that lay on the table before him.

Palming a handful of coins, he would have noticed that few were Spanish silver dollars or gold reals. Most were Portuguese gold and minted in the last two years. Still, it was possible that the Spaniards *could* have taken these from some unfortunate Portuguese before falling foul of the weather.

Quelch would have graciously explained that what lay upon the table was Colman's and the other owners' rightful shares of the shipwreck. Asked for an accounting of the remainder, he probably confessed that he had kept 20 percent (or thereabouts) for himself while dividing the remainder with the crew according to the accepted privateering formula. If this was the case, the alacrity of the division of the spoils—and without witness—was unusual, and Colman, being an official agent of the "tenths" or the duties for the Lord High Admiral Prince George, would have known this very well.

But equally, he would not have acted without first taking advice from the rest of the syndicate, particularly William Clarke. There was much to consider. In one fell swoop, he and his associates had gone from losing their shirts to regaining a small fortune— plus the brigantine, returned intact. But first, he and Clarke needed to know more. They needed to go to Marblehead. However, as he sent Quelch away, undoubtedly ordering him to return to Marblehead and await his arrival with Clarke, he kept the gold at his house. Moreover, he subdivided the treasure into shares for the other owners, keeping his own safe and separate. It was a decision that would nearly undo him. It was also a move that handed the governor a weapon that could be used against him and his higher-profile "brother" Colonel Hobby. Colman immediately went to seek out Clarke and possibly Paige or Gallop. They would make straight away for Marblehead, to see for themselves just what the state of the *Charles* really was and what had happened to her crew.

As for John Quelch, he departed Colman's with far less a burden than he had arrived with. As he prepared to spend the night in Boston at some inn or alehouse, holding close his own share of the treasure, he must have been counting on his gift of gold to ensure that the shipowners would not pry too deeply. He had little else to bargain with. Yet he had returned the vessel and had given over the fair share of the treasure. The hold of the sturdy little brigantine also held cloth and sugar to be consigned as well, adding more money into the pockets of the owners.

His own experience of the murky world of privateering out of the seaports of New England also influenced his decision to hand over the gold. Everyone benefited, from top to bottom, by not asking too many questions about captured ships and cargoes. It simply went against self-interest to do otherwise. So long as English vessels were not preyed upon, who cared what befell the Dagoes and the Portuguese? Seamen could actively count on being joined in this conspiracy of silence by the rising merchant class of coastal New England. In his own mind, Quelch had convinced himself that he was no murderous buccaneer but rather, a sharp man of enterprise who could play the game as well as the next man.

He still had one more task to accomplish in Boston before returning to Marblehead. He paid a visit to the shop of John Noyes, a Boston silversmith of some local renown who also did a brisk business in headstone carving when he wasn't making punchbowls or candlesticks. He is today probably more remembered for his artwork in stone: his trademark wilted flowers in a vase was unique at a time when most New England gravestones bore more austere imagery such as winged skulls.

Although Quelch may have known of Noyes, it is far more likely that he had inquired of the services of a silversmith and been directed there. Showing supreme faith in the avarice of the average Bostonian, he walked into Noyes's shop with a strange request. Quelch was keen to erase any trace of a connection to Portuguese gold and silver. He asked Noyes if he could melt down the coins into plate or bars. From the moment Quelch walked in, Noyes was probably under no illusions that the gold and silver were legitimate. Foreign gold and silver coins were legal tender in New

England, particularly Spanish ones. There was little reason for someone to want to melt down coinage, unless they were seeking to obscure its origins.

How did Noyes react to such a request? It appears that he complied—after a fashion. What exactly transpired that day in the shop remains unclear but Quelch himself set to melting down his coins in the presence of the silversmith. Was Quelch impatient to have the work accomplished or did he simply not trust Noyes (or anyone else) to the job unless it was under his own gaze? Or did Noyes feel too intimidated by the leather-skinned mariner to refuse him outright? Whatever the circumstances, it seems that Noyes stood by and watched while Quelch managed somehow to heat the coins in a crucible, and then poured them into small ingots.

Quelch quenched his ingots in a bucket of water and gathered them up, leaving some in payment to the silversmith for the use of the shop. The bizarre transaction came to an end and Quelch departed. Noyes did not alert the town authorities to his strange customer that day. Quelch's calculation about enlightened self-interest appeared vindicated. However, events were now in motion that Quelch had no knowledge of and even if he had, no ability to avert their course.

Chapter Ten

"Violently Suspected"

O nce Mr. Colman and Mr. Clarke had clambered up over the side and onto the deck of the ship they never thought they would see again, their eyes would have beheld a sorry sight. Sails that had been haphazardly stowed were flapping about in the breeze, rigging was fallen down, and lines lay strewn about the deck. Assorted rubbish was everywhere: broken jugs, scraps of biscuit, discarded bits of clothing, and probably a pile of human feces or two in the odd corner of the foredeck. The stink of a ship neglected wafted about the blistered and cracked deck rails of the *Charles*.

The two merchants and their accompanying party descended into the stuffy hold below deck, candlelit lanterns illuminating the gloom. It is not known if there were any crew members left onboard the *Charles* by this time as it sat at anchor in the little harbor at Marblehead. No specific mention was made of any contact with Quelch or his crew during the search. Of gold or silver they found not a trace. However, their search did bring to light several damning articles that the crew had left behind. In a sworn deposition, Colman and Clarke later stated that they found aboard the ship evidence that Quelch had attacked and boarded ships that were neither French nor Spanish. They brought up and laid out on the main deck several long *spadas* or rapiers, common weapons of the Iberian Peninsula but no longer fashionable elsewhere. While these could have been Spanish, other items highlighted a direct trail to the Portuguese.

These included several large "loaves" of sugar, wrapped in muslin and bearing labels written in Portuguese. They also discovered what were termed "prints" containing Portuguese writing. But most incriminating, the owners brought forth a Portuguese flag: a white ensign emblazoned with a golden crown and a red shield with seven golden castles. Holding the white ensign in his hands upon the main deck, Colman realized then that more than just failing to bring the treasure and captured cargo to legal adjudication in Boston, Quelch had preyed upon neutral shipping. Worse than that, by choosing the Portuguese, Quelch had attacked Queen Anne's newest ally in the war against France and Spain. Clearly, the owners knew they had an obligation to immediately report to the authorities an allegation of piracy against Quelch and his crew. Equally, they both had in their possession, as did the other syndicate members, large bags of gold coin and dust, a fortune far greater than any they had expected to come of the expedition.

In an age of dubious public morality and ethics, this must have created a quandary for Colman and his partners. They had sponsored the expedition in the first place primarily to curry political favor with the governor and to help rid local waters of French privateers who were taking a toll of their shipping. At most, they had probably expected only to just cover their costs and gain some small amount of silver. The question then, was who else knew about the Portuguese gold? Could the source of this largesse, this "sunken treasure," be kept disguised, the truth swept away by disinterested citizens, by more urgent news of Indian attacks, and by the payment, if necessary, of bribes?

One walk through the narrow streets, shops, and taverns of Marblehead told them a different story. There were still at least a dozen crew members hanging about the town, nearly a week after the return. They had bragged and spent their merry way from Marblehead to Salem and it was no longer a secret that Quelch's unlucky victims were not hapless Frenchmen or Spaniards. The town was full of talk of Captain Quelch's success off Brazil, providing more excitement than the inhabitants had had in years. Colman must have rapidly surmised that he had little choice but to report Quelch to the authorities, even if the average Marbleheader did not care a fig from where the money had come from. With tales spread near and far, Colman was leaving himself open to accusations of collusion with pirates and the receipt of stolen goods. The problem remained though, how could he and his partners keep hold of the gold while staying on the right side of the law?

It is surprising that Colman and Clarke found such an obvious trail of incriminating evidence in the *Charles*. More than one mariner had told of Quelch's harangue to the crew to dispose of anything linking them to the Portuguese and to Brazil. That none of these souvenirs were taken away by departing crew members seems to indicate that they were not really valued. Had this just been an unfortunate, but fatal, oversight on the part of Quelch and his quartermaster to erase all traces?

This does raise the possibility that some or all of the evidence was "planted" by the authorities some days afterwards to cement their case against Quelch. The sugar and swords could have been taken by the Spanish, but the presence of a Portuguese naval flag smacks of obvious convenience. The well-established trade between New England and Madeira meant that finding a Portuguese flag in Boston was not inconceivable. The same would apply to Portuguese printed tracts. But neither Colman nor Clarke would themselves have had a motive to fabricate evidence against Quelch. Indeed, by providing such weighty proof of wrongdoing they worsened their chances of keeping their shares of the gold. However, Governor Dudley and his son Paul, the Attorney General, would have had good motive to tamper. At a time and place where it was notoriously difficult to convict pirates for lack of hard evidence, the Portuguese flag was a fortuitous "godsend."

Hurrying back to Boston after taking steps in Marblehead to secure the *Charles* with some trusted men, Colman and Clarke decided to air their suspicions about Quelch with the government, if for no other reason than to cover themselves against future prosecution. It would not, however, be a fulsome disclosure.

On Tuesday, May 23, the two merchants walked into the main Town Square and up to the Town House at its head. The largest public building in Boston, the Town House had been built in 1657 at the high point of Puritan control during the time of Cromwell's Commonwealth. It was an unusual building by colonial standards, more like a late-medieval market town guildhall than provincial meetinghouse. A large clapboard structure, it was two stories high with a six-gabled roof topped with two pillared cupolas and a balustrade. Rectangular in shape, it spanned some sixty-seven feet long by thirty-seven feet deep with entrances at either end. The most striking aspect of the Town House was that it was raised up on pillars, twenty-one in all, ten feet high. This created a "market" space beneath the building where booksellers and other merchants would set up small wooden stalls to sell their wares. For this privilege the town charged them rent of a few shillings.

The Town House was the seat of provincial government—the place where locally elected representatives met, treated, argued, and governed—alongside the Queen's appointed representative: the Governor. They looked after the "prudential affairs" of Boston, meeting once each week when they would set rates for fines, regulate apprentices and commerce, authorize construction, and deal with the poor and the vagrant.

More than this, the Town House was a multipurpose focal point of public life. It housed the Province's treasury, a small library, the Governor's office, and the main meeting room of the Deputies of the General Assembly of the province (the prime legislative body). A small but vibrant bourse also was conducted on the main floor. At times, it was even used as a granary and an arsenal. Colman and Clarke would have been well familiar with the building as they ascended the wooden staircase and entered the huge open main floor, large brick fireplaces at either end. A great pewter chandelier hung suspended from the ceiling, dominating the room. The two continued upward until they reached the second floor, divided into two chambers to house the Governor and council members.

Here they met with the council's grizzled secretary, Isaac Addington, to tell of their news. Governor Dudley was not there. He was in New Hampshire conducting business as he served as governor of that colony as well as Massachusetts. Nor was he due to return for another week. Addington, however, took seriously enough the story they told and immediately summoned the Attorney General, Paul Dudley. When the younger Dudley joined them, he quickly seized the situation and orchestrated the draft statement of accusation. The two merchants were asked to sign, attesting to their suspicions about Quelch.

We *John Colman*, and *William Clarke*, of the Town of Boston, Merchants, and being part Owners of the Briganteen *Charles*, lately fitted out as a Private Man of War, under Command of Captain *Daniel Plowman*, (since Deceased) against Her Majesties Open and Declared Enemies of *France* and *Spain*, & c. The said Vessel arriving, from Sea some few Days since: By what we have observed of the Management of the present Commander and Company; as also by what we find on Board the said Vessel moves us to suspect, That they have Plundered and made Spoil upon some of Her Majesties Friends and Allies, contrary to Her Majesties Declaration of War, and the Commission and Instructions given them.

Neither merchant made mention of the gold *they* had received from Quelch. Rather, they emphasized that the pirates themselves had divided up a considerable sum, spending it as they went about the province. With the die now cast, they were walking a legal tightrope.

Paul Dudley, then twenty-eight, was every bit as ambitious as Dudley senior. More than fulfilling his role as chief prosecutor of the province, he recognized instantly the opportunity a pirate hunt would provide to show himself in a good light to his father and others even higher up the chain of rule. A slightly florid young man, leaning toward the plump, he was still new in his profession as barrister, having only been called to the bar in London in 1700. Thanks to his father's station, this bright, fourth-born son of the governor (and grandson of yet another) had received a commission from Queen Anne in 1702 naming him Attorney General and advocate of the Court of Admiralty in Boston. With just two years' experience he was the top lawyer in the province. Now, two years into his job and newly married to the daughter of an Ipswich merchant and militia colonel, he was about to prosecute the most sensational case of his career.

Dudley acted to put his "dragnet" into effect immediately. His first step was to inform the Lieutenant Governor, Thomas Povey, of the developments. Povey had been named at the same time Joseph Dudley had been selected governor in 1702, appointed directly by the Queen. In 1702 he had been a captain of the Queen's Own Regiment of Foot and he had high-level family connections in Whitehall going back some fifty years. His cousin was William

Blathwayt, the powerful Privy Council member and secretary of the Board of Trade and Plantations that oversaw all of England's colonies. A recent arrival to New England, he did not like it any better after two years there. Hoping to have improved his financial situation by this colonial office, he had been bitterly disappointed as the months went by that the Massachusetts General Assembly steadfastly refused to grant him an annual salary (nor would it grant one to the governor). Bored and frustrated, and very much subservient to the imperious Joseph Dudley, Povey only managed to get a grant of £200 for his pains. By the end of 1704 he would be on a ship to Lisbon, having resigned his office. From there, he returned to London, never to set foot in New England again.

Paul Dudley quickly convinced Povey not to wait for his father's return to Boston but to issue a proclamation against Quelch and his crew immediately. Every day wasted would mean more of the pirates could slip further away—along with their treasure. He found no argument from Povey, who gave the Attorney-General *carte blanche* to pursue the pirates. Armed with the statement of accusation from the merchants, Dudley was that very afternoon in search of John Quelch.

He had little trouble in finding him. Though it is not recorded where Quelch was taken, we know it was within twenty-four hours of Colman and Clarke going to the government. Colman or Clarke probably had an idea of where he could be found, and word on the street was easy to come by for the price of a coin or two. Moreover, at least three others of John Quelch's crew were also in Boston. These were rounded up within hours of Quelch himself.

These early days of the capture can only be conjectured. Frustratingly, there are no surviving records as to exactly when and where the crew was rounded up. Quelch, still in Boston conducting personal business with his newfound wealth, was likely in his old neighborhood of the North End. He had been resident in Boston before the voyage in the *Charles*, undoubtedly recruited by Captain Plowman on the very cobbled streets where he was captured by Dudley. Whether he was surprised at the Noah's Ark tavern, the Ship, the Swan, the Salutation, or the Red Lyon, the result was the same. Within hours, the news would have spread of the arrest across the town, creating a buzz of expectation and drama.

In anger and shock, Quelch was brought back to the center of the town, up present Union Street, past Dock Square, and westward over to Queen Street, a stone's throw from the Town House and the site of the jail since the foundation of the colony. Since the stay of its last most notorious resident, Captain Kidd in 1699, the jail had been further improved: enlarged and reinforced with even more stone, an imposing little fortress compared with the wood blockhouse that sat next to it.

Before 1700, the prison had the reputation of being less than secure. Escapes were commonplace, whether from shoddy wooden construction that could be forced or, more usually, doors that were mysteriously left unlocked by the jailer or his assistant. Indeed, jailer Caleb Ray had made a small racket of taking bribes for allowing special treatment or outright escapes, including conspiring to free Captain Kidd. He had, however, been caught out during the high-profile Kidd case, and dismissed from his post.

John Quelch found himself escorted by the town constables into the damp confines of the prison. He, and the members of the crew that shortly joined him, were not the only accused pirates in custody. The Frenchman Baptiste still paced his stone cell, hopeful of a prisoner swap in the near future. In addition to Baptiste, at least a dozen other French sailors were also incarcerated. Guided by the sputtering tallow-lit lantern of the new keeper, Daniel Willard, Quelch would have heard the taunts and insults hurled out by the Frenchmen as he trudged past. He was pushed into a stone cell, most likely alone, while the massive nail-studded door was bolted and locked. His cell held a bucket and a mat of straw, and possibly a wooden bench. The only light was from the narrow slit windows in the stone walls.

Within hours, he would have been alert to the sounds of new prisoners being ushered into the echoing corridor. Would he have recognized the voices of his former crewmates as they shouted their protests? Could he have glimpsed them or even cried out to them from the small iron grating in his cell door? When challenged by the constables, Matthew Pimer had gone with them willingly. Pimer had been shipped by Captain Plowman himself and later would claim to have been an unwillingly mutineer who went along with the rest to save his life. He may have even turned himself in to the authorities when he heard about Quelch. The others taken at Boston were: John Clifford, James Parrot, John Lambert, John Miller, John Dorothy, and William Wiles. These crew members may have shared the same cell. It would prove a convenient arrangement for them to get their stories straight.

Dudley too, probably realized that this first catch could prove useful to his prosecution. One was already willing to swear against his shipmates. Perhaps the others could be convinced to do the same. His interrogation of Pimer and the others yielded names, details, and clues to current whereabouts of further members of the crew. Combined with copies of Plowman's original ship's roster, they knew who made up the ship's complement.

Quelch was also probably questioned by Secretary Addington and Paul Dudley shortly after he was apprehended. He stuck resolutely to his story. He had done no wrong. He was, as he believed and probably vocally insisted, a privateer under legal commission.

As the light faded that early summer evening, gradually darkening his cell, Quelch would have been alone with his thoughts and fears for the future. He had gone from wealthy man to accused pirate in the blink of an eye. The constables had taken a pouch of coins from him but he still had the bulk of his gold coins and silver plate stashed safely. His sleep that night, if he slept at all, must have been fitful. Surely, the merchants would get him out of this. He had, after all, kept his part of the bargain.

The next day, Wednesday, May 24, Lieutenant Governor Povey issued a general warrant. It was shouted out by a crier in front of the Town House, after an initial trumpet blast to gather the crowd, then distributed and posted throughout Boston and surrounding towns.

By the Honorable,
Thomas Povey Esq.
Lieutenant GOVERNOUR and Commander in Chief, for the time being, of Her Majesties Province of the *Massachusetts-Bay* in *New-England.*

A Proclamation.

Whereas *John Quelch*, late Commander of the Briganteen *Charles*, and Company to her belonging, *Viz. John Lambert, John Miller, John Clifford, John Dorothy, James Parrot, Charles James, William*

79

Whiting, John Pitman, John Templeton, Benjamin Perkins, William Wiles, Richard Lawrence, Erasmus Peterson, John King, Charles King, Isaac Johnson, Nicholas Lawson, Daniel Chevalle, John Way, Thomas Farrington, Matthew Primer, Anthony Holding, William Rayner, John Quittance, John Harwood, William Jones, Denis Carter, Nicholas Richardson, James Austin, James Pattison, Joseph Hutnot, George Peirce, George Norton, Gabriel Davis, John Breck, John Carter, Paul Giddins, Nicholas Dunbar, Richard Thurbar, Daniel Chuley, and others; Have lately Imported a considerable Quantity of Gold dust, and some Bar and Coin'd Gold, which they are Violently Suspected to have gotten and obtained, by Felony and Piracy, from some of Her Majesties Friends and Allies, and have Imbezel'd and Shared the same among themselves, without any Adjudication or Condemnation thereof, to be lawful Prize. The said Commander and some others being apprehended, and in Custody, the rest are absconded and fled from Justice.

I have therefore thought fit, by and with the Advice of Her Majesties Council, strictly to Command and Require all Officers Civil and Military, and other her Majesties Loving Subjects, to Apprehend and Seize the said Persons, or any of them, whom they may know or find, and them secure and their Treasure, and bring them before one of the Council, or next Justice of the peace, in order to their being safely Conveyed to Boston, to be Examined and brought to Answer what shall be Objected against them, on her Majesties behalf.

And all her Majesties Subjects, and others, are hereby strictly forbiden to entertain, harbour or conceal any of the said persons, or their Treasure, or to convey away, or in any manner further the Escape of any of them, on pain of being proceeded against with utmost Severity of Law as accessories and partakers with them in their Crime.

Given at the Council Chamber in Boston the Twenty-fourth Day of May In the Third Year of the Reign of our Sovereign Lady ANNE, by the Grace of GOD of England, Scotland, France and Ireland, QUEEN, Defender of the Faith, &c. Annoque Domini 1704

By Order of the Lieut.
Governour & Council   T. POVEY
Isaac Addington Secr.

GOD Save the Queen

Addington, as the secretary of the Council, had previous experience with such matters. He had been closely involved in the arrest and interrogation of Captain Kidd four years previously. Like Quelch, Kidd had returned to his benefactors only to be arrested after a few days because he could not give proper account for his captures of neutral vessels. Now, four years on, Addington's warrant made specific mention that Quelch was "Violently Suspected" of having attacked allies of the Queen and had not followed proper procedure upon return to Marblehead by presenting his cargo to customs officials. Furthermore, it fired a shot across the bows to residents warning them not to harbor the fugitives (routinely how seaport folk responded to their own in distress). It was but the first, formal step in casting a wide net. From the moment the proclamation was announced, the race was on to round up anyone associated with the brigantine *Charles* before they could escape, and to find the treasure.

For his part, Paul Dudley was not wasting any time. That same day he assembled a small party of constables, and perhaps a militiaman or two, said good-bye to his young fretting wife, and rode out north to Hudson's Point to take the ferry to Charlestown. The information he had obtained said that most of Quelch's crew were strung out between there and Marblehead itself.

The Attorney-General of Massachusetts was going pirate hunting.

Chapter Eleven

The Governor Takes Charge

J udge Samuel Sewall climbed down out of his *calash*, a two-wheeled horse-drawn cart, and went to help his traveling companion, his daughter, dismount from her own horse. He was also accompanied by a young man, his son (and namesake) Sam Sewall. The three were stopping in the village of Lynn, just north of Boston to refresh at Lewis's Tavern after visiting relations for a week on the North Shore at Newbury, Ipswich, and Salem. Perspiring in the heat, the judge, a portly fifty-two-year-old and one of the Bay Colony's most prominent citizens, looked forward to a draught of beer to cool down. It had become so warm that he had taken his journey from Ipswich to Salem during the evening, not an unusual practice at a time when fashion dictated woolen coat and breeches, vest, linen shirt, cravat, wig, and hat. Sewall's burden of clothing was somewhat lightened by the fact that he never wore a wig, considering it a sin of gross indulgence to fashion.

A devout Calvinist and therefore accustomed to bearing the heavy weight of puritan introspection and guilt of sin, Sewall was also a conflicted man. He was wealthy by birth as well as by marriage. Tradition says that his father-in-law, Boston mint master John Hull, paid his daughter's dowry by way of the girl's weight in local silver "pine tree" shillings. Hannah, who tended to the Junoesque, apparently netted young Samuel a small fortune. Apart from his passable success as a merchant, he had been a Fellow at Harvard College and had briefly considered becoming a clergyman. As it turned out, he devoted his life to the more worldly concerns of politics. Although he had no training in law, he was appointed a judge of the Superior Court in 1692, eventually serving as Chief Justice from 1718 until 1728. He was also a longtime member of the Council, having served four royally appointed governors. He was, therefore, a defender of the *status quo*, a conservative in his politics as well as his religion.

But Sewall is best remembered as one of the judges in the notorious Salem witch trials of 1692. Appointed by Governor Phips as a special commissioner of *oyer and terminer* to investigate and try those accused, Sewall and his colleagues sentenced to death twenty innocent men and women for the crime of practicing "witchcraft." Although he had misgivings about the conduct of the trials as they occurred, he took no action to halt the proceedings. However, unlike the other judges involved, he was the only one to express guilt and remorse for his role. In 1697, he publicly declaimed a lengthy apology during a Sunday meeting, taking "the blame and shame" for what the court had done and begging pardon from the congregation. A day of fasting was then agreed to help make atonement, a day he personally honored each year for the rest of his life.

Yet this same man who had sent innocents to their deaths also authored the first antislavery tract written in America, *The Selling of Joseph, a Memorial*, in 1700. In 1705 he would fight tooth and nail in the General Assembly against a grimly racist miscegenation bill dealing with intermarriage between whites, blacks, and Native American peoples. It became law, but without the more onerous provisions that had been originally proposed. He always vigorously opposed strict interpretation of the treason laws that called for shipping the accused back to England for trial, believing that New Englanders had a God-given right to trial by their peers at home. In short, Samuel Sewall was a man who often struggled between his own strong innate sense of natural justice and the stifling confines of his creed and political class.

As he stood outside Lewis's at Lynn on May 24, brushing the road dust off his coat, he had little idea that he was about to be dropped into the middle of a new legal challenge that would again test his personal honor and ethics. As he recalled in his diary: "Refresh at Lewis's, where Mr. Paul Dudley is in egre pursuit of the Pirats. He had sent one to Boston; and seeing me call'd him back again; At such a sudden I knew not what to doe."

In his haste to run to ground Quelch's men, and not wanting to deplete his own party's strength, Dudley had asked Sewall to take personal charge of the prisoner and bring him back to Boston. Flummoxed by the young Dudley's excited request, and mindful of his daughter's and son's presence, Sewall quickly deputed two locals to take charge of the prisoner and deliver him to Secretary Addington in Boston. The task handed off, he took refreshment and then carried on his way home via Charlestown, his daughter's destination. It would prove to be but a temporary respite from the Quelch matter. Sewall would soon enough find himself at the heart of the government's relentless prosecution machine.

That Saturday evening, the governor returned from New Hampshire. He was quickly made aware that he had urgent business to deal with. Addington debriefed Dudley senior as to the amazing reappearance of John Quelch and the *Charles*, to the suspected acts of piracy against the Portuguese, and, of course, to the treasure. Only three days after Lieutenant Governor Povey made his proclamation, word arrived from neighboring Rhode Island that five suspected members of Quelch's crew had purchased a small, decked boat in Newport and had set sail, their likely destination: Long Island Sound. A sixth crew member had been seized by constables in Newport before he could get away. Governor Samuel Cranston was sending him straight to Boston, the unfortunate mariner being passed from constable to constable as he crossed jurisdictions along the way.

Despite the fact that his son was already off in pursuit of the pirates, Joseph Dudley was apparently dissatisfied with the efforts of his Lieutenant Governor to master the crisis. He immediately took control of the operation against the pirates himself. Thus, when he read the message from Rhode Island, it was very likely with total disdain and disgust. He was no friend of Governor Cranston, whom he believed was little more than a glorified pawnbroker for pirates. A long-time haven for buccaneers, the wayward colony of Rhode Island had been a thorn in his side for years. Indeed, it had infuriated his predecessor as Massachusetts governor, Richard Coote, the Earl of Bellomont. Given Rhode Island's spotted record for capturing and imprisoning pirates, he would not have been surprised if the five fugitives had bought their way out of Newport. Only nine months previously, Dudley had written to London that Boston privateers were returning to Rhode Island and not their home port to surrender their prizes. Once touched at Newport, these privateer crews were

> presently debauched, and the [Rhode Island] Government countenancing of them, refused to leave the place or to suffer their prize to come to Boston, and there they embessel'd the one halfe of the goods, and Cranston, the Governor, refused the Collector and the Receiver on behalf of H.R.H. to have anything to do, and all the letters and messages that I could possible write and sende, could get no answer from them to anything.

Dudley was greatly concerned with the unpleasantness concerning the *Charles Galley* (and this time on his own turf) for two important reasons, one obvious, the other less so.

The first and foremost was that the Quelch affair risked blackening the Bay Colony's reputation in London at a time when he was laboring hard to show its loyalty to the crown and the country. It was common knowledge that the Trade and Navigation Acts were openly flouted by American colonists. However, through the 1690s, Anglo-American privateers and pirates had been increasingly active in attacking neutral shipping in the Arabian Sea and off Africa. This was nothing less than pissing into the bathwater of the East India Company, jeopardizing their lucrative trade monopolies in the region as each new outrage to Mogul shipping unfolded.

In Dudley's eyes, New York and Rhode Island bore heavy responsibility for this lawlessness since their governors connived in issuing commissions to any scoundrel if the price was right. Captains Tew and Kidd had been bad enough for ruining New England's reputation (worsened by Lord Bellomont's own embarrassing involvement in having commissioned and bankrolled Kidd) but now Boston could be tarred with the same brush as wielded by Quelch.

In 1699, the governor of Rhode Island had been the subject of an official investigation by the Board of Trade at Whitehall, the Privy Council's arm that regulated the colonies. Governor Bellomont had been deputized to lead the inquiry. His findings gave even more credence to the suspicions against the Rhode Island government. Cranston refused to accept the credentials of the royally appointed Admiralty official in Newport and claimed such authority for himself as governor. In this he was supported by his own Assembly (being fiercely independent Rhode Islanders). Privateering commissions changed hands for bribes, stolen cargoes were declared legal captures for more bribes, and pirates walked in and out of jail in the colony as easy as entering or leaving a tavern.

Rhode Island faced the very real threat of having its charter revoked but fate intervened. Bellomont had sent to the Board in London a copy of Rhode Island's laws and statutes along with withering comments: "It seems that government have taken all this time to prune and polish 'em. And yet after all, I believe the world never saw such a parcell of fustian. I got Mr. Addington, the Secretary, to read 'em over and make some remarks on them."

Although the Board's damning report was passed on to King William, smooth talk from Cranston slowed down the proceedings. Fate also lent a hand to Cranston. Lord Bellomont died suddenly in office, London became focused on the renewed war against France, and Dudley quickly had a full plate in taking over as governor of Massachusetts and dealing with Indian attacks.

The latest case (which would have been very fresh in Dudley's mind) was, to him and his council members, typical of the rascals running—and ruining—Rhode Island.

In the spring of 1698, Robert Munday and George Cutler arrived in Newport aboard the frigate *Fowey*. Loaded with gold and precious gems they had stolen off Madagascar, they were arrested by local authorities on suspicion of piracy. Within a few days both men were out on bail, posted by the uncle of the recently retired Rhode Island governor, Walter Clarke. However, Governor Cranston held onto their treasure. The two pirates were not about to take their leave without their hard-earned gold. They stayed in Newport, openly carousing and abusing the locals for months as the government dithered. Finally, in March 1699, the Court of General Tryalls at Newport opened proceedings against the two men. Munday, recently reconfined to jail, managed to walk out and disappear. Cutler stood trial but not one person came forward to support the charges against him. The jury acquitted and the court ordered his treasure returned to him. Cutler quickly bought into Newport society, buying property and becoming a sponsoring member of the newly constructed Trinity Church above Thames Street.

Even more surprising is what befell Munday. After four years on the run, but coveting his fortune that Cranston still held, he returned to Newport and handed himself in for trial. Standing at the bar on April 3, 1703, he pleaded not guilty to charges of escape from jail and to piracy. The jury rapidly found him not guilty on either charge and he was released from custody upon payment of court fees. His story did not end there however.

With impressive bravado, Munday soon petitioned the Rhode Island General Assembly to return his confiscated gold. The legislators actually considered his demands, but, in the end determined "that all the monies, goods or chattels seized as aforesaid, was forfeited to his Majesty's use [at the time] ... wherefore, we find no cause to alter the aforesaid judgement, or any part thereof." The money ended up in the colony's coffers to be used as Cranston saw fit. Indeed, it was probably spent within months of being taken from Munday. A rough justice of sorts.

This was just the sort of mockery of the Queen's law that Dudley so despised. The case had been heard in a local criminal court, a trial by a jury of peers. Cranston's administration was in direct contravention of parliamentary law, passed under King William's reign, which directed acts of piracy to be tried by local admiralty courts—essentially military tribunals. These new parliamentary statutes, as yet untested ("Acts 11 &12 William III, For the More effectual Suppression of Piracy"), sought to accomplish exactly what they advertised to do. The intent was to circumvent trial by jury, thus bypassing sympathetic local courts, and gaining more convictions as well as confiscated treasure. Considered throughout the colonies as a violation of the freeborn right of all Englishmen to fair trial, the new Admiralty court powers created a stir similar to that of the recent U.S. Guantanamo Bay military tribunals for suspected terrorists. Then, as now, the tinkering with long-established legal conventions for reasons of judicial expediency was regarded with great suspicion and general hostility.

Nevertheless, Dudley realized that the Quelch case was his chance to run the first such Admiralty criminal court ever held outside of England. As the royally appointed Captain-General and Commander-in-Chief of New England, he firmly believed that it would be a dereliction of his duty not to proceed.

His second spur to alacrity in dealing with Quelch was equally important if somewhat more subtle. Though he was no economist in the modern sense, as a political creature, he understood the mechanics of public finance well. To his mind, the influx of what he knew was a significant amount of gold worth many thousands, could fundamentally undermine the creaky and besieged Massachusetts economy.

Massachusetts, like her sister colonies, had always been cash-poor. None of the colonies had the right to issue money, but in the 1650s Boston had begun issuing locally minted silver "Pine Tree" shillings. Although this was tolerated by London, New England money never traded at an equal rate to English sterling, which was always scarce in the colonies, nor were Pine Tree (or "Bay") shillings ever minted in truly significant numbers. The result was that by 1700, Massachusetts was totally dependent on external means for hard currency: Spanish silver "dollars" and gold. This was never available in large enough quantities to become a normal trade medium for most local people. The result was that New England operated under a barter economy that limited the development of commerce.

A New Englander had to possess a good head for arithmetic to survive daily commercial life in Massachusetts. As Madam Kemble noted in her journal:

> They give the title of merchant to every trader; who Rate their Goods according to the time and spetia they pay in: viz. Pay, money, Pay as mony, and trusting. *Pay* is pieces of Eight [Spanish silver dollars], Ryalls [Spanish gold *reals* or doubloons] or Bay shillings or Good hard money, as sometimes silver coin is termed by them; also Wampum, vizt. Indian beads wch serves for change. *Pay as mony* is provisions, as aforesd one Third cheaper than as the Assembly or General Court sets it; and *Trust* as they and the mercht agree for time [credit].

Although the General Assembly in Massachusetts set a rate of exchange that made a Spanish dollar worth six shillings, later sanctioned by the crown in 1704, in reality, the free market ruled. Two rates coexisted: the officially sanctioned "Proclamation" rate and the rate "on the street," which fluctuated according to circumstances and could be as high as eight shillings. But in many towns, household goods could be used as legal tender to settle tax bills. In Hingham, for instance, milk pails were offered up for payment— and accepted.

But Kemble fails to mention another form of currency, relatively new, but one that had gained credence since its introduction in 1690: paper money. Massachusetts was the first political entity in the western world to issue notes as legal tender. Not real money as such (the colonies could not mint currency), these notes were essentially bills of credit, issued by the government in expectation of tax revenue over a future period stipulated by decree. Issued in denominations of five shillings, ten shillings, twenty shillings, and five pounds, they changed hands at a discount compared to the hard currency rate. Nonetheless, they provided a convenient method of transaction and allowed the government to defer payment until revenue was collected. At the end of the term of issue, the notes would be "retired," that is, burned. Another issue would be authorized, and the whole process would begin again. Such a scheme could only survive in an environment where gold and silver remained relatively thin on the ground.

Dudley quickly realized that his government could be facing a serious devaluation of its bills of credit with Quelch's gold pouring into the Boston marketplace. And as he sat mulling his options, he did not yet know for certain the full amount of Quelch's treasure. Colman and Clarke reckoned that the haul was worth some £10,000 sterling. Given the prevailing wisdom that a pirate and his money are soon parted, Dudley saw that the province was balanced on the edge of a financial crisis. There was no "Bank of Massachusetts" with chests full of silver to honor the bills immediately and thus bail out the government. Governor Dudley needed to get his hands on every ounce of that pirated gold and confiscate it for the crown.

Staving off a financial meltdown and advancing the province's interests in the eyes of the Queen and her counselors were good enough reasons to be ruthless in proceeding against Quelch and his men. But Dudley also saw personal opportunity in the crisis.

For the past two years, he had been unsuccessful in convincing the General Assembly to vote him an annual salary. His subsistence was based on his family holdings, money in London, the stipend granted occasionally by the legislature in lieu of a regular salary, and whatever "fees" he could cream off from public administration through his position as governor. By recovering the pirate treasure and prosecuting the pirates, he would be well positioned to receive the reward of a grateful monarch. A large cash bounty could be reasonably expected, one that would help maintain him in the life of a gentleman.

His first move was to reissue the warrant against the crew of the *Charles,* slightly modified, in his own name. To his mind, Povey had not been firm enough in his language of denunciation and more importantly, had failed to grasp the urgency of retrieving the stolen gold and silver. This would require the instilment of fear in the local population. His new proclamation, issued on May 29, contained both carrot and stick: "Whosoever shall discover & Seize any of the said Pirates or Treasure concealed, and deliver them to Justice, shall be well Rewarded for their pains." But Dudley ended his warrant with a touch of menace: "And any who conceal or have in their custody any of the said Treasure, & shall not disclose & make known the same unto some one or more of the Council, with an Accompt of the Quantity & Species, & render the same unto the Commissioners appointed for that purpose, within the space of Twenty Days next after the Publication hereof at *Boston,* shall be alike proceeded against."

Slyly, Dudley had implied something of a threat to more than those who accepted pirate gold. His proclamation effectively cast suspicion on those Bostonians who transacted in *any* gold or silver. How could one tell the difference between Spanish or Portuguese coins once they had been melted down? At a stroke, he had buttressed his government's bills of credit by making it dangerous to use anything else. With the finger-pointing of the witch hysteria still fresh in local minds, it was logical to assume that many people understood the risks of being smeared by a neighbor with a grudge.

Three days later, Governor Dudley addressed the General Assembly at the Town House, chiefly about the state of defenses in the northern frontier from which he had recently returned.

However, he also used the occasion to lay out his course of action against Quelch and his men:

> The last Week has discovered a very notorious Piracy, committed upon Her Majesties Allies the *Portugal* [sic], on the Coast of *Brasil*, by *Quelch* and Company, in the *Charles* Gally; for the discovery of which, all possible methods, have been used, and the severest Process against those vile men shall be speedily taken, That the Province be not thereby disparaged, as they have been heretofore; and I hope every good man will do his Duty according to the several Proclamations, to discover the Pirates & their Treasure, agreeable to the Acts of Parliament in that case made and provided.

The speech and his proclamation were duly published by John Campbell in that week's issue of the *Boston News-Letter*. Dudley's proclamation also added a few valuable details about the case, namely, that some of the crew already apprehended had confessed, admitting that they had preyed upon the Portuguese and committed "divers Villanous Murders" during their piratical spree.

John Quelch's "Spanish shipwreck" alibi had collapsed like a wall of sand against a rising tide. He may not have realized it then, sitting miserably in the stink of his jail cell, but the most damning evidence against him was to be presented by his own men.

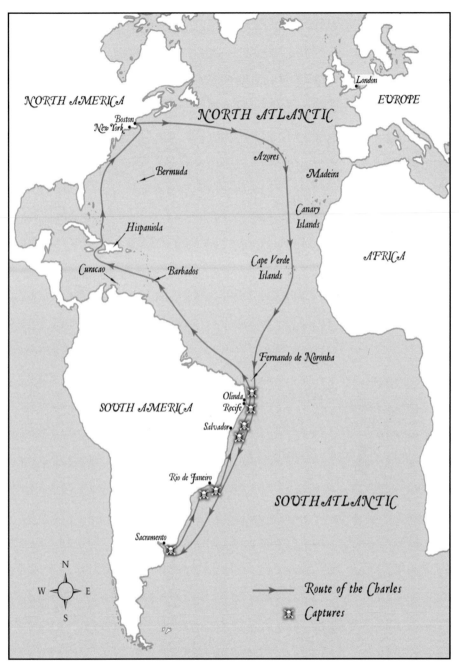

The Voyages of the Brigantine *Charles*.

18th Century South America

São Luís do Maranhão

Cabo de São Roque

PARAIBA
ITAMARACA
PERNAMBUCO
Olinda
Recife

BAHIA ● Cidade do Salvador

THE

SPANISH

VICEROYALTY

OF

PERU

S T A T E   O F   B R A Z I L

MINAS
GERAIS

ESPIRITU
SANTO

RIO DE JANEIRO
São Paulo ● Rio de Janeiro
SÃO PAULO ● Santos Cabo Frio
Ilha de São Sebastião
São Vincente
Paranaguá

RIO GRANDE
DE SÃO PEDRO
Ilha Santa Catarina

COLONIA
DO
SACRAMENTO ● São Pedro do Rio Grande

River Plate

Miles
0   500
Kilometres   800

N
W ● E
S

South America in the early eighteenth century.

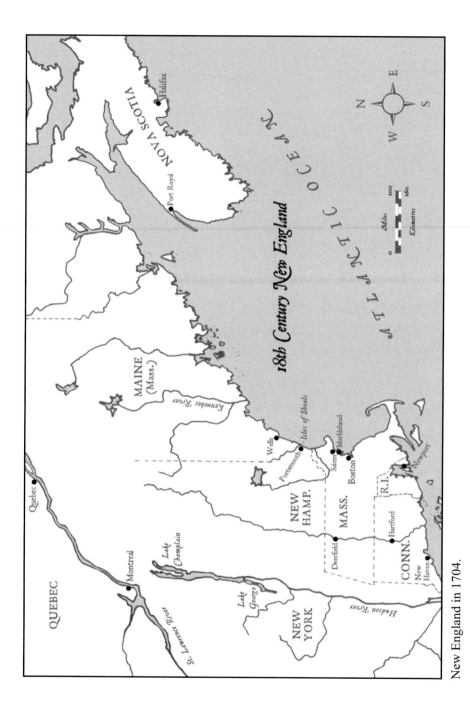

New England in 1704.

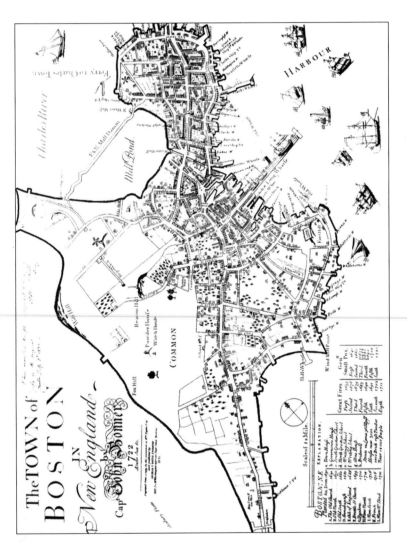

John Bonner's wonderfully detailed 1723 map of Boston shows its meandering streets and crowded seafront. The Town House lies at the top of King Street, a short distance from the Long Wharf seen jutting into the harbor. Bonner noted "Houses near 3000, 1000 Brick rest Timber." (*author's collection*)

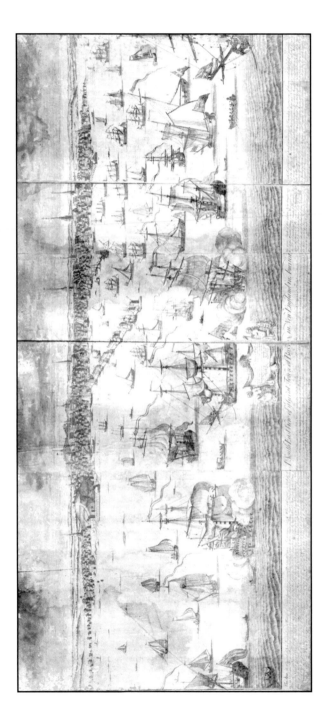

A 1725 panoramic view of Boston from the southeast shows a thriving seaport and a harbor filled with vessels of every shape and size. Wrote one visitor from England at the time, "Upon the whole, Boston is the most flourishing Town for Trade and Commerce in the English America." (*I.N. Phelps Stokes Collection, Miriam and Ira D. Wallach Division of Art, Prints and Photographs, The New York Public Library, Astor, Lennox and Tilden Foundations*)

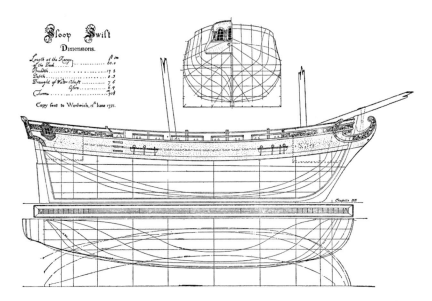

Sloop Swift
Dimensions.

Length at the Range
of the Deck 60.0
Breadth 19.2
Depth 8.3
Draught of Water Afore ... 7.6
Abaft 6.9
Tuns 90¼

Copy sent to Woolwich, 13ᵗʰ June 1721.

Hull plan of a Royan Navy sloop, the Swift, rigged out as a brigantine. The *Charles* would have been of similar dimensions. Note the "tholes" or oarlocks along the ship's bulwarks into which sweeps could be dropped for rowing in a calm. (*American Sailing Ships, New York, 1935*)

"Two Views of an English Brigantine" by T. Boon. The ship is from the late seventeenth or early eighteenth century but is rigged with a jib rather than the square spritsail that would have been used in Quelch's time. As the Union flag ensign is flying at the stern, the drawing must have been done sometime after 1707. (*National Maritime Museum London*)

Marblehead's Little Harbor around 1900. The sheltered cove from which the *Charles* departed for Brazil and to which it fatefully returned a year later. (*courtesy Library of Congress*)

A drawing of an early eighteenth century brigantine vessel showing its square-rigged foremast and the fore-and-aft rigged mizzen as on a sloop or schooner.

Sir Charles Hobby, owner of the Boston-built *Charles* brigantine and the most high-profile member of the privateering syndicate. (*courtesy Boston Athenaeum*)

Samuel Sewall, infamous as a judge at the Salem witch trials, also played a major role in the trial and conviction of John Quelch and his crew. A portrait from later life with Sewall was 76. (*courtesy Massachusetts Historical Society*)

Governor John Dudley, Massachusetts-born, London-educated, and an astute politician, used the Quelch episode to curry royal favor and secure his power base in Boston. (*courtesy Massachusetts Historical Society*)

Paul Dudley, the governor's first-born son and chief enforcer of royal policy in Massachussetts. As Attorney-General, he led the pursuit, capture, and prosecution of Quelch. (*courtesy Boston Athenaeum*)

Boston Town House
Built 1657

Boston's Town House was the center of public life in the colony. The seat of the governor, his council and assembly, storehouse, library, and marketplace, it was also where the Quelch trial was held. (*courtesy Boston Public Library*)

The oldest surviving prison in America, the Old Gaol at York, Maine, was constructed in 1917 based on the plans of Boston's stone jail. The plank-lined cells mask a stone wall some three-feet thick. Note the seventeenth century saw blades on the grating as an extra security measure. (*courtesy Old Gaol Collection, Old York Historical Society, York, Maine PYV12/F.29*)

The execution of pirate captain Stede Bonnet in Charleston in 1718; the scene of the death of John Quelch would have looked much the same. Bonnet's head is shaved as he normally wore a gentleman's periwig. Onlookers crowd in and watch from nearby ships. (*A General History of the Robberies and Murders of the Most Notorious Pyrates, London, 1724*)

THE

Arraignment, Tryal, and Condemnation,

OF

Capt. John Quelch,

And Others of his Company, &c.

FOR

Sundry *Piracies, Robberies,* and *Murder,* Committed upon the Subjects of the King of *Portugal,* Her Majesty's Allie, on the Coast of *Brasil,* &c.

WHO

Upon full Evidence, were found Guilty, at the *Court-House* in *Boston,* on the Thirteenth of *June,* 1704. By Virtue of a Commission, grounded upon the Act of the Eleventh and Twelfth Years of King *William, For the more effectual Suppression of Piracy.* With the Arguments of the QUEEN's Council, and Council for the Prisoners upon the said Act.

PERUSED

By his Excellency *JOSEPH DUDLEY,* Esq; Captain-General and Commander in Chief in and over Her Majesty's Province of the *Massachusetts-Bay,* in *New-England,* in *America,* &c.

To which are also added, some PAPERS that were produc'd at the Tryal abovesaid.

WITH

An Account of the Ages of the several Prisoners, and the Places where they were Born.

LONDON:

Printed for *Ben. Bragg* in *Avemary-Lane,* 1705.

(Price One Shilling.)

A censored transcript of the trial was published under the authority of the governor after the convictions in an attempt to justify Dudley's aggressive actions and thus stem the public outcry. (*The Arraignment, Tryal and Condemnation of Capt. John Quelch, London, 1704*)

Early twentieth century popular illustrator Howard Pyle vividly brought to life scenes from pirate life during the Golden Age. This post-battle parley on deck, with a privateer captain holding court on the bulkhead, might well evoke the real drama aboard the *Charles* off Brazil. (*The Book of Pirates, New York, 1903*)

Sir Isaac Newton, scientist, mathematician, alchemist, Master of the Royal Mint and first man in England to see and assay Quelch's gold. (*courtesy of Hulton Archive/ Getty Images*)

A 1705 Queen Anne gold guinea coin, quite possible minted from the treasure of Captain Quelch. The hole probably indicates that this piece was used as jewellery at some point. (*courtesy of the Governor and Company of the Bank of England*)

Chapter Twelve

Trail of Gold

By June 4, as John Quelch began his third week of incarceration, any hopes of a quick release under a bail bond or even via a quiet deal allowing him to "disappear" in return for his gold, must have evaporated fully. The shipowners had apparently disavowed his reckless undertaking off the Brazilian coast and neither Mr. Colman nor Mr. Clarke had interceded on his behalf as far as he could tell. He was on his own now and he knew it.

Quelch's personal discomfort after two weeks in prison would have also sapped his confidence and fed his fears for the future. The weather in Boston in June can go either way: mild and rainy or broiling. The summer of 1704 was the latter. As Braintree mason and militiaman John Marshall remarked in his journal: "As to this June past the weather was very hott ... especially toward the end of the month."

For those prisoners committed to the older, wooden portion of the jail, mainly debtors or petty delinquents, the quarters began heating up fearsomely during the day, the air close and stale, stinking of wood fire and the pungent odors of the privy. However, debtors often had the luxury of periods out of doors in the prison yard, under the watchful (or not so watchful) eye of the jailor or a constable. Food or a few personal possessions could be brought in from well wishers on the outside, to help soften the discomfort of their miserable situation.

But for felons or prisoners of war, the circumstances were altogether different. These unfortunates, whether convicted or accused awaiting trial, would be committed to the stone prison where little light or fresh air penetrated its perpetually damp three-foot thick walls. Cooler perhaps, but all the more noxious due to the concentration of unhealthy men and the most rudimentary sanitation, normally a bucket in the corner of the large communal cells. These conditions were exacerbated by poor standards of food and water. Unless well bribed, the jailers would have no incentive to provide a good meal or favors of any sort. Archaeological evidence from the old jail at York, Maine, built in 1719 under instructions from Boston (and still standing), points to a diet of lesser cuts of meat and shellfish, the latter cheap and plentiful. After gnawing on crusty bread and pig's knuckles or boiled mussels and clams, walks in the yard were out of the question. Normally prisoners would be shackled day and night. The thirty-seven French sailors who made up the largest percentage of the inmates, were unlikely to have any benefactors in Boston. For the accused of the brigantine *Charles,* the matter was somewhat different. Unless their money had been confiscated by the authorities, an accomplice could have bought, his comrade some amenities or better treatment, the result of a shady agreement made with a constable in a nearby tavern. In Boston as in London, it was common practice for jailors to supplement their meager income through extorting prisoners or accepting bribes. It is not known if Quelch or any of his men managed to improve their lot this way, though a few years later, accusations of extortion by the authorities were raised publicly, to the embarrassment of the Dudleys.

The arrival of the mariners had complicated the primitive logistics in operation at the prison. It was so drastic a situation that by the middle of the month, the governor's council recommended that action be taken:

> Upon consideration of the great number of French prisoners of War now within the Prison at Boston, and the danger of Infection by their close confinement, now in this hot season of the year. Ordered . . . to rayse the fence about the Prison yard next the street, between the Stone Prison and the house of Mrs. Eyre. And at both ends of the old wooden prison, and make up a shed within the sd yard, that the said Prisoners may have the benefit of the aire in the day time, as *his Excellency the Govr shall direct.* (Author's Italics)

Even a breath of fresh air would come only at the express command and largesse of Governor Dudley.

Council minutes for the period between February 29 and June 5, 1704, have not been found in modern times. They resume beginning June 6, and from these it can be gleaned that the whereabouts of the pirate gold was at the top of the agenda. It is also clear that Dudley's scare tactics against the populace had borne some fruit. The minutes noted the delivery of several parcels of gold from locals eager to avoid prosecution. Joseph Hearne of Marblehead brought in nearly three ounces received as a pledge from one of the crew "but before any Proclamation was issued out against them."

A militia colonel, one Hathorne, also brought in over thirteen ounces of gold he had received from concerned inhabitants at Marblehead. Local goldsmith Jeremiah Dummer turned up to relinquish some six ounces "bought of several woomen before the Proclamation was Emitted against Quelch and Company or their piracy discovered."

All the confiscated gold was weighed and then turned over to the province treasurer for safekeeping. Despite this small success, it was noted that "there is considerable of the sd Gold and Treasure lying in the hands of several persons at Marblehead who have not yet disclosed and delivered up the same."

Although the Council records are lost, we know from Sewall's diary that on May 29, the first of the gold had been rounded up. Sewall recorded, "Several bring in Gold; Capt. Tuttle brings three parcels; two given him by Wm Clarke *de Johane* [the younger]; one by Capt. Quelch." This is the only proof found that Dudley had not only managed to get the owners' shares of the Treasure (presumably Clarke's honesty put Colman on the spot) but also some or all of Quelch's personal fortune. Moreover, this was nearly a week after the capture of Quelch and the other crew members in Boston.

Quelch had probably been interrogated in the first few days of his imprisonment by members of the council, possibly even by Governor Dudley himself. No records of these meetings, if any were made, have ever been found. All we know for certain is that Quelch must have divulged the location of his treasure. Whether it was through duress or the promise of leniency will never be known. Had Quelch given over all of his gold to the governor? If he had done so, he had surrendered up his last bargaining chip. Given that he steadfastly maintained his innocence of piracy, it may have been a desperate gamble to prove his sincerity to the authorities.

On June 7, more parcels of gold dust and coin thumped onto the conference table in the Council chambers at the Town House. Constable Thomas Foster had managed to round up nearly forty ounces while a William Browne, esquire, turned over some six ounces. Colonel John Legg, the commander of the South Essex militia regiment at Marblehead, delivered a small packet of "seven penny wt." Most revealing though was the appearance of John Noyes, the silversmith at the council chamber. He brought in "sixty eight ounces & halfe silver plate, being coyne run downe." It is highly unlikely that this was just Noyes's fee for helping out Quelch. This was in all likelihood part of John Quelch's treasure, held by Noyes for safekeeping. Now, this too, was in Dudley's hands.

During the council meeting on June 6, Governor Dudley decreed that a "Commission of Inquiry" be instituted and sent to Marblehead immediately. He personally nominated two judges (and council members), Nathaniel Byfield as judge of the Admiralty, and Samuel Sewall. Also appointed, though not by name, was the Attorney General, the governor's son.

The stated purpose of the special commission was "to send for and examin all persons of whom they shall have Information or just ground of suspicion, do conceal and detain the same, either at Marblehead, or parts adjacent, and to take what they shall find into their hands; as also to secure any of the Pirates."

Clearly from this wording, the chief mission was to secure the gold; the capture of the pirates only a secondary matter. Dudley already had snared the captain and some of the crew to put on trial; the priority had to be getting his hands on the remaining treasure.

Following his announcement of the creation of the commission, the governor produced copies of his royal instructions in order to make it clear under what authority he was proceeding against the pirates. The first of these was a note relating to the prosecution of individuals under the new parliamentary act for the "more effectual suppression" of piracy that directed him to proceed against any accused to the "Intent of the Act." This was Dudley's open declaration that unlike previous trials held in the colonies for piracy, this one would be handled very differently. He also produced a note that directed him to secure all goods relating to those accused of piracy.

With Paul Dudley presumably still on the road, perhaps even still in Marblehead, Byfield and Sewall lost no time and departed that same day for Salem. The council deputized as constables James Noyes and Joseph Gerrish and ordered them to accompany the judges on their mission north. The party reached the town of Salem by about eight o'clock that evening as the light began to fade. Sewall knew Salem well and no doubt Salem remembered him well too. A decade earlier he had ridden into town to examine and try those accused of witchcraft. Now, in 1704, with the full awareness of his central role in that miscarriage of justice uppermost in his mind, he was back again to mete out the law.

But he also had family connections locally. His brother, Stephen, a major in the Essex County militia and a clerk of the court at Salem, had married into a Salem family of good standing. He was a frequent visitor and indeed had first learned of the Quelch matter on his way back from a visit just two weeks previously.

After ensconcing themselves at an inn, they probably linked up with Sewall's brother and took refreshment before they received another visitor, one who carried some alarming news. This was Sam Wakefield, the "water-bailey" who served as the customs and revenue officer for the port. Wakefield excitedly informed them of new developments concerning the pirates. He had that day heard a rumor that two of Quelch's crew were over near Gloucester at Cape Ann, planning to join the crew of another privateer who was in the final stages of fitting-out. The privateer in question was Thomas Larrimore, well-known for his military service to the province. Byfield and Sewall immediately drew up a warrant for the arrest of these Quelch fugitives and dispatched Wakefield around midnight to carry out the order.

The next morning, Thursday, dawned refreshingly wet. The party left the inn at Salem, joined by Major Sewall, and proceeded the short distance to Marblehead in the pouring rain. When they arrived at the town, they made for the house of Captain John Brown, a leading citizen, and there opened their "court" by the fireside as their sodden boots raised wisps of steam on the hearth. Unfortunately, Sewall provides no color of the proceedings that day; the diary rarely delves into the details of official meetings, his comments most often swirled about the more mundane aspects of his day. It is likely that Byfield and Sewall, now joined by Paul Dudley who was already there, interviewed a parade of witnesses through the afternoon, all attesting to what and whom they had seen or not seen. Dudley had no doubt been typically thorough in the week past. He would have ferreted out any active accomplices in the town and intimidated the locals to turn in anything they had received of Quelch's men. He had also probably coordinated the deliveries of confiscated treasure from Marblehead to the council chamber in Boston on June 7.

Samuel's brother Stephen returned that evening for Salem while the others stayed on to take their evening meal and raise a mug or two of buttered rum. However restful their sleep may have been that night, the house was awoken by a loud hammering on the front door at six in the morning. It was an express rider carrying news from Gloucester. The situation facing the commissioners was about to become more complicated.

Sewall's jaw must have dropped as he read the letter, hastily scrawled by Wakefield in the middle of the night. Some "9 or 11 Pirats, double arm'd" had been spotted holed-up in an isolated house on Cape Ann. No longer just a simple "mopping-up" operation, the Boston officials now faced having to subdue a gang of very desperate men. Their response, not surprisingly, was to muster overwhelming force. Straight away they sent word to Col. Legg to summon the "northward" or outlying companies of his regiment, the Essex South, and call out what parties as he could raise and send them to Cape Ann "upon this Extraordinary occasion." Secondly, they drew up another letter to Col. John Wainwright, commander of the Essex North at nearby Ipswich, a few miles northwest of Salem, to do the same with his regiment, the commissioners "intimating that we were moving thither our selves to be Witness of their forwardness of Her Majesties Service."

The Province of New England rarely had even a few regular English troops billeted upon it at the beginning of the eighteenth century and although the crown sometimes helped pay for cannon and forts, Massachusetts was on its own militarily. Instead, Boston had a provincial army comprising one or two uniformed foot regiments, usually drawn up from volunteers from the more numerous militia bands of the province. These might number only 100 to

200 men and were usually activated for specific periods of time to defend the province. The regiment at Boston more often than not served as a paramilitary unit to enforce public order in the town. The chief responsibility for New England's defense therefore fell upon the shoulders of the local town and county militias. Since every able-bodied man between the ages of sixteen and sixty was bound to serve a few months a year when required, and to appear at local musters quarterly, theoretically at least, this afforded Massachusetts an army numbering some 40,000 or more.

In 1701, militiamen were directed to own a serviceable musket, a "snapsack" for supplies, a bandoleer of twelve measured charges or a cartridge box, a pound of black powder, twenty musket balls, twelve flints, and "a good Sword or Cutlash." In reality, the supply and coordination of the *entire* assembled force would have entailed an expense and effort beyond the capabilities of the Boston authorities. Even the few large expeditions to Canada assembled during these years normally only numbered a few thousand soldiers at most. Militia colonels were sanctioned by the governor (and sometimes had to supplement their troops' equipment) while captains, lieutenants, and ensigns were elected by the local men. Generally, militia officers were leading citizens and merchants and their rank carried enormous cachet in town and country life. The militias were motivated and dependable forces when they were needed— defending their towns from Indian attack, but less so when sent off far from home for extended periods. Training was inconsistent and haphazard, as was discipline, and officers rarely had any professional military experience. In short, their effectiveness was highly dependent upon the situation they faced and where they were going. Sewall and Byfield must have been well aware of these limitations.

They sent James Noyes off with the letter for Wainwright, telling him to show it to Captain Fiske at Wenham on his way. The three commissioners were taking no risks. If enough militia officers could be rousted they stood a fair chance of cobbling together at least *some* number of militiamen. Their fears for the success of this emergency muster would soon prove to be well-founded.

Rushing about Captain Brown's house to ready themselves, Sewall and Byfield eventually saddled up and took to the rocky rutted road northwest to Salem. Paul Dudley, the younger and more adventurous of the commission members, decided to accompany Col. Legg to Gloucester by boat from Marblehead. Under sail, he was bound to reach the fugitives faster than by land. Once Sewall and Byfield were back in Salem, they sought out a resident, Dr. Francis Gahtman, to take an affidavit "for some better foundations for our Actions." Gahtman apparently possessed information that Captain Larrimore, far from being tricked into accepting the Quelch runaways, was actually in the process of turning pirate himself.

Thomas Larrimore was a master mariner of Salem and a war hero with a well-earned reputation for loyalty and daring. What would make him turn to piracy? He had served as quartermaster on three separate privateers during King William's War: the *Dragon*, *Dolphin*, and *Salem Galley*. In 1702, under a commission issued by Governor Dudley, he had given valuable service to Boston under command of his own vessel against French raiders. At the start of January 1703, again under special commission, he was sent aboard HMS *Gospir* in charge of a company of foot comprising fifty-nine volunteers, many of them his old sailing mates, to aid the colony of Jamaica against the Spanish. Outfitted and sent out at Dudley's expense, they had been promised not only soldiers' wages, but also a share of riches from captured enemy ships and forts. Dudley paid each man £1 as a bounty for signing up. The second-most expensive outlay for the expedition was £24 to pay for a few dozen casks of rum to keep the troops happy on the voyage to the Caribbean. Wrote Dudley to his opposite number in St. Jago de la Vega:

> Capt. Larrimore and his officers and most of his men have been abroad this summer upon this coast, and have taken five good ships, and have shewed themselves of good courage, but will fall short in their appearance and discipline of the regular troops you do receive from England ... but that may be in a few weeks taught them, and in real service I hope they will show themselves Englishmen.

Dudley went on to comment:

> They are the first men in armes that ever went out of this Province, or from the shoar of America, and if at first they meet with discouragement I am sure I shall never send from hence one file of Volunteers more. I therefore humbly pray on their behalf that they may be kindly dealt withall and provided so that I may have a good account of them to be made public here, and it will satisfy everybody.

As events transpired, Larrimore and his men became volunteers in the truest sense of the word. The governor of Jamaica and his council noted in their records that "there is noe establishment remitted hither yet for their pay or subsistence." Dudley had passed the buck—and the bill—onto Jamaica, whose council, in turn, stonewalled on paying the men. The New Englanders were bustled onto a Royal Navy flotilla engaged in Caribbean operations. The survivors of the company eventually ended up transported to Newfoundland, broke and diseased, before making it home to Boston in November 1703, still unpaid for their service. Despite Larrimore's entreaties to the government that winter, no pay materialized. It was small wonder that, with his patience at an end, bitterness overcame him and he decided to turn rogue with the remnants of his company.

Sewall and Byfield now realized that they were facing not just a dozen pirates on the run, but Captain Larrimore and the crew of a large sloop or brigantine armed with heavy cannon. This vessel's name, *Larrimore Galley*, was probably chosen less out of the captain's vanity and more by wounded pride for the dishonor done to him. The commissioners immediately dispatched Gahtman to Boston to inform the Governor of what was taking place.

Despite the new odds, Stephen Sewall also fell into the spirit of the hunt that his older brother was orchestrating. He managed to commandeer a local fishing shallop, the *Trial*, as well as Salem fort's pinnance to transport him and twelve of his company to Gloucester to buttress the gathering force. Meanwhile, Byfield and Samuel Sewall linked up with the Sheriff of Essex County, William Gedney, and then proceeded overland to Cape Ann and Gloucester town (a ride of some twenty miles) accompanied by a small troop of dragoons (essentially mounted militia) under the command of Captain Turner. On the way they passed the town of Beverly where they mustered Lieutenant Robert Briscoe and his troop of horse. The everswelling army continued on toward Cape Ann. Halfway to Gloucester by the coast road, they came to the town of Manchester. Word had already spread of the *posse* and when Sewall, Byfield, and the troopers rode in, they found the local militia already assembled and drilling on the top of a large flat granite outcrop on the edge of town.

After some hurried greetings and introductions, these militia-men joined the party and carried on toward Gloucester. The force was within sight of the town when a lone rider hove into view, pounding up the road to greet them. He delivered a letter from Paul Dudley and Col. Legg that carried disappointing news: Larrimore had that very morning sailed to the head of the Cape and picked up all of the pirate fugitives. The messenger, recalled Sewall, "seem'd to discourage our going forward."

Sheriff Gedney was sent to post Dudley's note to the governor in Boston while the Salem troopers were told that those who wished could return home. Dudley's note also urged the Ipswich regiment to turn back. One can easily imagine the scene on the roadside; mixed feelings of relief and disappointment that the quarry had flown, the various townsmen debating whether to continue on or go home, some eager to press on but most happy to call it a day having had their fill of excitement.

The commissioners, along with a much-reduced party, pressed on to Gloucester to await the arrival of Stephen Sewall's little navy. Samuel would have been forgiven for thinking it was just as well that his brother had missed intercepting the *Larrimore Galley*. The fishing boats would have been shattered in minutes against a broadside of shot from the privateer. The *Trial* and its compan-ion pinnance showed up in port sometime midafternoon. Reunited with his brother and the other commissioners, Stephen Sewall sat down to dine with them at the home of Captain Davis.

Talk was heated as the arguments flew back and forth what to do next. It was finally resolved that Larrimore ought to be pur-sued. But this meant, of course, pursuit by sea only. That was, un-fortunately, where the town militia drew the line of duty. Captain Herrick "pleaded earnestly" that his troopers not be coerced into sea battle. The commissioners cajoled in vain to get men to carry on the chase. At length, just like in some fictional tale, one voice spoke up above the mutual recriminations.

"At last, Brother offer'd to goe himself," wrote Sewall, "Then Capt. Turner offer'd to goe, Lieut. Brisco, and many good Men; so that quickly made up Fourty two; though we knew not the exact number till came home, the hurry was so great, and the vessel so small for 43." Major Sewall's bravado challenged the others into making the leap into the unknown. With a seasoned pilot found to guide them (and the four fishermen sticking with their little vessel despite the risk), the volunteers piled cheek by jowl into the tiny *Trial*, jostling and stumbling, muskets, powder horns, and bandoleers all clacking together as the group sought places on the shallop. The remainder climbed aboard the pinnance, the small, narrow, craft probably tied by a length of cable to the shallop.

Without uniforms, dressed in everyday wool kersey breeches and jackets, leather waistcoats, latch shoes, riding boots, and moccasins, knit fisherman's caps or brimmed felt hats, they would have looked more like a hunting party than a military unit. Their arms were equally eclectic: firelock muskets of differing lengths and calibers (old and new), well-worn single-edge cutlasses, wood-handled axes, an Indian tomahawk or two, and at Major Sewall's hip perhaps a proper officer's small sword. "Men gave us three very handsom cheers," recalled Samuel, "Row'd out of the Harbour after sun-set, for want of wind."

Sewall does not record how they knew where Larrimore was headed. Perhaps someone in port had given intelligence to them, possibly fishermen that had been passing the opposite way back to their moorings. The *Larrimore Galley* already held a head-start of several hours on them, a lead that to bystanders must have seemed everwidening as they watched the slow rise and dip of the oars as the overburdened *Trial* made her way out into the harbor and north toward the open sea.

As they lost sight of her in the gloom, Sewall, Byfield, and Dudley turned back to the town. The Attorney General had decided to return to Salem that night accompanied by the Beverly militia. Sewall and Byfield spent the evening in Gloucester, fortified not by drink but by prayer led by the town's minister, John White. The commissioners were up at dawn and on their way back to Salem, which they reached by nine that morning. Sewall immediately went to call on his sister-in-law to break the news that her husband was gone to sea on a hunt for pirates. Unsurprisingly, she took the news hard. "The Wickedness and despair of the company they pursued," wrote Sewall, "their Great Guns and other war-like Preparations, were a terror to her and to most of the Town; concluded they would not be Taken without Blood. Comforted our selves and them as well as we could."

Chapter Thirteen

To the Isles of Shoals

Stephen Sewall was without doubt a brave man, but he was no sailor. Without the handful of mariners onboard the shallop—just four fishermen and a pilot—the little expedition would never have had a chance of pushing off from the wharf. It is difficult to imagine what Sewall actually thought he could accomplish with his vessel and volunteers. It is unlikely that any had seen naval action. All carried long muskets, a weapon of limited use in a shipboard fight. Worse still, they had no cannon with which to engage the enemy. Still, Larrimore himself would have probably found it inconceivable that a boatload of landsmen militia could have had the daring to pursue him to sea in a commandeered fishing boat. The element of surprise, if little else, was in their favor.

Once out of the channel and into the open sea, the boats would have started to toss about depending upon how large the swell. Among those militia farmers not used to open water, the experience must have been both unnerving and nauseating. As soon as the breeze picked up, the fishermen told the soldiers to ship their oars while they themselves then set about raising the single large lateen sail on the shallop. Instantly, the craft would have shot forward, the churning bow wake audible as the canvas filled out. Assuming the sky was free of cloud that night, they would have had a waxing half-moon to illuminate their way until just after midnight. Not terribly good visibility but enough for experienced local mariners to gauge the coastline and consult their brass compass, aided by a dimly flickering tallow lamp. Sailing along any coastline in darkness is dangerous business and something the crew would be well aware of. The North Shore, like much of New England, is strewn with jagged outcrops capable of ripping out the bottom of a boat. The pilot directed the *Trial* nearly due north, this course edging them further away from the coastline that lay behind and to their larboard (or port) side.

Somehow, Sewall had learned that Larrimore's destination was a small group of rocky islets that lay about ten miles off Portsmouth, New Hampshire: the Isles of Shoals. This was not a surprising destination; since the early seventeenth century the Isles had been a favorite waypoint for people looking to disappear. They were also largely ungovernable: For some seventy years, Massachusetts Bay, New Hampshire, and the Province of Maine had been unable to establish any real form of authority on the five islands. This was a lawless outpost, predominantly male, and chiefly comprising poor fishermen who lived there year-round. Though hardly a town in the mainland sense, the inhabitants named the settlement on Star Island "Gosport," and it possessed a relatively calm anchorage on its northern shore, sheltered in part by Smuttynose and Cedar Islands to its east and by Hog Island due north.

Named not because they were grass- and scrub-covered rocks that barely stood out above the waves, but instead for the vast shoals of codfish that surrounded them, most of the islands' 600 or so inhabitants lived in wood or stone hovels clustered largely on Star Island and Smuttynose. Scandalously libertine by puritan standards, they had neither church nor chapel to worship in. Ministers had occasionally set up shop from time to time over the past decades, only to give up when faced with the Herculean task of the salvation of the islanders' souls, and instead returning to the more devout *terra cognita* of the mainland. Murderous brawls were commonplace and many Shoalers lived in a near permanent state of rum-induced inebriation.

To gain supplies and drink, they would trade fish with anyone who happened by, be they pirates, English, French, Spaniard, or Portuguese. Even among the poor, hardscrabble fishing villages of the coast, the Isles of Shoals had a reputation as the last refuge of the ungodly, a place to escape a shrewish wife, taxes, and all social responsibility. It was a reputation that was set to last.

During the War of Independence, New Hampshire and Boston forcibly evacuated all the islanders to the mainland, not for reasons of their safety but because they feared that the Shoalers would provide willing refuge and replenishment to the British navy.

Captain Larrimore, having hastily departed Gloucester, had chosen to finish fitting-out at the Shoals, obtaining the last of his supplies and fresh water, and perhaps recruiting additional crew members from among the more bellicose or bored denizens. It was a safe harbor and certainly he need not worry about any Shoalers asking too many questions or raising the alarm as in Salem and Gloucester.

Stephen Sewall's shallop made the dangerous night voyage without incident. As the sun arose low in the east, the men aboard *Trial* found themselves looking at the low silhouettes of Star and Lunging Islands. Making their way cautiously to the western approach, they neared the cove at Gosport. Two tall masts poked up above the ragged and rock-strewn shore—a large vessel was tucked into the port, sitting at anchor.

Militia officer Sewall may have been only a county clerk, but his next steps proved a certain innate tactical prowess. Having no cannon, his only hope was to catch Larrimore and Quelch's men by stealth. He was in the perfect vehicle to carry out an ambush. What better than a fishing boat to enter a fishing community unsuspected? Sewall gave orders for all the men to lie as flat as possible, concealing themselves below the gunwales of the vessel. They ranged themselves to cover both sides of the *Trial*, muskets loaded and primed for a volley once the order was given. Only the four fishermen remained standing, hauling on the sail and lines, and manning the tiller. Slowly, the *Trial* glided into Gosport cove, the fishermen quietly conversing while the militiamen kept silent. Skillfully, the pilot nudged the helm, guiding the vessel close to the *Larrimore Galley*, which sat lazily on its cable and anchor.

Peering over the gunwale, Sewall spotted a longboat with half a dozen men just running onto the shore from Larrimore's ship. Here was a stroke of luck indeed or as his brother Samuel would later put it "a singular good Providence of God." Only a few sailors remained on the deck of the ship, shouting and laughing to one another. The sight of the little fishing shallop edging ever closer did not cause concern and they ignored it until it came practically alongside them, sitting just a few yards away. But once it had drawn up amidships to the *Larrimore Galley*, the game was up. A shout went up from one of the privateer crewman and the half dozen or so on deck began scurrying for the cannon, yanking off tarpaulins and pulling the *tompions*, or wooden plugs, from the mouths of the guns.

Sewall's men rose up precariously from their crouch in the wobbling shallop, leveling their muskets at a slack-jawed Thomas Larrimore and his skeleton crew. Larrimore, no fool, had but seconds to decide upon his course of action. In an instant, the options must have raced through his mind. He was outnumbered but he still held the "high ground" on his ship. Could he depress his guns low enough to sink the shallop before the Boston men could scramble aboard? On the other hand, he had not *yet* committed any crime— including piracy. However, once blood was spilled, he would be a felon. His men on shore had not yet realized what was happening and even if they had, would probably not make it back in time to make a difference.

Both sides held their fire during this frozen flash of indecision. But Sewall refused to cede the momentum his surprise had afforded. He immediately called out to Larrimore to come aboard the *Trial* to talk. Larrimore demurred, saying that he could not, his boat having rowed ashore. Sewall instantly shouted back that he would come to Larrimore, and without waiting for assent he stepped into the pinnace along with Captain Turner, Captain Abbot, and Lieutenant Brisco, and pushed off to the side of the privateer ship. He and the other captains had managed to scramble up and over the rail but Larrimore or one of his officers swore that no other armed men should come aboard. Brisco let himself back down into the pinnace.

A tense standoff ensued on deck between the two commanders. After a few civil words from Sewall, Larrimore consented to a parley on shore. As the others waited, Sewall's arguments managed to win over Larrimore. The privateer quickly signed two orders as Sewall demanded; the first directing Larrimore's lieutenant, Joseph Wells, as well as one of Quelch's men, to leave the galley and come ashore. The second was an order giving over command of the galley to Captain Abbot "till they return'd." Had Larrimore's courage failed him or had he shrewdly calculated that he could avoid any prosecution through his cooperation and by dint of his previous record of loyal service to the province? Whatever the motivation, Stephen Sewall's surprise and fast action, combined with a little luck, had secured Larrimore, the galley, and seven of Quelch's fugitive crew. The whole business had been carried off "without striking a stroke or firing a gun," as Samuel noted in his diary.

While the fate of Larrimore and his own crew remained open to question, Quelch's seven men could have been in no doubt where they were headed. Sewall and his militia secured them for the journey back south and in the process relieved them of a total of some forty-six ounces of gold. But had Major Sewall recovered all of the treasure? Had more of it been left on Star Island, hidden or left with someone else for safekeeping? Considering that a share of sixteen ounces of gold is known to have been given out of generosity to just one sick crew member, it is likely the confiscated forty-six ounces was just a fraction. Sewall didn't push his luck by antagonizing the Shoalers with a search of the place, a search that no doubt would have been fruitless. He and his officers well knew the reputation of the islanders and wisely, he departed with his ships and prisoners before the Shoalers could decide whether he was friend or foe. He was also lucky in that two New Hampshire justices were conducting business on Star that day, further buttressing the show of authority.

With he and most of the militiamen transferred to the *Larrimore Galley*, Sewall took the *Trial* in tow with the pinnance and guided the vessel out of the cove and south, headed for Gloucester. The next morning, June 11, they were back at Gloucester where they dropped off some of the militia on Eastern Point. Sewall and his officers had learned on the voyage back that two more of Quelch's crew, William Jones, a twenty-four-year-old Londoner, and Peter Roach, a thirty-year-old Irishman, had missed the pickup by Larrimore on Cape Ann and were still hiding out in the area. As he waited for the wind to pick up again so that he could continue on to Salem, Sewall gave instructions for the militia to organize a search party and to spread the word to townspeople and farmers throughout the area. The two mariners were indeed found the next day and apprehended without a fight. The *Boston News-Letter* boasted that the manhunt was "performed very industriously" by the townspeople and that the two men "Being strangers and destitute of all Succours, they surrendered themselves this Afternoon, and were sent to Salem Prison."

There they joined their former shipmates as well as Thomas Larrimore, Joseph Wells, and Daniel Wormmall, the latter the master of the *Larrimore Galley*, all of whom had been delivered safe and sound by Sewall on the afternoon of June 11. On the previous day, at Boston, Governor Dudley had issued a warrant for Larrimore's arrest, presumably on the charge of aiding the escape of Quelch's men. As he heard the key and lock tumble and click home in his cell door, Larrimore must have been cursing himself for not having made a different decision at Star Island. No doubt his second-in-command and ship's master were harboring a grudge or two against him for his foolhardiness as well.

Major Sewall's homecoming at Salem, in which he rejoined his anxious family and accepted the congratulations of the locals, was short-lived. He and his men set out the next day overland to deliver the prisoners to the authorities in Boston. Reward money was uppermost in their minds.

On Monday, June 12, Samuel Sewall was awoken by constable Gerrish knocking on his bedchamber door. Gerrish excitedly told him of Major Sewall's astounding bloodless victory over the pirates at the Isles of Shoals and of his impending arrival in Boston with prisoners and treasure in tow. Samuel was soon afterward over to the Town House to inform the Governor and council of "Brother's good success." Dudley, both father and son, had not been idle during the drama that had unfolded over the past few days out on Cape Ann and in New Hampshire waters. Two more of Quelch's men had been rounded up in Boston: Benjamin Perkins a twenty-four-year-old bargeman from London and John Templeton, a fifteen-year-old Scottish boy. From Piscataqua town in New Hampshire, came a messenger with word from Deputy Governor Usher that James Austin, though still ill and weak, was on his way to Boston under guard along with "a considerable quantity of gold" that he had tried to conceal "in a girdle about him." Usher was wise enough not to leave himself open to future allegations. Accompanying the prisoner and the gold was an affidavit signed by Usher attesting that the gold delivered was the exact amount seized from Austin and not a pennyweight less.

Dudley's threats to charge receivers of pirate treasure, as accessories to the crime were being heard and believed, if not by all then
by many.

On the receiving end of the governor's invective in the last
week had been John Colman. When Clarke or Quelch had admitted to the premature division of the spoils amongst the ship owners, Colman had boldly asserted that it was his right as an official
receiver for the Admiralty's "tenths" to hold on to the gold himself. Dudley, who was well within rights to seize the gold under
his Queen's commission, not only refused this insolent demand
but also ordered Colman to sign a statement swearing that he had
turned in *all* of the treasure that Quelch had handed over. Colman
had reluctantly given over his and Hobby's share amounting to
eighty-four ounces and ten pennyweight each (worth over £420).
That same amount had been allocated to each of the investors and
even poor dead Captain Plowman was allocated eighty-five ounces
(whether by Quelch or Colman it is not known). The rest of the
owners remained quiet. They knew that if the governor chose to
pursue them, the facts could be damaging. They had all concealed
the treasure in what should have been a clear case of an undeclared
cargo, not yet legally condemned, and awarded by Nathaniel Byfield, the local Admiralty judge at Boston.

Dudley's failure to indict or publicly humiliate any of these
wealthy merchants at this time seems to indicate a desire to "bank"
the information as possible ammunition against his critics and enemies in the future. He may also have been worried by reports that
Bostonians in the street were grumbling about what was befalling
honest seamen returned home. Despite the fact that gold was being
turned in, this did not mean people accepted the principle behind
it. Routinely at loggerheads with the General Assembly, he had to
move carefully. As the biographer Everett Kimball noted, "A royal
governor attempting to carry out the policy of England could not
hope for the support of the province; rather must he be prepared to
encounter bitter opposition in the performance of his duty."

Dudley had learned through his interrogations that Quelch had
imported treasure worth some £10,000. According to the council
records, as of that moment Dudley had only recovered a little less
than half. Where did the rest lie? Given what he and the Council had taken off of individual crewmen, it stretches belief that the

thirty or so who had fled justice had done so with over £5,000 among them, but this does remain a distinct possibility depending on what kind of a share system Quelch used. If Dudley *did* learn how shares were divided, he never made this apparent in the commission proceedings. Moreover, Dudley would shortly mention the figure of £10,000 in a July letter to his master and political sponsor, William Blathwayt, at Whitehall. To officially quote such a sum when he had only managed to collect just about half of this treasure was an embarrassment for both he and Blathwayt. Dudley had no reason to inflate the amount of treasure taken by Quelch, and indeed, had every reason to minimize his reporting of the size of the haul.

As he quizzed Colman, he must have harbored considerable doubts that the man (who he held in poor regard anyway) was being completely truthful about the shares the owners had received. Until he obtained some proof of this, however, there was little else he could do.

Governor and son, lawyers both, restrained as they were with the merchants, had been busy in the past week rapidly building their legal case for the prosecution of Quelch and his men. This they set about doing by singling out those mariners that could be tempted into betraying their comrades for the sake of a pardon. The first, Matthew Pimer, had surrendered himself early in the drama at Boston. Shipped originally by the unfortunate Captain Plowman, he had never agreed with the actions of Lieutenant Quelch but had stayed the course for fear of the consequences. Two other of Quelch's men agreed to talk freely about the voyage: John Clifford, twenty-three years old and a Dublin malt-maker by trade; and James Parrot, twenty-years-old, a born and bred Yankee who had trained as a tanner but had succumbed to the promise of adventure and treasure at sea.

After the three men had been examined, they were undoubtedly moved to a separate cell to protect them as witnesses against the others. Paul Dudley called in a Town House scrivener, Edward Weaver, to take detailed statements from the prisoners. Dudley was keen to mine them for as much detail as possible concerning the voyage. How was Captain Plowman treated in captivity? Who were the ringleaders? What was Quelch's role as the new captain? What ships had they attacked, when had they attacked them, and where? Pimer's testimony would be crucial since he had kept the ship's logbook, later torn to shreds by Quelch near the end of the cruise. Would he be able to recall the details from memory?

Intimidated by the grilling from finely dressed gentlemen in periwigs, the three mariners must have realized there was no going back. Once separated from the others for any length of time, it would have been obvious that they had betrayed the crew. From this moment on they entrusted their lives to the Governor; any backsliding in commitment would see them returned to the main dungeon with the others—a prospect that must have frightened them witless.

Sitting in the gloom, shackled in irons along with the remnants of his crew, John Quelch somehow convinced the others to keep up their courage and stick to their story. Quelch either believed he truly was acting as a privateer albeit a loose one, or else he reckoned that no real evidence could be mustered against him in court, the testimony of codefendants not being enough to condemn a man under English Common Law. He may even have received word that the Boston mob was agitating for his release, egged on by what was perceived as royal high-handedness and greed. But the camaraderie of shared deprivation and misfortune is no substitute for sound advice. Quelch was in the dark both literally and figuratively.

Before the afternoon of June 12 had ended, Governor Dudley sent a messenger from the Council chamber scurrying over to Postmaster Campbell just as his printer, Benjamin Green, labored to place type blocks in the wooden frame for the week's issue of *The Boston News-Letter*. The messenger carried a statement that the Governor wanted included before Green inked up the press. Campbell dutifully obeyed, ensuring that those in the coffee houses and taverns that evening and in the morning would read the very latest news: "His Excellency intends to bring forward the Tryal of *Quelch* and Company now in Custody for Piracy within a few days."

But even this, like everything else in Dudley's methods, was calculated. The trial of John Quelch and his crew was set to begin in just hours.

PUNISHMENT
AND REWARD

Chapter Fourteen

"Plain Matters of Fact"

W hile Stephen Sewall had put to sea in search of Captain
Larrimore and Quelch's runaways, Paul Dudley had ridden back to Boston to report to his father on what the
commission had learned out at Marblehead. As Attorney General,
his job now was to prepare an ironclad prosecution brief against
Quelch. Given his father's desire to have things handled with utmost speed, he had little time to accomplish this.

Between his arrival at Boston on Saturday, June 10, and the
opening of the trial on the following Tuesday, he buried his nose in
the sheaves of notes that Secretary Addington and his assistant had
taken during their examinations of the prisoners. Much of the force
of his arguments would require bolstering with specifics of the actions about which Quelch and his crew had been accused. Dudley
would have spent a few hours in the "library" of the Town House
consulting an atlas in order to match as best he could the longitude
and latitude of the places where the various captures had occurred.
This could only be informed guesswork; memories of crew members differed on exact locations so many months after the events
had transpired. Still, to have specific coordinates (whether accurate
or not) would give the public a subtle perception that the Crown
saw all—nothing could he hidden from the eye of the governor or
the Admiralty that he served.

Dudley would himself have spent time interrogating several
of the prisoners, particularly, Parrot, Pimer, and Clifford. We also

know that Samuel Sewall, according to an admission in his diary, also spoke with at least some of the prisoners at this time in his capacity as First Judge of the province. Unfortunately (and somewhat strangely), Sewall's voice goes quiet after the return from Marblehead. He does not resume his diary entries until June 27, long after the trial is concluded. Apart from a few brief allusions to the Quelch case, he chooses not to enlighten the reader with any insights or reflections into his own role as council member, investigator, and judge in the case. Given the legal precedent that Captain Quelch's prosecution constituted and the public uproar it unleashed, Sewall's silence is almost deafening.

Tuesday, June 13, in Boston town began with excitement as word spread from north to south that Major Stephen Sewall had arrived with his prisoners and treasure. Winding their way through the narrow streets toward the prison, Sewall must have been sitting tall in his saddle as he guided his horse slowly to the Town Square, leading a sizeable party of troopers that followed up behind. Secured in chains and probably stuffed like livestock into a large cart, the accused pirates, sullen, surly, or frightened, would have been the subject of stares and shouts from the populace. These last crew members of the *Charles* to be apprehended, Erasmus Peterson, Charles James, John Carter, John Pitman, Francis King, Charles King, and John King would soon be at the end of their journey, joining the already overcrowded and noxious cells of the new stone prison. Sharing their public parade was a shackled Thomas Larrimore, Joseph Wells, and Daniel Wormmall: the officers of the *Larrimore Galley*. Larrimore must have been appalled at his own situation and flushed red with embarrassment as he stared back at the Bostonians that gawked at him. He was well known and somewhat of a local hero given his exploits of 1702 and 1703. To enter the town in this way was a fall from grace both dramatic and unprecedented.

With no apparent crime yet committed, the crewmen of the *Larrimore Galley* had been allowed to disperse and go their own ways. Undoubtedly, many remained at the Isles of Shoals to eke out other work—or wait for a new privateer captain to arrive. The officers, on the other hand, were complicit in the harboring of fugitives and would have to answer for their actions. Pirates and privateersmen all were handed over to the keeper of the prison while the gold was formally presented to Treasurer James Taylor who duly signed for it.

Meanwhile, on the second floor of the Town House, Governor Dudley and his Council gathered to convene the morning meeting. It was, by necessity, a short one. The council minutes record only one order of business: "The Court of Admiralty for Tryal of the Pirates being opened this morning, the Members of the Council being Commissioners for the holding of that Court . . . Adjourn'd unto tomorrow at ten in the morning."

With that, the twenty or so officials filed down the staircase and to the large open room below, normally reserved for the General Assembly. All was in readiness for the proceedings. Long dark tables laid end to end for the members of the court, and benches in front at a respectable distance for the prisoners and their guards. And with this quick change of venue, the character of the Council took on an entirely new—and hitherto unknown—guise: that of the first legally constituted court of English Admiralty to judge a case of piracy outside of England. It was, however, a role that none of the players, even the lawyers among them, knew the lines for; the conduct of the trial would have to be improvised in the extreme.

When all were seated, one of the constables in attendance was directed by Governor Dudley to call for silence, pounding his staff onto the thick oak-planked floor. The parliamentary statute "An Act for the more effectual Suppression of Piracy" was read aloud in its entirety for those assembled. John Valentine, Boston's Notary Public, was then sworn in as Register of the Court by the governor. Valentine immediately administered the oath of office to Dudley as President of the Court who, in turn, administered oaths to the rest of the commissioners present. That accomplished, Dudley read out the existing instructions of Whitehall for the trial of pirates, directing that such proceedings be governed according to the relevant acts of Parliament including the new act (which had never before been invoked).

The governor passed around a warrant for signature, summoning John Quelch from the prison along with Clifford, Pimer, and Parrot, in order to answer "several Articles of Piracy, Robbery, and Murder, exhibited against him and Company." These formalities taken care of, Dudley declared the Court adjourned until three that afternoon. It was time for the main meal. He and the commissioners left to walk the short distance past the town dock to the Star Tavern at present-day Hanover and Union streets in order to dine and fortify themselves for the judicial rigors of the afternoon.

They returned to the Town House, fed and watered, and sat down to begin their task. As soon as the court was again called to order, Dudley set about lining up his three star witnesses for the prosecution. Clifford, Pimer, and Parrot were all stood before the bar and formally arraigned on nine charges: one for each vessel taken with the ninth article also including a charge of murder for the killing of the Portuguese captain, Bastian. As arranged, all pleaded guilty to the charges. Governor Dudley immediately ordered that the three be "received into the Queen's Mercy" and declared and sworn as witnesses on Her Majesty's behalf.

Finally, John Quelch, who had been standing in the vestibule at the entrance to the main chamber, was escorted in by the constables, his leg irons clanking as he hobbled toward the bar to face his accusers. The worse for wear after three weeks of close confinement, his body odor carrying across the room, Quelch looked upon the velvet and brocade-attired and bewigged panel that sat arrayed in front of him, the governor at its center. If he had not been aware before that moment, he would have certainly known now that he was not facing an ordinary criminal court or a jury of his peers. This was something altogether different: a tribunal of local officials. He stood as each article against him was read out, each a lengthy and detailed account that described the place and the time, the nature of the capture, and the amount and exact value of booty seized.

Defiantly, Quelch pleaded not guilty to all charges against him. He asked that he be given more time to prepare for his trial. Governor Dudley agreed, allowing him until that Friday morning at nine o'clock. Quelch then requested that he be given legal counsel "upon any Matter of Law that might happen upon his Tryal."

This was grudgingly obliged, Dudley churlishly remarking to Quelch that "The Articles upon which you are Arraigned, are plain Matters of Fact; however, that you may have no Reason to complain of Hardship, Mr. James Meinzies, Attorney at Law, may assist you." Quelch was handed a copy of the articles against him and sent from the courtroom back to prison. Next, the twenty apprehended members of his crew were brought out of the prison and lined up before the bar to face the charges. For those who had only that morning been delivered up by Major Sewall, their heads must have been still spinning at the frenetic pace of Massachusetts justice. The disheveled state of the coughing and shuffling mariners probably only further confirmed their guilt in the eyes of the Boston worthies that sat in judgment upon them. Guided by their captain, they pleaded severally "not guilty" after the charge list was read out. Like Quelch, they requested legal counsel and more time to prepare for trial. Again, Dudley acquiesced, telling them to stand ready for the Friday morning.

With that, the court adjourned for the day.

On Wednesday morning, Dudley resumed his duties as governor and not as Vice Admiral. Province business went on as usual: civil officers were nominated and consented, the prison was ordered improved, soldiers' pay authorized, and a justice of the peace who had lately admitted his adherence to the Quaker faith was summarily dismissed from his post by reason of being "unfit for that station." Finally, the governor and council had Major Sewall escorted into the chamber where he gave his story of the pursuit and capture of Quelch's crew and the taking of their gold dust. After his tale was told, he presented the council with his account of the expenses incurred by the expedition. This was duly allowed for and "With an addition thereto made for gratification of Major Sewall, Capt. Turner and other Officers amounting in the whole to one hundred thirty-two pounds five shillings to be paid out of the Treasure imported by the said Pirates."

How this bounty was divided is not recorded but Sewall must have been pleased with such a generous reward for his initiative and diligence in pursuing Quelch's men, especially since he had been the only one brave enough to push on against the odds while his comrades balked.

Meanwhile, a stone's throw from the Town House, Attorney Meinzies met with his assigned clients in the stone prison to pull together what defense arguments he could. Meinzies was a Scotsman and lawyer of good reputation who had been resident in Boston for several years. He knew from the start that acting as defense counsel in a trial without a jury drawn from the farmers, fishermen, and merchants of Suffolk County, would require every ounce of his skill since he could count on no element of sympathy from the court's president and commissioners. His strategy would ultimately rest on calling the court's authority and procedures into question. If Quelch insisted that he had taken the gold from Spaniards, Meinzies would have precious little evidence to prove it.

It would appear that he and his clients had some difficulties in constructing the case, or in at least establishing the facts of it. When Friday morning came, and the court was again convened, Quelch found himself once more set before the bar. As soon as the proceedings began, he immediately submitted a petition "on behalf of himself, and the rest of the Prisoners, praying for further time." The petition was allowed. Dudley ordered the prisoners "Peremptorily to come upon their Tryals" beginning first thing the following Monday at nine o'clock. Before President Dudley could push back his chair and stand to end the session, Meinzies spoke up to make a motion.

Not unreasonably, he argued that the Queen's Witnesses—Clifford, Pimer, and Parrot—should be kept separated until the prisoners' trials actually began. Although in reality this was like shutting the barn door after the horses had bolted, Meinzies was attempting to forestall any collusion among the witnesses to prevent them from agreeing on a single version of the "facts" of the case. Massachusetts's most seasoned lawyer, Thomas Newton, as Queen's Counsel and chief prosecutor, quickly moved to cut off this avenue of defense. He agreed that witnesses should be kept out of each other's hearing during the *giving* of evidence to the court, but was adamant that to separate the witnesses before they came upon their trials was simply "unprecedented." Dudley senior, not surprisingly, agreed with the prosecution and the motion was denied. The court then adjourned, leaving Meinzies and Quelch less than forty-eight hours to make final preparations.

Monday morning, June 19, John Quelch was once again marched up the steps of the Town House and ushered into the main chamber *cum* courtroom. Standing at the bar, the president ordered that his chains be removed for the duration of the session. Joseph Dudley then permitted the prosecution to lay out its case.

As Attorney General and Advocate for the Court of Admiralty, Paul Dudley led the attack with the blessing of Thomas Newton. He launched into his opening statement to the court:

May it please Your Excellency, and the rest of the Honourable Commissioners of this Court: The Prisoner at the Bar stands Articled against for, and charged with several Piracies, Robberies, and Murder
committed by himself and Company upon the High Sea, (upon the
Subjects of the King of *Portugal*, Her Majesty's good Allie) the worst
and most intollerable of Crimes that can be committed by Men.

Dudley then proceeded to outline the justification for the proceedings, by invoking previous jurisprudence in such cases, particularly the need for the latest acts in light of the difficulties in obtaining convictions. He began his legal salvo by stating that pirates
"Are not Entituled to Law ... Captors are not obliged to bring them
to any Port, but may exposs them immediately to Punishment, by
Hanging them at the Main-Yard." However, he went on, Quelch
and his men "Being then suffered to live ... they are to by used,
treated, and tried as the Laws of *England*, and our own Country do
direct."

Under previous laws pertaining to the trial of pirates, particularly before the *Statute of the 28th, Henry VIII*, although Admiralty
courts might be convened, these were to operate under the principles of Civil Law: prisoners had to confess they committed a crime
and all witnesses against them had to be indifferent. Since the in-
ception of that statute, however, piracy trials were to be conducted
along the lines of Common Law. This meant that the accused had
the benefit of a trial by jury in England in criminal court. These facts
Dudley duly noted in his address.

Then, he moved to discuss the nub of the legal conundrum that
faced the country. Captain Kidd had been tried in 1701 under the
statute of Henry VIII, shipped from Boston to London where, after a lengthy and expensive trial, he was found guilty and hanged.
This was too impractical a regime to be followed in perpetuity in order to combat the scourge of piracy, or so the Parliament believed.
It was, therefore, that the new Act of King William for the more
effectual suppression of piracy, was enacted, allowing trials to be
convened in *any* of the plantations. It was this new Act, claimed
Dudley, which allowed the present court to be assembled.

It is by Virtue of this Act of Parliament ... that your Excellency
and this Honourable Court are now Sitting in Judgment upon the

Prisoner at the Bar, and his vile Accomplices; and though it may be thought by some a pretty severe thing, to put an Englishman to Death without a Jury, yet it must be remembered, that the Wisdom and Justice of our Nation, for very sufficient and excellent Reasons, have so ordered it in the Case of Piracy; a Crime, which as before I observ'd, scarce deserves any Law at all.

Such a cavalier interpretation would have been received as alarming news by most Englishmen, be they in London or in Boston. For Dudley's argument essentially made the case for the new courts on the grounds that the burden of proof was just too *difficult* for the state to make under Common or Civil law. It was a chilling prescription for "show trials" that would pull the rug from beneath centuries' worth of hard-fought civil rights, chiefly, that a man was innocent until proven guilty.

The Attorney General prefaced his remarks concerning the various articles against the defendants by noting the circumstances of the crime. These "Vile men," he remarked, had led a mutiny, treated their rightful captain to "Murderous usury," and although armed with a lawful commission and "A sword to fight the open and declared Enemies of Her Sacred Majesty ... instead of drawing it against the French and Spaniards, they have sheathed it in the Bowels of some of the best Friends and Allies of the Crown of England at this Day." Dudley pressed home to the members of the court the clear intentions of Quelch and his coconspirators by saying that in their "Perfidious Impudence" they had robbed not once but many times until "they were glutted," putting into various Brazilian ports where they confessed friendship only to set sail and plunder "some of the Neighbours and Friends of those they had seen the Day before."

Quelch, he suggested, who would have been entitled to "at least double" of any crew member in taking just and lawful prizes, would now reap "the same measure" in his share of the guilt. In making his case, Dudley proposed to put forward proofs that he termed "partly presumptive, partly circumstantial, and partly positive and downright."

The first to testify were John Colman and William Clarke. They brought with them the rapiers, two skins of sugar, and the Portuguese naval ensign they had recovered from the *Charles*. Two local merchants who knew Portuguese were sworn as interpreters and told the court that the skins of sugar were addressed to a recipient in Lisbon. Colman and Clark swore under oath that the articles had all been retrieved from the ship after she had returned to Marblehead.

Next up was the silversmith, John Noyes. He testified that Quelch had brought in to him a considerable quantity of coined silver money, much of it Portuguese, and that Quelch himself had set to melting it down. Following this, the remainder of the treasure recovered from the crew was brought into the court, one bag after the next, and piled onto the table. Colman was asked to identify his parcel of gold and to tell the court from where he had received it. Colman replied that he had received it (and all the other owner's shares) from Quelch. He added that upon examining some of the gold coins, he noticed that they were Portuguese, many minted in 1703.

Joseph Dudley, upon hearing this, noted aloud that "the Money being Coined so lately, it was very improbable it should ever have been out of Portuguese hands, Inhabitants of Brasil."

Finally, the last of the physical evidence was brought forth by the prosecution. These were the few broadsides or pamphlets found onboard the *Charles* that were printed in Portuguese. While there was little doubt that the exhibits were Portuguese in origin, on their own they comprised only circumstantial proof—they could have just as easily been taken from a Spanish ship. Paul Dudley now moved to call forward his star witnesses to link the physical evidence with the defendant who now stood before him. This would constitute the "positive and downright proof" that Quelch and his men were guilty of the charges.

The first of these was somewhat unexpected. Joachim, the young black slave taken during the attack on the brigantine off Mora, was brought into the courtroom. "Cuffee" as the crew had nicknamed him, no doubt terrified, was made to stand before the austere commissioners where he was questioned through the interpreters. Joachim, like the gold, had been confiscated by the constables from one of the ship's crew either at Marblehead or Boston. He was put into the care of Captain Edward Brattle, a prosperous merchant, who had looked after him while the trial preparations were made. The young Brazilian was, in effect, stolen property, and until the fate of Quelch and his men was decided, his own status was in limbo.

Under examination, the first thing he made clear to the court was that he was a baptized slave. This was a crucial point: "heathen" were prohibited from testifying in a court case, particularly a criminal one. Although no proof other than his own admission was put forward as to his status as a Christian, the prosecution and commissioners did not mention it and attorney Meinzies failed to pick up on the fact himself. He was then asked if he had ever seen the prisoner at the bar. Joachim looked over to Quelch and replied that he was indeed onboard the ship that had boarded him. President Dudley then asked the interpreters to address the boy in both Spanish and French. It was found he understood neither tongue. Joachim was led off to the side.

John Pimer, Captain Plowman's ever-loyal skilful mariner, was next to testify. The other two crewmen witnesses were taken out of the room as the examination began, as had been earlier agreed upon. Pimer told his entire story, guided by Paul Dudley's questioning, detailing each of the nine captures from the first victim seized in November until the last in February. He offered no accusation against Quelch in the death of Captain Plowman, stating that Anthony Holding had barred the captain's cabin, but he made it clear that Quelch was the acting commander throughout the voyage. Pimer provided many details from memory concerning the nature of the ships taken, their ladings, and locations. Most damaging was his statement that Quelch had ordered him to alter the ship's logbook and tear out pages before admonishing the crew to silence and giving them their "Spanish wreck" cover story.

To bolster Pimer's account of the taking of the last ship off the River Plate, another witness was brought forward. It was the young slave Emanuel. Under questioning he gave his name, told the court that he was baptized, and that his owner had been Captain Bastian. Although he said that one of Quelch's company had shot and killed his master, the murderer was not Quelch himself. Fingering the grim and silent John Quelch, he said that he saw Quelch board his ship "arm'd with a Cutlace and 2 Pistols."

Pimer had concluded his evidence by recalling the moment when Quelch told the crew to say they had salvaged the gold with the help of friendly Carib tribesmen. On this he set the court to rights: "Whereas we never had any Gold from any Indians, it being but once that any of them were on Board of us, and then we did not trade with them."

As Pimer stepped down, President Dudley adjourned the court for the afternoon repast. At four o'clock, it was back in session and John Clifford was brought forward to be sworn (while James Parrot was led out of earshot). Clifford, when asked by the court to acquaint them with what he knew relating to Quelch, replied that although Quelch had not been aboard when Holding and the others subdued Captain Plowman, he had not objected to the turn of events when he did finally arrive onboard.

Paul Dudley proceeded to question Clifford on each successive article of piracy. Clifford corroborated Pimer's testimony in the main, recalling each vessel seized, the cargo it carried, and the fate of its crew. Finally, James Parrot was brought in and set before the commission. When prompted, he too corroborated the detail of the previous two witnesses although he could not recall anything relating to Quelch's dealings with Plowman. "When the Captain was thrown overboard," he told the court, "then he took upon him the Command, and ordered us to Sail to Sea." When questioned about the ninth capture, Parrott could not say for certain who had killed the Portuguese captain although it was said to be Christopher Scudamore who dealt the blow. Clifford contradicted this, saying that several had claimed credit for the deed. Before the witnesses were set down, they were asked jointly if any had anything further to add. Obviously coached for this moment, Clifford and Pimer provided additional details concerning the alibi that Quelch had concocted for them and his rage when one of the crew had let slip to a prisoner that they were New Englanders and not Frenchmen.

As the damning accusations piled on, Quelch must have struggled to contain his frustration and anger. Mr. Newton rose to hammer in the final prosecution nail: he produced copies of the *London Gazette*, dated May and July 1703, and read aloud the announcement of the treaty of amity between England and Portugal signed at Lisbon on May 16. This proved, he said, "Though there be no necessity for it" that the alliance had been sealed "long before" the said piracies occurred against the Portuguese ships.

Governor Dudley directed his gaze to Quelch. "Captain Quelch, This Court is now ready to hear what you have to offer for yourself."

The words were meant literally. In eighteenth century courtrooms, the accused conducted their own defense. Indeed, this is how the term "legal counsel" got its name; the defendant's lawyer could only comment to the court pertaining to points of the law. The defendant had to shoulder the burden of refuting witnesses and bringing his own arguments forward to the judge and jury. For a weatherworn sailor, more at home on a heaving deck at sea than on dry land, this was a formidable challenge against very overwhelming odds. Quelch had not an ounce of legal training; his opponents—in sharp contrast—were the best London-educated lawyers in America at that time.

Addressing the court for the first time, Quelch immediately deferred to his counsel to raise "Sundry matters of Law" on his behalf. Attorney Meinzies prefaced his remarks by first distancing himself from any perceived justification of "the horrible Crimes that are charged upon the Prisoner" but reminded the court that "'Tis equal Justice to acquit the Innocent as to condemn the Guilty."

Meinzies first objected to the admission of the *London Gazette* (presumably on the grounds that the news could not have made it to Boston before Quelch sailed) but Joseph Dudley immediately quashed this defense by stating that the "Stress of this matter does not lye upon the Alliance . . . *Kidd* was hang'd for Robbing the Great *Mogul*."

Meinzies apparently chose not to labor the point and moved directly to his second objection, namely, the assumption that the gold dust was Portuguese. To bolster his argument, he asked that David Jess, a goldsmith, be sworn to testify. Jess challenged the court that no expert could distinguish the difference between Portuguese gold dust and Spanish gold dust. This clumsy challenge too fell on deaf ears, the governor dismissing it angrily:

You attempt a very vain thing, for had the Dust been dug in *Mexico*, yet if our Friends have it in keeping, it is Piracy to take it from them. Besides, what answer can you give to all the Coin'd Gold shewn in Court . . . plainly to be *Portuguese*.

Unperturbed, Meinzies moved to challenge that the witnesses had disagreed as to the places where the vessels were taken and as to the number of persons that were on board. Dudley countered this by claiming that the differences were "very immaterial" and that Pimer's details would have been more exact had not Quelch falsified and defaced the ship's journal.

"'Tis plain," responded Meinzies, "That none of the Witnesses understand the *Portuguese* Language, and it ought to be very positive Evidence to take away a Man's Life."

Governor Dudley was unmoved. "I believe Her Majesties Commissioners now present will think they have very positive proof, however they are the Judges of that."

Meinzies continued down his list of objections, pointing out that under the civil law, Quelch could not be charged with the murder of the Portuguese captain because it was well known he was not the man that did it and the prosecution had recognized this. Newton allowed this, but countered by saying that under common law, all assisting at the scene of a murder can be treated as principals. Matters of piracy, he maintained, were to be tried according to common law as stipulated under Statute 28 of *Henry VIII*. Meinzies was no doubt beginning to realize the pick-and-choose nature of jurisprudence that was being applied in the tribunal and the size of the mountain he had to climb. However, he had saved his most compelling legal objection for the last.

Meinzies challenged the court proceedings on the grounds that the witnesses were ineligible to testify for the prosecution being interested parties. Nor were they competent witnesses for they had not yet received the Queen's Pardon. Even more to the point, he asserted that the very act of Parliament that made their court legal, Statutes 11 and 12 *Wm III*, made it quite clear that the trial of pirates was to be conducted under the *Civil Law* as well as the methods and rules of the Admiralty. As such, no accomplice could serve also as a witness. In essence, the prosecution had presented nothing that legally proved John Quelch's guilt in mutiny, murder, or piracy. To back up his argument, he liberally quoted from the said Act and bolstered this with quotations from *Coke's Institutes*, a foundation work of English law.

Newton stepped up to salvage the proceedings before Meinzies could unravel them totally. He cleverly sidestepped the matter of the witnesses' testimony by referring to them as *approvers*. This was a medieval and largely legally obsolete form of accusation that *did* permit accomplices to crimes to testify—but under strict conditions. But these had not been met. An appeal to become an approver had to be subject to an inquest by a special judge or coroner, while the approver himself was held on indictment. Newton failed to mention this and, unfortunately, Meinzies did not either.

"It has never been thought convenient to give Approvers their Pardon, until they have actually convicted their accomplices ... This is the Opinion of Lord Coke ... and so has the practice been since," said Newton.

But it was Paul Dudley who rose up to refute Meinzies' claim that the trial was being conducted under the wrong set of laws. First, he accepted Meinzies' arguments pertaining to trials conducted by the civil law. However, he went on to explain that the very strictness of the methods tended to let pirates escape justice. The statute of *Henry VIII* recognized this problem, asserted Dudley, directing instead that common law be used in such cases. Of the lack of disinterested witnesses, he opined "There happens to be no other way to bring Criminals to their just Punishment, but by singling out some of their Company, that may be the least guilty, and make use of them to convict the rest."

Meinzies was under no illusions as to where the proceedings were headed, but he stood his ground against the younger Dudley. His sense of honor as a barrister demanded that he play out the drama until the end.

"I don't take myself to be thoroughly answer'd by Mr. Advocate, as to what I offer'd in the last place, for I take the case of Pirates, thay may be try'd in *England* upon the Statute of *Henry VIII* to differ very much from the case of Pirates that are try'd in the Plantations, by vertue of the New Statute." Meinzies emphasized his remarks by pointing out that whereas under the Common Law his clients would be entitled to the benefit of a trial by jury, the new parliamentary statute took this right away and so therefore directed commissioners to proceed under the Civil Law and Admiralty methods as a means of providing some legal balance.

Dudley's reply was little more than sophistry. He maintained that the methods of the Admiralty had been conducted under the Statute of *Henry VIII* for some 160 years using the common law. The new law, he submitted, merely strengthened and established the preexisting one. "And it would be very odd to suppose," he said, "that what the first Act ... had rejected and condemn'd, the method of the civil Law in the tryal of Pirates ... the second Act of Parliament should ... restore and set it up in the Plantations especially when the Title of the New Act, is an Act, *for the more effectual Suppression of Piracy.*"

According to the trial transcript, Newton, the senior prosecuting attorney, said not a word to refute Meinzies. It is likely that he was content to let Dudley suffer the professional shame of basing a legal argument on political expediency over justice. Newton must have known—at the very least—that the new law was ambiguous and that Meinzies was correct in his summation. More disappointingly, Meinzies did not press his objections further. He had done only the bare minimum to raise the points on behalf of his client; it would have been detrimental in the extreme to his future career to explode the case against Quelch and embarrass the entire provincial government.

But is this the whole story? There remains considerable doubt that the version of events described in the trial transcript is an accurate one. The only transcript that has ever surfaced was one that Governor Dudley and his son prepared and released for public consumption. This appears to be highly abridged; illogical gaps occur in questions and responses, particularly those relating to Meinzies' objections. Had the legal sparring been bloodier— and the proceeding more slipshod—than the transcript makes it sound? Even more suspicious, it was this printed, public version of the trial that Governor Dudley later submitted to the Admiralty in London as the *official* record, not the original transcription that notary Valentine had dutifully labored over in the courtroom. Valentine's unedited transcript of this trial has never been found.

The peculiar cadences of the trial transcript became more obvious after Captain Quelch spoke in his own defense. He was permitted to do this as soon as Paul Dudley had airily dismissed Meinzies' procedural objections. It was an exchange that vividly conveyed the mariner's desperation, anger, and ignorance of what he should do.

Govr. Dudley: Capt. Quelch, if you have anything further to offer for yourself, or if you would Cross Examine the Witnesses, the Court will hear you.

Capt. Quelch: I desire Pimer may be ask'd, Whether there was any Bolt upon the Captain's Cabbin Door, when we first sail'd?

Pimer: It was fastened with a Marlin Spike.

Capt. Quelch: Was I then on board?

Govr. Dudley: The Witnesses have answered as to that already.

Capt Quelch: I desire the Witnesses may be ask't Whether they know the Gold Dust, to be Portuguese Dust?

Govr. Dudley: This is not material, Capt. Quelch.

Capt. Quelch: I desire Pimer may be ask'd, how he knows the first Prize was taken the Fifteenth of November?

Pimer: I say it was on, or about that Day, I sat down the very Day in my Journal, but 'twas torn out, I cannot now swear to a Day.

Capt. Quelch: How many Tun was the second Vessel that was taken?

Govr Dudley: Capt. Quelch, This is not cross examining the Witness, but rather examining him over again; if you would say any thing to the purpose, You should acquaint this Court, where you took those Quantities of Gold Dust, and Coyned Gold, those Negroes that have been shewn to this Court; if they were taken from the French or Spaniards, let us see some of them here, or some Evidence of their being so taken?

According to the transcript, Quelch did not answer the governor, and indeed, spoke no more during the remainder of his trial, which in any event, was short. The court was cleared while the commissioners deliberated their verdict. Just one hour later, the court was reconvened. Governor Dudley spoke up and addressed the prisoner who stood before him.

Capt. John Quelch, 'tis now Six Days since this Court first sat, by Her Majesties Special Command to myself and these Gentlemen

Commissioners ... This Court hath weighed and considered the several Evidences that have been produc'd on Her Majesties Behalf against you, and your own Allegations for you, and upon the whole have found and adjudge you Guilty of the several Articles of Piracy, Robbery and Murder, where with you are charged, and have agreed that Sentence should be Pronounced against you for the same accordingly.

The registrar ordered a proclamation of silence and the town crier duly bellowed across the room. "All manner of Persons are Commanded to keep Silence, while Judgement is giving, upon Pain of Imprisonment." A grim-faced John Quelch looked into the eyes of Joseph Dudley, the Vice Admiral, and the Governor of the Province of Massachusetts Bay. Although he knew what was to come, the words nevertheless must have numbed him. Governor Dudley made the pronouncement, one he had never had the opportunity to make before:

You the prisoner at the Bar, you have been tried by the Law of the land, and convicted ... nothing now remains but that Sentence be passed according to the Law. And the sentence of the Law is this: You shall be taken from the place where you are, and be carried to the Place from whence you came, and from thence to the Place of Execution, and there hang'd by your Neck until you be dead. And the Lord have Mercy on your Soul.

Chapter Fifteen

"Where Is Your Gold?"

John Quelch was now tried and convicted. But even as his shackles were once again clamped upon his wrists and ankles and he was led away, the weighty work of Boston's first-ever court of Admiralty was not yet finished. The fate of the remaining crew members had still to be decided. The Dudleys had, in their own fashion, divided the accused according to shades of complicity, based upon the examinations of the crew members turned Queen's witnesses. The remainder of the trial appears to have been conducted as little more than well-rehearsed theatre; there is not much in the transcript record to indicate that these men were given equal justice under the law. Some were selected to stand upon their trials individually, while others did so collectively. It was a choice made by the court based upon the degree of their sin, as attested by Matthew Pymer and in all likelihood abetted by Meinzies. When the court resumed its business on Tuesday, it began with the deliberation of the guilt of the lowliest on board the *Charles*: its three black slaves.

Caesar-Pompey, Charles, and Mingo were led into the chamber around ten o'clock and set before the bar. They were read the charges against them whereupon they pleaded not guilty. Paul Dudley was soon on his feet to make his case for the prosecution.

May it please your Excellency...The Three Prisoners are of a different Complexion, 'tis true, from the rest that have been

Arraigned...but it is very well known that the First and most Fa-
mous Pirates that have been in the World, were of their Colour; and
Negroes, though Slaves, are as capable of taking away the Lives and
Estates of Mankind, as any Freemen in the World.

He concluded by saying that if the circumstances proved that
"these Fellows" were as active in the crime as the rest of the company, they should be judged equally guilty. Pymer was asked to
give his account of the conduct of the slaves during the voyage.
Looking upon the men, he replied to Governor Dudley, "Those
Three Negroes were on board during the whole Voyage, but were
not Active nor did they any thing but as they were Commanded:
[they] were the Cooks of the Briganteen, and Sounded the Trumpet...but handled no Arms." Clifford and Parrot affirmed the same
when asked. Pymer spoke up again to say that Mingo had been
Captain Plowman's slave, purchased in Guinea. Next, John Colman was brought forward again to testify that the other two were
the personal slaves of Colonel Hobby, his brother-in-law. He made
it clear that the two men were not runaways having been lent for
service upon the voyage under Plowman.

Dudley cleared the court while the commissioners deliberated
for less than half an hour. After the court reassembled, Caesar-
Pompey, Charles, and Mingo were led forward to hear their fate.
For these three reluctant mariners, the news was good. Governor
Dudley told the slaves that the commission had considered the
matter and found them not guilty of the charges. "Whereupon,"
says the transcript, "they were ordered upon their Knees, & c."

Though their station and duties had directly led to their salvation from death, the three now were essentially nothing more
than adjudicated property. Caesar-Pompey and Charles could be
returned to Colonel Hobby, while Mingo, as the slave of a deceased
master, would now face the prospect of being sold again—or the
tantalizing possibility of gaining his freedom. The latter would de-
pend on whether Captain Plowman had left a will or expressed
his wishes before his last voyage. Unfortunately, there are no further mentions concerning Mingo in the province records; however,
neither is there mention of his resale into bondage. For Emanuel
and Joachim, the slaves captured by Quelch and his crew, there was
never any question concerning their fate. Within weeks of the trial

they were sold at auction in Boston, apparently below market value at £20 each, one of them to none other than Paul Dudley. This transaction would spark allegations of corruption against him, fostered by John Colman. This political attack, just one of the many aftershocks resulting from the eruption of the Quelch case, still lay several weeks over the horizon. For the moment, all interested parties worked together in an unspoken truce to lay blame squarely on the mariners in order to gain legal status for the confiscated gold, silver, captured weapons, and supplies, and indeed even the *Charles* itself, now impounded at the wharf in Boston.

After the three slaves had been dispensed with, Meinzies moved for further time to prepare the prisoners. This was granted and the court adjourned until three o'clock that same afternoon.

Governor Dudley, his son, and most, if not all, of the council then left the Town House for lunch, venturing out into the humid air of the square. The governor and a few others would have climbed into his coach while the rest would have mounted their horses or walked, the destination of all the party being the Star Ale House, about half a mile away. Stephen North, the taverner at the Star, had given over his large upstairs room to the governor and council for the duration of the trial. There, the government (as well as the prosecution's witnesses) could meet in privacy to discuss the trial and the next steps in the drama. For North, it turned out to be a lucrative catering contract: the council later paid him the sum of £28 and twelve shillings and sixpence, all out of the pirate treasure. Lying at the intersection of Union and Hannover streets, the Star was just one of several taverns and inns near the Town Dock, all popular with Bostonians regardless of class and where the political and social pulse of the metropolis was strongly felt. Across from the Star was the Green Dragon, an equally large clapboard and stone inn later to be the regular meeting place of Samuel Adams and the Sons of Liberty.

After dining on their roasted fowl and quaffing their ales and Madeira wine, the commissioners, now sated and fortified, made the short journey back to the Town House. Once the court was reconvened, six more of the accused were set before the bar: John Lambert, William Wilde, Christopher Scudamore, Peter Roach, Benjamin Perkins, and Charles James. After some short discussion between Meinzies and the prisoners, Lambert and James made it known that they wished to be tried by themselves and not as part of the larger group, as had been planned. This was the case because, once they had heard the sentence on their commander, most of the others were now desperate to change their pleas.

Dudley agreed to the request, and Lambert and James stood still while the other prisoners were escorted out of the chamber. Immediately, Governor Dudley began his questioning of the Queen's witnesses as to the actions of these two prisoners who were maintaining their innocence. Pimer and his companions swore that both Lambert and James had been active in the captures off Brazil and that both had taken their shares without complaint. Offered the chance to cross-examine, Lambert and James, both flustered at their condemnation, seemed able only to deny their acquiescence of the voyage, but little more. "I was sick down in the Gun room when they bolted the Door upon the Captain, and never gave my Consent to go to the Southward," protested Lambert, who was forty-nine years old and one of only three of the crew born in Massachusetts: "What I did I was forced to."

Charles James followed the same line but to little avail, despite the fact that at fifty-four years of age he was the oldest of the crew and ancient for a merchant sailor. "I was constrained against my Will to go to Sea, and was deluded by false Pretences," he told the commissioners. When asked why they accepted their share of the treasure, and where it had come from, James could only plead. "It was the Commander did it . . . the reason we accepted of our Shares was because otherwise they would either have killed us or set us upon some desolate Island."

For his part, Lambert maintained his innocence: "You may be sure I would never have come home in the Vessel if I had thought I had done any thing amiss, or that I should have been Arraigned for't." It was a reflection that was shared by many of the crew and no doubt Quelch himself. Indeed, the commissioners themselves must have labored the point behind closed doors. Why did this crew return home?

The court again cleared and both "in some small time" were sentenced to death.

Next, whether he liked it or not, Christopher Scudamore, the twenty-eight-year-old ship's cooper was ordered to stand trial on his own. He was hit with a barrage of accusations by his former shipmates following which, Paul Dudley told the court that the prosecution would further prove that Scudamore was "The only man who gave the Mortal Wound" against the Portuguese captain. When Pimer was asked to corroborate this, he could only reply that although Scudamore *had* taken the credit for the slaying, *another* crew member had also claimed to have done it. Dudley, undeterred, brought back the young Brazilian, Emanuel, to finger Scudamore. Speaking through an interpreter, he pointed out the prisoner at the bar and said that it was he who had slain his master with a pistol shot. Scudamore, according to what the transcript says, appears to have been resigned to the outcome.

Govr. Dudley: What say you, Scudamore?
  Scudamore: I did not kill the Captain of the Portuguese Ship.
Govr Dudley: Where is your Gold?
  Scudamore: I can't tell. What I said upon my first Examination about it is false.
Govr Dudley: Have you any thing farther to say?
  Scudamore: No.

Most of the remaining prisoners, who were still present in the chamber to hear the proceedings, now realized, if they had not before, the dire situation they faced. Immediately, through Meinzies, they submitted a petition to alter their pleas to guilty and in so doing, throwing themselves upon the Queen's mercy. Governor Dudley warned them that this was no guarantee of safety. "We don't take your pleading Guilty now to be any submission, nor will it of itself entitle you to Mercy. This Court can make no Bargain with you." These fifteen men were each in turn asked by Valentine how they now pleaded. Fifteen times the word "Guilty" echoed across the high-ceilinged chamber.

Governor Dudley now turned his attention to the three remaining men who still protested their innocence: John Miller, John Templeton, and William Whiting. It was Miller who first stood at the bar to face his accusers. As before, the prosecution witnesses gave oath that Miller had been an active and eager participant in every capture of the Portuguese vessels. Miller, a forty-year-old shoemaker born in Yorkshire, first claimed he was sick most of the cruise. When Pimer countered that Miller was well enough during all the captures, and boarded the last bearing "sword and pistol,"

Miller changed his tack, claiming that because the vessels showed no colors, he had no idea what they were. But the court's president was saving his last attack as a *coup de grace*. Governor Dudley asked Pimer if he had ever heard any of the company say that Miller had been one of Avery's crew. A murmur must have rippled across the chamber at Dudley's question. Captain Ben Avery or "Long Ben" was probably the most successful pirate of the Golden Age. After taking more than £600,000 worth of plunder in the Red Sea in 1695, he had avoided capture and disappeared into obscurity in Ireland while most of his crew returned to England, were captured, and hanged.

Pimer answered as arranged: "I heard some of them say they heard him say so himself, so said Clifford."

Miller immediately denied the accusation, but the character assassination by insinuation was complete. He was sent back to the rear to rejoin the others while John Templeton, a fifteen-year-old Scot, was stood up before the bar. Pimer and his comrades told the court that although Templeton had borne arms on some of the captures, because he was a boy, he had chiefly served as a cook aboard the tender and had no vote as the rest of the company had. The mention of voting, if true, affirms that the crew was indeed sailing under articles of piracy, though at this point in the proceedings, the fact made little difference.

What saved young Templeton's life was the testimony of the apprentice's master, Henry Franklyn, who had shipped the boy under Captain Plowman's request. For his part, John wisely played the ignorant when asked by Dudley what he had to say for himself. "I have nothing to say, but that my Master sent me out," he told the court, "and I knew not whither we were going."

The court moved on to deal with Whiting. Whiting, like Templeton, also had friends who stood ready to aid him. All the prosecution's witnesses agreed that he had been ill virtually the entire voyage, taking no part in the acts of piracy (although he had been granted a share of the plunder). Samuel Sewall then interposed on the twenty-two-year-old's behalf, saying that Whiting had told him during the course of examination that he had known Captain Plowman from his days in New York and had accompanied him to Boston out of respect. William Clark came forward, was sworn, and stated that Plowman himself had recommended Whiting to serve as ship's clerk, that he had written most of the captain's letters to the owners, and, had been in a "very low condition" while ashore at Boston.

Whiting himself denied taking part in any action and said he did not discover the crew's piracy even when he had been brought ashore at Marblehead "Because I was then very sick and like to die." Dudley and his colleagues had heard sufficient testimony. The hour was growing late. The court was adjourned until the following morning. All that remained to be accomplished was the pronouncement on the remaining defendants and the sentencing of those found guilty.

On Wednesday, June 21, at nine o'clock in the morning, the court of Admiralty opened for its final session in the case against Quelch and company. The business of the court was short and sharp as the prisoners were escorted, in groups, to the bar in order to learn their fate.

Called forward first were John Templeton and William Whiting. Dudley told Templeton that the court had been indulgent in regard to his youth and found him not guilty. Turning to Whiting, Dudley said that the court had considered his case and found him also to be not guilty of the charges. The two youths sank to their knees in relief, thanking the court for its judgment. Rising, they walked to the back of the chamber, undoubtedly on weak legs, but now as free men once again.

The news for Scudamore and Miller, next marched up to the bar, was dark but certainly no surprise. Dudley pronounced them both guilty as charged and asked them if they had anything to say why the sentence of death should not be passed upon them.

"I had no Hand in altering the Voyage," protested Scudamore, "nor killing the *Portuguese* Captain." Miller too, was adamant of his innocence: "I was never Active after the Voyage was alter'd."

Unmoved, Dudley sentenced them both to hang.

Finally, in two groups, the remaining fifteen prisoners who had changed their pleas were ordered forward. There was silence as they were asked, according to convention, if they had anything to say before sentence was passed upon them.

Dudley spoke the words of the formal sentence, each of the mariners receiving the dreaded invocation to their own personal horror as they stood dumb before him and the other grim-faced, bewigged, betters of the province: "Hang'd by your Neck until you be dead."

The verdict and sentence may have sounded final and unremitting, but the governor and a few close members of his council, in truth, had yet to decide the final lottery among the convicted pirates. Some they would spare the noose. The question was: Who?

Chapter Sixteen

The Last Voyage

On June 30, 1704, John Churchill, the first Duke of Marlborough, was on the march south into the German lands,
just hours away from what would be a bloody and hard-
fought battle at Schellenberg on the Danube River in Bavaria. Despite the stiff resistance of the French and their Bavarian allies, it
was to be a victory for Marlborough, a robust prelude to his even
greater masterstroke at Blenheim a few weeks later in which his
forces and those of his Austrian allies would defeat an even larger
enemy force, one of the epic English feats of arms and the first major defeat inflicted on the all-conquering Louis XIV.

Half a world away, in Boston, the provincial government was
striking its own blow in the War of the Spanish Succession. It was
that day to carry out the execution of several men found guilty
of preying upon ships of the Queen's newest ally in the current
struggle, the Portuguese. As patriotic an act as this was to officials
of the crown, it was not viewed with any favor by the citizens of
Boston. After the convictions had been handed down a week earlier by Dudley and his council, assembled as a court of English Admiralty, word of this trial without jury had spread from square to
square, coffeehouse to tavern, ordinary to cookhouse, and wharf to
wharf. Bad enough to most common folks that Englishmen (some
local-born) were tried for bringing in foreign gold, it was worse still
that they would be *hanged* for it with such unseemly and suspicious
haste.

Dudley, already distrusted by the rank and file for his callous aloofness and London ways, found himself in an invidious situation: by enforcing the law against piracy as he interpreted it, something that he believed was not an option; he was also weakening his position in the province. Already, rumors were spreading about the town that Dudley's greed, combined with the fact that he had not been able to squeeze a salary out of the General Assembly in over a year, had driven him to seize upon Captain Quelch and his windfall of gold. Had Dudley really proved it was from the Portuguese? Testimony from Negroes? Surely, Matthew Pimer must have been paid to wag his tongue against his comrades.

For his part, Dudley must have been anxious to have done with the entire matter. He had managed to claw back about half of the plunder (which would please Whitehall) but the majority of the crew had evaded capture and would probably never be found. Still, he had upheld the honor of the province by running the court according to the new parliamentary law against piracy. While life was momentarily uncomfortable for him, he had still succeeded in feathering his nest: When word reached the Board of Trade and the Admiralty, his career would be given a strong boost, made more pleasing by the heightened prospect of a generous reward from the Queen. Dudley's strategy would be to hold firm, keep the town's rabble at bay, and continue his search for the remaining gold dust.

John Quelch, on the other hand, along with his condemned men, was that week suffering under a relentless rant from the town's preachers. This was more than just a race against the clock to obtain salvation for the condemned. Personal egos were also on parade as the leading clergymen, Cotton Mather and Benjamin Colman, sought to gain the highest exposure for their oratorical skills and boost their own congregation's standing in the community by tending to the spiritual needs of the celebrity prisoners. Sewall made note in his diary on June 27: "In the morning I heard Mr. Cotton Mather, Pray, preach, Catechise excellently the Condemned Prisoners in the chambers of the prison." How the mariners reacted to these ministrations is unfortunately not recorded. Since before the trial, they had been subjected to fire-and-brimstone harangues; now, in light of their condemnation, they were forced to listen to the clergymen every day.

In this era, it was usual for convicted murderers to be escorted from the prison a few days before their execution to Mather's church in the North End so that they could be viewed by the congregation, while being the central subject of the reverend's weekly sermon. Part and parcel of the very "communal" aspect of crime and punishment in colonial New England, this spectacle served as a reminder to all that the path of the sinner was a perilous one. This time, however, the practice was not carried out with Quelch and his crew. Evidently, as "maximum security" prisoners, it was far too risky to transport them across town to church—Dudley probably feared the mob might try a rescue attempt. Given the public mood, he certainly had grounds to sustain this fear. Calling out the militia regiment to escort the prisoners would also cost the treasury, something else he was loath to do.

Although he was deprived (for the moment) of a public performance with the condemned men in front of him, Mather wasted no time in milking the event to better educate his flock. The very day after the trial, he offered up a lengthy sermon to the congregation at the all-important Thursday Lecture, entitled "Faithful Warnings to prevent Fearful Judgements."

From the high pulpit of the whitewashed North Church, just a few streets up from the wharves, Mather regularly preached to the largest congregation of churchgoers in New England. With members numbering around 1,500, there was likely a huge audience that afternoon for his sermon, these normally lasting some ninety minutes or more. Forty-one years of age and just entering the height of his influence and power, Mather's style was emphatic—almost staccato—as he drove home his admonitions to the faithful. The curls of his periwig bouncing as he raised his hand skyward, his words rebounded from the rafters and carried across the packed pews below him: "But I say unto you, *Sinners* can't be *Pursued* with a greater Evil, than a Soul insensible of the Evil, that *Sin* is bringing upon them! There have been *Sinners* actually seized by a Law of Death, for *Capital Crimes*; These Criminals in their very Chains, have been so stupified, as to flatter themselves that there was no Danger near unto them; They have spent their Time in Drinking, in Gaming, in Profane Frolicks, when every Jingle of their Chains would have wrung that Peal in their Ears, *Wretch, Thy Damnation slumbers not.*"

Mather was relentless in his zeal to save others from a similar fate. As he ran down the long list of evils that waylay men, he strove to impress on his congregation that each had a duty to save their fellow. And he warned how easy it was for men to be led astray from privateering to piracy: "But there is Especially One [trap] that leads into all the rest; One that has proved signally Fatal to the poor Sinners that are now going to Dy for Piracy . . . Alas, They have *Ruined one another*; The Sinners Enticed one another; They said, *come with us, Let us lurk privily for the Innocent without a Cause. We shall find all precious Substances.* You see what *Evil* it has brought them to. *My Son, walk not thou in the way with them.* Oh! The Snares of Death, which are laid in *Wicked Company!*"

No doubt, Quelch and his men would have heard some version of this in the week that followed during their own private audience with the Puritan divine. Benjamin Colman too, took his turn administering to the condemned, though his Anglican-leaning ways may have been less apocalyptic than Mather's. Other ministers may also have visited Quelch and company, indeed, it seemed as if a war for their souls was being waged by the various denominations of the town. The parade of black-clad churchmen must have consoled some of the pirates but many too must have been terrified by the message that was brought to them. The very presence of the clergy, bibles in hand, was a vivid reminder of where they were soon headed.

For whatever reason, the governor had decided not to hang all the condemned pirates at the same time. Some of his subsequent letters to London indicate that he had never meant to carry out the execution of all of them anyway, asking that the lesser of the prisoners "young and ignorant fellows" be granted clemency. That left, however, the choice of exactly who would face the hangman.

It is not known exactly when those selected to die on June 30 were told of their fate. An announcement of the pirate execution was probably made on the Tuesday or Wednesday from the Town House by the crier, once the death warrants had been penned and signed by Dudley. He, along with a few members of the council and his son Paul, had made their selection of who was to die. While the prisoners were preached at on Thursday, carpenters out in the North End were busying themselves down on the mud flats near Hudson's Point, just a stone's throw from the Charlestown ferry landing. Two large wooden uprights, roughly twelve feet high, were set into the fine sand just at the low-water mark of the tidal Charles River. A large pine log was raised up into place, to serve as a ridgepole, lashed or nailed into place. About four or five feet up from the base, a wide plank was attached to the uprights with ropes such that it could be released quickly with a tug, dropping to the beach with a thud. It was a well-established English Admiralty custom that pirate executions take place between the high and low tide marks, a position signifying the limit of the jurisdiction of the Admiralty court. It was also tradition that executed prisoners must hang long enough that three tides pass over their bodies as they swung. For those passersby going about their business on the wharves or taking the ferry over the river, it was obvious what this rude stage was designed for.

By Friday, Boston was in a tense state. As in London, executions were high entertainment. And this execution, given the political circumstances, had the town in a minor frenzy. The last execution of a pirate had occurred back in 1690. At that time, eight men had been condemned under Massachusetts's law after being tried by the Superior Court. However, thanks to influential merchants (and second thoughts by several court members about the legality of the proceedings), seven out of the eight were reprieved and eventually released after paying fines. The sole pirate to hang, Thomas Johnson (known as "the limping privateer") was unfortunate in not having friends in high places. Prior to this, pirates had not been hanged since 1673. Boston had never liked hanging its more enterprising mariners but under Governor Dudley, official attitudes at least, had hardened. Boston's citizens were now about to witness a vivid demonstration of the changing times.

Those that were able had probably traveled in from outlying areas, staying at inns or with relations so as to get a good place for the drama. By late morning, crowds were beginning to converge on the North End, spilling out on the grassy slopes of Copp's Hill (then called Windmill or Broughton's Hill), overlooking the river and docks. The weather was fine and dry, and as the sun climbed higher, so did the temperature. Fishwives and merchants' wives alike pulled their linen bonnets forward or donned wide-brimmed straw hats to shield their faces from the heat. Little business was being conducted in Boston on this Friday as show time drew near.

For not just one poor soul was to be "turned off" that Friday at three o'clock in a public spectacle: seven men were condemned to hang simultaneously. It was to be Boston's largest mass execution to date.

Not even the Council would get much work accomplished this day. In the morning, shortly after Dudley convened the daily session, a messenger arrived bearing sad news. Dudley's niece, Anna Paige, had died suddenly after a short illness. Not only a relation of Dudley, she was the wife of Nicholas Paige—part-owner of the brigantine *Charles*. As Sewall later wrote, Dudley "clap'd his hands, and quickly went out, and return'd not to the Chamber again; but ordered Mr. Secretary to prorogue the Court till the 16th of August."

Although he was clearly moved and upset by the death of his niece, it seems curious that he would declare a six-week stop to the important business of the province. Were the ongoing events and the imminent pirate executions preying upon his mind? Perhaps the memories of when the Boston mob attacked his home and carried him off to prison in 1689 were all too fresh. Those events, sparked when news of the "Glorious Revolution" reached Boston, had led to him being roughed up and thrown into a jail cell as a supporter and official of the now deposed James II, his house ransacked and robbed in the bargain. He was later put under close confinement, receiving comfort and aid, at the home of his niece, Anna Paige.

Shortly after midday, the execution party arrived at the prison. The prison keeper turned the heavy iron key in the door and the officials stepped into the stinking cells. Giles Dyer, sheriff of Suffolk County led his constables into the main chamber, joined by Henry Franklin, the Marshal of Admiralty (and saviour of young Templeton) and by Reverend Mather. Outside the prison, forty musketeers stood at the ready. Once inside the muffled stone walls, one of the officials would have called out the names of the seven who were to be hanged, reading out the death warrant against them. It is not known if this was met by silence or, perhaps, by a mixed explosion of English and French cursing and shouting from the inmates. One by one, the condemned were unshackled and led out into the fresh air, shielding their eyes from the bright sunlight. Whether or not those remaining behind shouted words of encouragement to

Quelch or cursed him is not recorded. Some must surely have resented and blamed their captain for having led them to this dismal end but it is disappointing that neither Sewall nor Mather made note of how he took his final leave from his shipmates.

Quelch was followed by six others that Dudley felt were deemed not worthy of reprieve: John Lambert, Christopher Scudamore, John Miller, Erasmus Peterson, Peter Roach, and Francis King. With the exception of Peterson, a Swiss-born sailor of twenty-five, all the others were over thirty years of age and age did seem to have been a determining factor in deciding who would be the first to the gallows. Experience, at least according to Dudley, was the chief indicator of moral corruption. Simply put, longtime mariners ought to have known better than to turn pirate; younger men were naïve and inclined to follow their elders. Just how the oldest convicted crewman, Charles James, avoided the noose is unclear.

The prisoners would have had their hands bound behind their backs with rope before being conducted out into the street outside the jail. With the red-coated musketeers, firelocks, and swords at the ready, forming a cordon around the prisoners, the party began its march into the center of the town, via the Town House and then Dock Square. Leading the procession was Henry Franklin, who as Marshal of the Admiralty, bore a miniature silver oar measuring about three feet long—the symbol of naval authority and equivalent to the mace of civil authorities. For the condemned, it was to be their last walk alive, a half-mile trudge eastwards through the widest streets toward their first destination: Scarlett's Wharf. Followed and shouted at by crowds of townsfolk, young and old, the musketeers warning off those who approached too closely, the mood must have been one of noisy support for the prisoners. Others spectated from indoors, hanging out of their upstairs windows to see the parade. For their part, the mariners, some petrified, others resigned, would have kept their eyes forward, their ears filled with shouts, whistles, the jangle of soldier's weapons and harness, and the clop of all those shoes and boots upon the uneven cobblestones. To this was added the constant slow beat of a single muffled drum, providing the cadence of their sad march.

From Fish Street the party turned onto Ship Street and then out onto Scarlett's Wharf, covered with warehouses and boatbuilder shacks. Here, the prisoners were put into a longboat, escorted by their guards. Other boats carried the officials of the Admiralty, the town constables, and the clergymen. Pushing off from the wharf, the boats were rowed out and around the peninsula, headed up the Charles estuary. Around them, the river was covered by small craft of every sort. Large merchant ships at anchor had their crews climbing masts and spars to get a better look. The longboats passed another dozen wharves as their oars raised and dipped; crowds waved their hats to give the pirates a proper send-off.

The half-hour boat trip ended at Hudson's Point. Pushing their way through the confusion of canoes, shallops, and rowboats, and cursing loudly (probably wielding an oar or musket barrel at those who impeded them), the officials beached the longboats on the mud flats where the gallows stood waiting.

Samuel Sewall was one of the people there. He wrote: "Many were the people that saw upon Broughton's Hill. But when I came to see how the River was cover'd with People, I was amazed: Some say there were 100 Boats. 150 Boats and Canoes, saith Cousin Moody of York."

Hundreds of spectators pushed and shoved to get a better view of the condemned as they were escorted up the beach. Quelch would have had a good view of the Charlestown ferry, from where he had made the fateful decision to enter Boston just one month before. The town guard (presumably having made their way on foot while the execution party traveled by boat) spread out in front of the gallows, muskets gripped across their chests, in order to keep the multitude at bay. Joining the officials at the gallows, was John Campbell, the postmaster, pencil in hand and taking notes for what would be the first "extra" of an American newspaper. Herded together, the seven pirates were once again subjected to preaching by Mather and Colman: "As we have told you often, ye we have told you Weeping, That you have by Sin undone yourselves . . . that your Sins have been many and mighty; and that the Sins for which you are now to Dy are of no common aggravation . . . We have told you, What Marks of Life must be desired for your Souls, that you may Safely appear before the Judgment Seat of God . . . We can do no more but leave you in His Merciful Hands!"

The scaffold was hoisted up to the proper height and made fast. With this, the prisoners were assisted up onto this wobbling plank, the constables and executioner spacing them equally apart and steadying them on the creaking boards. Quelch showed no fear. He doffed his hat and made several bows to the crowd, which responded with a roar of approval. Ropes were thrown up over the crossbar and made fast, the nooses dangling just at shoulder-level.

Reverend Mather, taking advantage of one of the largest audiences of his career, was not found wanting for a prayer to the masses assembled. After a proclamation for silence was made, Mather's voice boomed out across the beach and up the slope opposite. He began: "O Thou most Great and Glorious LORD! Thou art a Righteous and a Terrible GOD. It is a Righteous and an Holy Law that thou hast given unto us. To Break that Good Law, and Sin against thy Infinite Majesty, can be no little Evil."

John Campbell struggled to keep up with the oration due to the speed and the surrounding burble of the crowd (and later made apology in print for any problems with the text). This prayer was not meant so much for the condemned as for those yet-to-be-condemned out in the vast crowd. "Great GOD," invoked Mather, "Grant that all the Spectators, may get Good by the horrible Spectacle that is now before them!" The exhortation lasted some ten minutes or more. All the while, the condemned stood upon the stage, contemplating their impending deaths, some near nervous collapse.

Mather gathered up his voice for his final blast: "And now, we fly, we fly to Sovereign Grace, Oh! That the Poor men, which are immediately to appear before the awful Tribunal of God, may first by Sovereign Grace, have produced upon their Souls, those Marks of thy Favour, without which 'tis a dreadful Thing to appear before that awful Tribunal... God be Merciful to us all, for the Sake of our Lord Jesus Christ... Amen."

Franklyn, the serving provost, stepped forward and pulled out an order from the governor. It was a reprieve for Francis King. King, no doubt a shaking wreck, was pulled down off the stage and delivered over to the constables. Dudley's mercy was a calculated move, one intended from the beginning to help allay public anger.

Franklyn stepped up to the gallows and faced the remaining prisoners. Beginning with Quelch, he asked if they had any final words before they were to be turned off. According to the broadside that Campbell published a few days later, Quelch was to have confided to Mather that he was "Afraid of a Great God, and a

Judgment to Come." This seems out of character given the words that he subsequently shouted out to the crowd. It was not unusual for broadsides to take artistic license in such things for the greater public good. Given Dudley's role as censor, it may have been insisted upon.

Campbell found Quelch "Not concerned, nor behaving himself so much like a Dying man as some would have done." Mather had urged him to make a testimony of his sins to the crowd, and to glorify God. Quelch was in no mood to comply.

"Gentlemen, 'tis but little I have to speak: What I have to say is this, I desire to be informed for what I am here, I am Condemned only upon Circumstances. I forgive all the World: So the Lord be Merciful to my Soul."

John Lambert "Seemed in a great Agony" wrote Campbell, "and pleaded much of his Innocency: He desired all men to beware of Bad Company."

Quelch joined in at that point, shouting over Lambert's voice.

"They should also take care how they brought Money into New-England, to be Hanged for it!"

Lambert broke down into repeated calls for God's mercy and asking for forgiveness. Christopher Scudamore, "very Penitent since his Condemnation" was quiet and prayed aloud. John Miller was overwrought, crying out of his "great Burden of Sins" and asking how he could be saved.

Erasmus Peterson could scarce contain his bitterness at what had befallen him. He called out to the crowd that "It is very hard for so many mens Lives to be taken away for a little Gold." Speaking of the injustice done him, he said his peace was made with God but that it was "extream hard" to forgive those that had wronged him. Turning to the executioner his last words were forthright. He said he was a strong man and prayed to be put out of misery as soon as possible.

The last of the men, Peter Roach, "seem'd little concerned and said but little or nothing at all."

Sewall's diary entry captures the horror of the next moment with compelling simplicity: "When the Scaffold was let to sink, there was such a Screech of the Women that my wife heard it sitting in our Entry next the Orchard, and was much surprised at it; yet the wind was sou-west. Our house is a full mile from the place."

It is highly unlikely that their deaths were quick. Unless the executioner had left sufficient slack in the ropes, and unless the stage was high enough to allow a long drop, the condemned would have found themselves suspended when the plank was dropped. Instead of a mercifully quick death of a broken neck, they would have suffered a slow strangulation under their own weight. The scene was common enough in London at the Tyburn gallows where the spectators would watch those executed dance the "Tyburn jig," legs kicking spasmodically until death, often ending in defecation from stress. Depending upon how the noose gripped the neck, death could take several minutes. This led to condemned men getting their friends and relations (or paying a stranger) to pull on their legs once they fell in order to hasten death.

Once John Quelch and his companions had stopped their twitching, the official party would have returned to the longboats and put back out into the river. The town guard would have remained behind to prevent the corpses from being cut down, as it was now necessary for them to be swirled and washed about by three successive high tides. Eventually, the crowd must have lost interest and dispersed back to their homes or to the taverns to discuss what they had witnessed. More than a few were grumbling about injustice.

Although he was not attending to official business, Governor Dudley was worried enough about the public mood to order Campbell to immediately publish the censored transcript of the pirates' trial. Paul Dudley had spent the last few days in writing this up and the governor had collaborated in this effort. Perhaps by showing the people the nature of the crimes that Quelch and his crew had committed could assuage their anger; particularly a version of events that had been given some progovernment "spin." Such a move was unprecedented. Until the Admiralty and Board of Trade in London had seen and approved the transcript, it should not have been released. Dudley would soon be facing down an angry Whitehall over his decision to do so.

For his part, Samuel Sewall, appeared to have been moved by what he had witnessed that afternoon. Shortly after the execution, he was approached by family members of the Salem resident John Lambert, including his son. They made suit to Sewall, as the senior judge of the province, to allow them to take Lambert's body and bury it respectfully. This was something that Sewall was not bound to do, pirates normally being buried in unmarked graves or, more commonly, left hanging in chains on a gibbet to rot and be picked at by gulls and crows. Even in death, captured pirates would remain a warning to mariners entering Boston that the province was tough on crime.

Sewall agreed to release Lambert's body to his widow. But more than this, he also ordered the diggers of Anna Paige's tomb in the Old Burial Ground across from the Anglican Church to dig a grave for Lambert as well. Before the three tides could cover him, Lambert had been cut down and taken away, his relations burying him around midnight that evening under lantern light near where other relatives lay buried. It was an extraordinary act of compassion but was Sewall alleviating his own guilt for the botched trial, or was he doing his part to cool down the tempers of the townsfolk by giving the local pirate a decent burial. Sewall never confided his reasoning to his diary.

The fate of Quelch's body, and that of the others, is not recorded. Future pirates tried at Boston, William Fly among them, were gibbeted out on Nix's Mate in Boston Harbor. Quelch and the five others were probably spared this and buried in unmarked graves in the North Burial Ground above Broughton's Hill. Such a move would have fitted in with Dudley's strategy of calming the waters after the unpopular trial.

In a strange coincidence, Sewall records how the very day after the execution, news came in on a merchant ship bound from New York that under an act of Parliament, it was now legal for the colonies to trade with the colonies of New Spain in South America. As Sewall remarked, "This comes in seasonably upon Quelches Spightfull admonition yesterday." Since the act would have been announced in London before the trial had even begun, this meant that even Quelch's alibi was no defense of his actions.

That mattered little now. Captain Quelch was now a waterlogged corpse along with five of his crew, while the others waited in prison upon a similar fate. But the fate of Quelch's gold, and those that had a stake in it, was yet to be determined. In fact, the struggle to root out, calculate, divide, and profit from the pirate treasure was only just beginning.

Chapter Seventeen

Doubts and Recriminations

T he trial and execution was the great drama of the summer. John Marshall, who lived in Braintree, and therefore was one level removed from the scene at Boston, made this clear in his diary: "That of most remark in this month was the tryall and condemnation of Capt. Quelch and his Company to the number of 20 or more who weer found guilty of piracy and murder on severall of the queen's allies . . . to which they weer condemned to dy—6 of them executed the last day of the month."

In Marblehead and Salem, towns that had played a central role in the pirate excitement and where many residents had been forced to turn over the gold they had received in payment for services, one local wag composed a bit of doggerel to commemorate the adventure:

Ye pirates who against God's laws did fight,
Have all been taken which is very right.
Some of them were old and others young,
But on the flats of Boston all were hung.

In Boston itself, anyone remotely connected with the episode was lining up to claim reward or compensation from the governor. Stephen Sewall's troop had already received their reward for capturing the last of Quelch's crew. The new petitioners encompassed the social strata of the province all the way from Attorney

General Paul Dudley down to the men who lashed the gallows and hammered the leg irons. Some of the money doled out of the pirate treasure was to reward civic mindedness, but most of it was reimbursement for expenses incurred. Almost every sheriff, constable, or customs official in the region managed to make a few pounds for their services. Stephen North, publican of the Star, charged £28 and eleven shillings for his catering services; Paul Dudley was handed £36 for leading the prosecution case; but Meinzies received only £20 for handling the defense. John Valentine, Registrar of the province, received £13 for his diligence in taking the transcript, while Captain Edward Brattle charged the province £1 and five shillings for looking after the slave Emanuel.

Henry Franklyn, as Marshal of the Admiralty in Boston, charged £29 and nineteen shillings for supplying the gibbet and guards and for conducting the executions. The town's blacksmith, James Jarvis, was gratified with a sizeable payment for fabricating the prisoners' chains and for putting them on and taking them off during the trial. The jailor, who carried responsibility for some of his inmates until the end of July 1705, received £112 and fourteen shillings for "diet and keeping." Five of the commissioners divided a £100 stipend for their services in receiving and securing the gold but, not surprisingly, the largest disbursement went to Governor Dudley. For his services as Judge of the Court, he put in for 5 percent, calculated at forty-four ounces at £5 an ounce, netting him a handsome payment of £220. In all, over £750 was paid out of the treasure for charges relating to the capture, trial, and execution. It was a huge sum and one that would not go unquestioned by the Board of Trade at Whitehall. Yet seen from a Boston perspective, and particularly from Dudley's, it was all about keeping the lid on the simmering pot of public unrest.

On July 12, the General Assembly of Massachusetts sent a letter to Queen Anne (or more probably Dudley himself since he had already prorogued the Assembly until August) that carried substantial reference to the recent Quelch trial. It was the first communication to openly pledge the province's support in the war against piracy.

"We crave leave also humbly to express our just resentment and detestation of the piracies and robberies lately committed by Capt. Quelch and Company, and we hope the speedy justice that has been done upon those vile criminals will vindicate the Government from the imputation of giving any countenance to, or favouring of, such wicked actions." Not stated, but implied, was the intent to distance the province from its sister colonies in Rhode Island and New York and their dubious commercial dealings.

The following day, Governor Dudley penned a letter to his masters in London, giving details of the Quelch case and justifying his handling of it. He also made clear his logic in how he chose from the twenty in custody those who were to face the gallows.

> Have executed six of them that is to say, the captain and master who were the ringleaders, the person that kept Plowman close and would suffer no man to speak with him, the man that shot the Portuguese Captain after he got on board his ship, and there are yet fourteen condemned left in chaines that are young and ignorant fellows, objects of Her Majesties mercy if she please.

He was also at pains to explain the difficulties he faced in carrying out the duties of his office: "The whole proceeding is enclosed which I ordered to be printed it being a very new thing and seeming very harsh to hang people that bring in gold to these provinces."

The new law against piracy that permitted local admiralty courts did not cover accessories to the crime of piracy. As such, Dudley was duty-bound to send these men back to London to stand justice, along with any witnesses to carry the case against them. "I have also sent home," he wrote, "Captain Larrimore and his Lieutenant John Wells who have made themselves accessories after the fact by hideing, concealing and carrying away seven of the sd Pyrates."

Finally, to reinforce his own position, he again made mention of the peculiarities of dispensing justice in the provinces. "The executions past I hope will forever be a warning to such evil men here . . . *I pray I may be pardoned for any mistake in the Tryalls*, the proceedings here being wholly new, and that I may have Her Majesty's direction for what remaines in this affair." (Author's italics)

To deliver his letters, the court's proceedings, and Larrimore and the witnesses, Dudley chose a local merchant and sea captain, Nathaniel Cary, to conduct the mission to London. Cary, who lived across the river in Charlestown, was well known to the governor and his council and a dependable choice.

What Dudley chose *not* to send back is obvious: the money. His motives were mixed. The outgoings had probably not yet all been accounted for and these would have to come out of the treasure if not the strained provincial Treasury. Secondly, he knew that once shipped out, he would never see the gold again. With a rebellious Assembly digging its heels in on paying for troops and fortifications (not to mention his salary) Quelch's gold was manna from heaven—if he could get the crown's blessing to use it for such. To further his plan, he provided Cary with detailed drawings of the major fortifications around Boston and on the frontier at Pisquataqua in New Hampshire and Pemaquid in Maine. These sketches made clear the need for additional cannon to fend off French incursions. He also told Cary to make his plea for financial aid to the Board of Trade or to members of the Queen's Privy Council. Withholding the treasure for a few months might cause some irritation back in London, but he was within his rights to be prudent until he received direct orders from Whitehall telling him how to dispose of it.

Cary sailed out in the sloop *Sea Flower* about the third week of July. Larrimore and Wells, both in irons, found themselves unwilling passengers to London but given the justice machine they had witnessed in Boston, probably felt better for a hearing in England. Even more shocked at having to make an unscheduled trip to London were four local men of Marblehead and Salem, including Dr. Francis Gahtman. Had they known that their civic-mindedness meant an eight- to ten-week voyage over the Atlantic, a leave-taking of family, and a loss of trade that would not be compensated, they may have thought twice about fingering Larrimore to the authorities. Indeed, the £5 that Gahtman had already received as reward from the treasure would have to stretch considerably in order to support him during an enforced holiday of more than seven or eight month's duration (and at London prices). It must have been a joyless trip indeed across a wide, rolling sea.

Samuel Sewall, sitting back in Boston, may also have had cause for second thoughts about the events of June gone by. Immediately after the trial, he had posted out a few of the mass-produced printed copies of the trial and executions to correspondents back in

England. A reply several months later from Sir William Ashurst, MP, a friend of the province and former lord mayor of London, seems to have put Sewall on the defensive. Ashurst's letter does not survive, but the tone of Sewall's reply indicates that Ashurst had questioned the legality of the proceedings against Quelch.

"As to the compentency of the Witnesses," wrote Sewall, "the Grounds I went upon was the province Law ... unless they prov'd the Men and Treasure to be Taken from the Queen's Enemies, they were Pirats and when I gave my voice against Capt. Quelch, I caused the Law to be read. The Court did not stand in any absolute Necessity of the testimony of the Approvers that was made use of *ex abundanti*." Sewall's explanation still did not address the way the commission had applied civil and common law willy-nilly as it suited, nor did it mention how no independent evidence was produced to prove the guilt of the men. Everything Dudley had put forward during the trial was circumstantial. To many on the outside looking in, it smacked of judicial convenience at best, mistrial at worst.

Perhaps Sewall's conscience bothered him more than he was willing to admit. He confided in his diary on February 13, 1705/6, "Last night I had a very sad Dream that held me a great while. As I remember, I was condemn'd and to be executed."

Worse still, even as the *Sea Flower* plied its way to England, carrying the details of the Quelch trial, the Board of Trade in London had come to the conclusion that a few administrative details were seriously lacking concerning the war on piracy. The Board had recently received word from the governor of Barbados that, in the opinion of that island's Attorney and Solicitor General, the governor could not legally try pirates under the *Act of 11 and 12, William III*, chiefly because William III was now dead. When the Board of Trade submitted this legal objection to the Attorney General of England for *his* review, they found that the Barbadian interpretation was indeed correct. In effect, Dudley's commission (and that of all governors in the plantations) to try pirates locally under Admiralty authority was invalid. John Quelch and his men had been tried and convicted illegally. Quietly, the Privy Council redrafted commissions under Anne's name and shipped these out to the plantations around January 1704/5. Governor Dudley received his on April 20. He later wrote to the Board of Trade: "The next day after the receipt of the Commission for the tryal of pirates, I publish'd it in the proper Court, and it is of record in the Offices." Quelch's condemnation stood and no legal objection was ever lodged to overturn it—simply put, it was not in the interest of anyone aware of the legal foul-up to do anything about it.

The owners of the *Charles*, ignorant of the wrongful prosecution of the recent trial, were not happy about the denouement of the Quelch affair either. Their gold was confiscated by Dudley, their ship impounded, and all stores removed to be auctioned to the public. Declaring Quelch a pirate had the effect of declaring everything he had touched to be stolen goods and now property of the crown. As men of business, there was but one solution: start again. The syndicate was forced to buy back the *Charles* (at £200 this was well below the real value of the vessel and a bit of good fortune). They would now try to refit her, crew her, and send her out again before the weather turned bad in an attempt to salvage some profit from the ill-starred enterprise. Colman managed to hire a new captain for the ship, one John Halsey of Boston. Halsey had led two highly successful privateer voyages in 1702 and 1703 around Barbados and seemed a wise choice. The problem though, was that they now needed a new privateering commission. Dudley, however, would not be moved.

Stating that the province could hardly spare mariners from commercial shipping to go out privateering when Boston was preparing a convoy to sail to the West Indies, Dudley found support in his decision from other prominent merchants who did *not* have a stake in the *Charles*. Undeterred, Colman and Clarke, supported by Charles Hobby, made a beeline for Rhode Island to see Governor Cranston. Although Cranston had no clear royal authority to issue privateering commissions as Dudley did, Cranston certainly believed that he did. His government had for years done a brisk business in licensing pirates and privateers in a dizzying revolving-door fashion, skimming off substantial profits in the process.

For a fee, Cranston was delighted to give Colman and Captain Halsey the paper they needed. To the fury of Dudley, and with half her crew comprising Massachusetts men, the *Charles* was plying the sea off New England in November, destined for the Caribbean to hunt the French and Spaniards.

With their investment back out to sea and in earning-mode, the owners now turned their efforts to regaining the fortune they had lost through Dudley's zealousness. A necessarily lengthy letter-writing campaign to London would begin in 1705, chiefly to get back their share of the gold, but also, one designed to destabilize Governor Dudley's position.

Meanwhile, Dudley was waiting for some word from Whitehall regarding Captain Cary's mission. In a reflective mood, he wrote to the Board of Trade at the end of January 1704/5.

> Captain Lawrence [sic] and Lieutenant Wells the accessories whom I am commanded to send home, have these two last years done good Service. The first year Lawrence [sic] took five prizes, since commanded a Company of Volunteers to Jamaica ... and did a good service there & returned, but fell unluckily into this folly. I pray it may consist with Her Majesty's Honour he may obtain his pardon.

He might just as well have saved his ink. Calamity had overtaken the *Sea Flower*, a fact that Dudley would not be aware of until March. The previous September, off Brittany, *Sea Flower* was overhauled by a large French warship and forced to strike her colors. Cary desperately tore up all of the governor's letters and the plans to the province fortifications and tossed them over the side before the French could board. Taken into Brest and condemned as an enemy prize, *Sea Flower* was now French and Captain Cary, along with his charges, was stranded. When all the crew and passengers were immediately released from custody, Larrimore and Wells took the opportunity to make a swift exit. The French naval authorities, after all, had no business with any of them.

All Cary could do was to gather up an exasperated Dr. Gahtman and the other three witnesses, and make his way to Portsmouth on the next neutral ship. Finally making it to London, Cary wrote to the Board about his misadventures. Gahtman, too wrote to the Board, evidently fed up with his situation. "I was obliged to quit a profitable Employment in that country to attend this service," he wrote. "That in my voyage hither I was taken into France by which I lost all that I had with me, that I never yet received any consideration for my Services."

It was spleen worth venting. By the end of March he had been compensated by HM Treasury with £50, which allowed him to sail home on the *Guernsey* that spring.

Once he reached London, Cary chose a more enterprising way of getting compensation. Having secreted a printed copy of the pirate trial on his person, he immediately sold it to a London broadside printer, rather than presenting it to the Board of Trade first. Dudley, in turn, would get a sharp rebuke for his messenger's cavalier approach. But Cary did his best to convey Dudley's need for money, meeting with the Board in early 1705.

> The expences of the war are now above 20,000*l.* sterl. Per annum; the distresses of it are so great that the 10th man in the Province was last summer constantly under arms to defend it ... we are at present utterly destitute of either fund or credit to answer the cost ... *Prays* that the money seized on the Pirates, exclusive of the charges in their prosecution, may be bestowed on the Province to enable them to purchase small arms and ammunition, etc.

Secretary Blathwayt and his colleagues did finally convince the Queen to send over twenty cannon for the forts. Cash grants, however, proved more problematical. A small minute in the Privy Council records for March 29, records: "Petition of Nathaniel Cary merchant in behalfe of New England, read and nothing done thereupon." But Blathwayt was more than annoyed that no accounting of this pirate treasure had been sent over. He fired off a missive to Dudley informing him of the grant of twenty guns but demanding duplicates of the plans for the fortifications. Blathwayt also chastised Cary for his printing of the pirates' trial while also rapping Dudley's knuckles. "We have not received the account you mentioned to have sent us of the pirates's treasure, and therefore we desire you not to omit it in your next [letter]." Finally, they demanded that security be set for the gold with crown receivers in the colonies and that it be sent over to England at the earliest opportunity.

Dudley's later replies (spread over at least two letters to ensure delivery) clearly put the blame on Cary. He told the Board that he would not have ordered the trial to be printed in Boston, "But to satisfy and save the clamour of a rude people, who were greatly surprised that anybody should be put to death that brought in gold into the Province and did at the time speak rudely of the proceeding against them, and assisted to hide and cover those ill persons."

As for Cary's actions, "I am very sorry that Cary should offend your Lordships in printing those tryals before he had done his duty ... or neglect his [duty] referring to the Prisoners sent home by him, or trouble himself about the pyrat [treasure] to obtayn it for this Province.... But with the loss of his papers, I think he lost this prudence also."

The governor also assured the Board that Cary's letters had also contained a full account of the treasure "every pennyweight of silver or gold taken" and that a duplicate of the accounts were now on their way. "The recovery of the money out of the many hands where it was scattered was a great drudgery, and hard to steady the people in their obedience ... if H.M. shall be pleased to bestow any part thereof upon me ... it will justify my proceedings against those ill men."

A previous letter to London, written on March 10, had also conveyed Dudley's frustrations with the people he ruled. "By the *Gospir* I gave your Lordship the account of the pyrates ... since which six have broken prison notwithstanding constant Guards upon them, our prison being so full of French prisoners and some people that are offended that any such proceeding should be had against those that bring in money though never so ill-gotten, have taken care to hide and carry them off which I cannot discover, and one of them is dead in prison so that there are but six left."

Dudley could not have received a clearer signal of the unpopularity of his administration. Some six months after the trial, public feeling remained so stirred that citizens had risked incarceration themselves by helping to spirit away the remnants of Quelch's company. The crew had undoubtedly forced the wooden fence that surrounded the prison yard while townsfolk helped pull them through and out to freedom. Yet another prisoner, William Wilde, broke out in June, but was later recaptured.

Loathed in Boston, Dudley, through no fault of his own, was slipping in estimation in London as well. Moreover, his political enemies at home and in England were probing for weaknesses.

Charles Hobby had powerful friends in Whitehall. In 1705, they would gain him a knighthood and agitate for him to replace Dudley as governor. In Boston, this plan was being fostered by the

Mathers who had had their fill of the governor's increasingly royal grip on power (and his decidedly Anglican ways). Colman too, would leverage his connections as a receiver for H.R.H. Prince George, the Lord High Admiral and royal consort, in order to challenge Dudley's confiscation of the gold while at the same time insinuating that the prince's financial interests were being diverted into Dudley's pockets.

In May 1705, Hobby wrote to the Board of Trade to press his suit: "The owners having at the request of the Governor and purely for the service of the country at their own charge fitted out the vessel, it will be a very great hardship unless they have some compensation for their loss. Prays that the Board will not make any report until H.R.H. shall have made some determination herein."

Unfortunately, the petition fell on deaf ears at the Treasury, which responded somewhat curtly: "These effects are already ordered to be sent to England and to be applied to the public use as they ought to be." Moreover, the Admiralty itself was at a low of influence having been politically gelded by politicians on the Privy Council. In fact, orders frequently were issued by the Queen's cabinet directly to admirals at sea without even being seen by the Admiralty office. Prince George had little say in London, much less in Boston.

The struggle between Dudley and the *Charles* syndicate (now in common cause with Dudley's numerous other enemies) intensified rapidly in May 1705. Ironically, the catalyst was the renewed success of the brigantine *Charles*. When Captain Halsey brought in a Spanish prize ship worth £5,000 to Newport in May 1705, Dudley made sure that his ally, Nathaniel Byfield, the judge of the Admiralty for New England, blocked its condemnation on the grounds that Cranston's granting of commissions was illegal. A furious spat ensued that nearly saw the cargo seized by Halsey, his enraged mariners, and Rhode Island officials. Dudley relented, belatedly recognizing that Halsey had operated in good faith as a legal privateer. He allowed Byfield to condemn the prize in order to defuse the crisis, but he also took a cut of £50 (as was his right as Vice Admiral of New England) while Byfield earned £150 for his services. The legal tangles and dubious sincerity of customs officials in Boston and Newport left a lasting and bitter impression on John Halsey, one that would eventually lead him down a new path.

For his part, John Colman showed little fear of the governor. When the syndicate's interests were blocked by Dudley's veto over Cranston's authority he successfully lobbied the Rhode Island Assembly to issue a proclamation supporting that colony's right to issue privateering commissions independent of Boston, based upon *their* interpretation of their charter. Once he had secured the prize after paying off Byfield and Dudley, Colman then lashed out in a series of letters to the Board of Trade during the summer of 1705. His accusations were serious ones. In addition to complaining about being "oppressed" by the governor in his demand for a percentage cut of the Spanish prize ship (after having refused them a privateering commission), he strongly hinted that the Admiralty under Dudley was inflating the value of captured cargoes in order to boost his own cut as adjudicator. Hoping to stir trouble at the level of the Queen herself, he went on to claim that Dudley was interfering in his rightful collection of the "tenths" or duties owed to H.R.H. Prince George. He then accused Paul Dudley of obtaining one of Quelch's Brazilian slaves at a private auction for a price that was half of what would have been obtained at open market.

He then twisted the knife by bringing up the subject of Quelch's treasure, stating his alarm at how the province had paid out over £1,500 in charges from the gold. Some of this, he alleged, was due to the fact that Dudley paid a huge sum to send Captain Cary over in *Sea Flower*—a task he would have put the *Charles* to for much less "and they [the owners] would run the risque of her" themselves. He concluded his letter by saying how "very much slighted" he was at having been made to relinquish the gold (despite the fact that he held security for the sums back in England) and put it into the hands of others, "kept in the dark . . . am not capable to render any account about it but what I am beholden to others for." It was a carefully worded, but very clear accusation that the gold was being embezzled by Dudley and his cronies.

Dudley, annoyed by the episode, wrote to his masters before learning of Colman's attack upon him. "There was no danger of the Prince's tenths," he protested to the Board of Trade, "but of Mr. Coleman's own halfe or thereabouts." Dudley voiced his concerns that a receiver for the crown's interests should also be engaged in profit-making by privateering because of the temptation to fraud: "I have nothing personally to charge Mr. Coleman with of any

neglect." But once Colman's letters brought forth the inevitable demand by Whitehall for an official response from Dudley, the governor would prove a formidable warrior under siege. A skilful prac-
titioner of the verbal duel, Dudley's rapier-sharp justifications to
Whitehall demolished the rather clumsy and blunt-edged petitions
that Colman was churning out to the Board of Trade.

"That I refused him the Pyrates' gold is most true," Dudley
wrote in October 1706. "H.M. Instructions commanding mee to do
... which I have strictly obeyed.... He saith he was much slighted
when that treasure was taken out of his hands. I do not know
whether your Lordships were advised that 700*l.* or 800*l.* of this
pyrates' gold was upon a secret division amongst the owners of that
unfortunate vessell carryed home to Mr. Colman's house." He went
on to say that Colman had taken the money without any judgment
by the Admiralty in Boston, essentially accusing Colman, Hobby,
and the other owners of accepting stolen goods.

He concluded his report on the matter with a final thrust at his
tormentor: "I humbly submit myself to your Lordships' censure in
everything, but pray not to be left to the calumny of Mr. Colman,
who is of no further consideration originally here than the son of a
poor Ale-house keeper yet living, and, as they say, not able to pay
his debts."

In early 1707 the Board lost interest in the complaints of Colman
and company. Colman had never presented any evidence of his
claims while Dudley's letters had been generously appended with
documents backing up his version of events. In retrospect, Colman
was lucky not to have lost his position as a receiver of the prince's
interests in New England. Although Dudley had fought off this particular attack, others far more serious were about to break upon his
office, one—involving allegations of treason—would nearly topple
him as governor.

As for the treasure itself, on October 27, 1705, after the last of the
petitioners had been paid, the governor and council finally closed
the account book. In the presence of the two naval officers tasked
with carrying the treasure to England aboard the frigate *Guernsey*,
the gold was again weighed, placed into five large leather bags,
and then placed into a wooden chest that was nailed, corded, and
sealed. After all charges, it weighed in at 788 ounces and three
pennyweight. Captain John Huntington and Lieutenant Simon

Lyon signed for the treasure and personally escorted it down to the wharves and onto the *Guernsey*. Braving the impending autumn Atlantic storms, the ship and what was left of Quelch's gold, set out for home. Joseph Dudley was finally relieved of the burden of responsibility for the treasure, yet he had been unable to secure any of it for the use of the province. Moreover, in a calculated move, he had given back his own percentage cut as admiralty judge leaving it to the Queen and her councilors to set his rightful reward instead. This was a gamble. He was no Duke of Marlborough bathing in the generosity of a grateful monarch. He was an American-born colonial official a very long way from the center of power, beholden to men who had far greater concerns.

Beset by his political enemies, his actions over the past months, including his handling of the Quelch affair, had only served to further estrange him from the people he administered. As the winter of 1705/6 slowly settled upon Boston, the governor's prestige was dealt another blow: He was personally involved in an early eighteenth century "road rage" fracas.

In December, while on his way out of Roxbury in his coach, and accompanied by his younger son William and other members of his household, he found his way barred by two carts laden with cordwood. The lane divided, offering the option of a short detour to the governor and his party, and the cart drivers had pulled up short, waiting for the coach to take this route. The governor's son demanded that the cart men veer off the road to allow their passage. When the farmers politely indicated that it would be far easier for the governor to take the detour around rather than they having to maneuver their heavily laden team-drawn wagons, William Dudley struck the horses and then threatened to run them through with his sword. The altercation quickly flew out of control. One of the farmers placed himself between his team and William Dudley and defended himself with a stick while the other farmer sought the intervention of the governor. He got it.

Joseph Dudley leapt out of the coach shouting, "Run the dogs through!" and while the second farmer had turned back to rescue his horses that were rearing up in fear, the governor stabbed him in the back. As the farmer, John Winchester, wheeled around in pain, the governor struck him on the head. Winchester, not seriously hurt, wrenched the governor's sword from his hand and broke it before falling to the ground. As he warded off the continued blows of a seeming madman in a massive periwig, he called out to bystanders to witness that he was "in defence of my life."

Dudley, still flailing, replied: "You lie, you dog, you lie, you divell." William Dudley, meanwhile, wounded the other farmer in the hip and then was joined by his father who set upon him as well. It was an appalling incident and one probably fostered by Dudley's siege mentality. Knowing full well the lack of esteem in which common people held him, in all likelihood he probably thought it was an ambush. A Justice of the Peace made his way to the scene and Dudley ordered the two farmers clapped up in the jail. In his subsequent statement to the court, the governor claimed that the cart men had refused to yield and then had affronted him, saying, "I am as good flesh and blood as you; I will not give way; you may goe out of the way." Independent witnesses saw it otherwise. Justice Sewall, clearly shocked by the entire incident, worked to get the men bailed after a few days, despite Paul Dudley's best efforts to frustrate this in his capacity as Attorney General. "I am glad," Sewall wrote in his diary, "that I have been instrumental to Open the Prison to these two young men, that they might repair to their wives and children and Occasions."

When the case finally came to the Superior Court, nearly a year later, it was dismissed immediately, both farmers being "discharged by solemn Proclamation." The authoritarian Dudley, ever eager to press the royal prerogative in governing the province, was finding he could not always have his own way. The months that followed would compound his troubles further.

Chapter Eighteen

Flotsam

L
ike a large stone pitched into a mill pond, the ripples of the Quelch affair spread far beyond Massachusetts, rolling over individuals both high and low. His own demise withstanding, John Quelch's gold was still making a remarkable journey. It had traveled from Brazil to New England and from there, some of it stuffed into the pockets of fleeing mariners, moved along a myriad of paths down the seaboard colonies of America; the remainder traveled across the Atlantic again to England, intended for higher purposes. Still more of it, no doubt, lingered in Boston or thereabouts, secreted away until a safer day.

In the first week of March, 1705/6, a sixty-three-year-old Sir Isaac Newton watched as his assistants lugged a large, securely nailed and corded wooden chest into his draughty office at the Royal Mint, then a ramshackle and tumbledown series of rooms wedged between the inner and outer walls of the Tower of London. He would be the first person in Europe to touch Quelch's gold.

Newton, having made his fame as a mathematician and astronomer, had become Master of the Royal Mint in 1699. The father of modern physics, who shaped our notions of light and motion, time, and space, also dabbled in alchemy and the occult. It was from alchemy's spurring that he developed a keenness for metallurgy and this, in turn, made him particularly well suited for the job of Mint Master. Applying his innate genius to the mundane world, Newton sought to improve the coinage of the realm. The position was traditionally a *sinecure*, normally bestowed as a mark of royal or political favor and requiring no active involvement, but Newton's administration of the mint was memorable for his hands-on approach in perfecting the minting process while combating counterfeiters. It was no surprise then that he personally took charge of assaying the gold dust that Governor Dudley had shipped to Portsmouth.

"It was 1oz ¼ above weight [as recorded at Boston]," wrote Newton to the Lord Treasurer Godolphin, "but the Dust Gold was very foule and being examined with a Load Stone [magnet] was found full of Iron filings & therefore in the Melting lost something more than 2 lbs in weight and remained very brittle. . . . The standard Weight after Melting & toughning is 65lbs: 10oz: 11: 5gr & being Coyned it made 2,944 Guineas & 22 grains . . . amounts to 3,164:19:8 [sterling]."

Sir Isaac concluded his report by requesting compensation for the expenses in retrieving the gold from Portsmouth and melting it down and "Without allowing the Officer anything for his Trouble who in Modesty would make no demand on that Acct," asked Godolphin for a reward for the fellow's diligence. The Lord Treasurer readily agreed to these payments (with a reward of £12 and eighteen shillings), making the father of modern physics and astronomy (and his assistant) the first men in England to profit from Quelch's treasure. Newton's machine-struck guinea coins, all bearing the stern and jowled likeness of the sovereign Anne, were placed in receipt of Her Majesty's Exchequer for what use the public purse would put them to.

The "wreck" of John Quelch's daring enterprise in 1704 left much human flotsam bobbing and drifting in the transatlantic maritime world. Those most directly concerned with the misadventure suffered the greatest.

Back in June 1705, Governor Dudley had received a letter from the Board of Trade, penned in April. Sir Charles Hedges, secretary to the Board and Privy Council member, wrote, "We have laid before Her Majesty what you write us in relation to the pirates and to Captain Larrimore." He went on to request a full account of the treasure and ordered that it be shipped back to London. Despite the determination by the Crown that the parliamentary act authorizing local prosecution under courts of admiralty had expired before Dudley conducted his trial against Quelch and crew, the Board of Trade never questioned the proceedings, the outcome, or Dudley's methods, even after their lordships had read the transcript. So much water under the bridge is how the affair was viewed from London; the *intentions* had been honorable even if the commission had been in error. But the letter to the governor contained an element of mercy as well. Hedges directed Dudley to pardon the remaining mariners languishing in Boston's jail.

This mercy, however, was not without its conditions. The six convicted crew members (a seventh had expired in the cells that winter) had their chains struck off but were then immediately frogmarched down to the Boston docks where they were pressed into service aboard HMS *Deptford*, a navy frigate bound for patrol against the French in Canada. It was no small irony that these six mariners who had made the journey from privateers to pirates, now found themselves hunting down the same. *Deptford*, with Quelch's men aboard her, took an active part in the Port Royal (Nova Scotia) expedition of 1707, an ill-planned and even worse executed campaign that ended in embarrassing failure for its chief architect: Governor Dudley.

For the five Africans who had been caught up in the affair, the future was equally cloudy. On October 6, 1705, Joachim and Emanuel found themselves on display at the Swan Tavern where they suffered the indignity of public sale. Paul Dudley's well-timed nod to Shannon, the auctioneer, gained him one of the men for £20. A few months later he was forced to provide a copy of the sales receipt to prove legal purchase after Colman complained to London that the "auction" had been a sham. These men, having endured slavery in Brazil, now found themselves the property of wealthy Bostonians, destined to be house servants or stable "boys" for the rest of their lives. Mingo, who had been enslaved in Guinea and acquired there by Captain Plowman, may have had the good fortune to be declared a free man (this was not unusual at this time, particularly in the northern colonies) but equally, he may have fallen into Colonel Hobby's hands if Plowman's personal property had passed to the shipowners.

As for Caesar-Pompey and Charles, the two slaves that Hobby had lent to Plowman for the voyage, they undoubtedly returned to duties in that gentleman's household on Rawson's Lane in the

South End. Both slipped back into obscurity except for one tantalizing reference in Sewall's diary for New Year's Day 1704/5: "Col. Hobbey's Negro comes about 8 or 9 mane and sends in by David to have leave to give me a Levit [trumpet blast] and wish me a merry new year. I admitted it: gave him 3 Reals. Sounded very well." Could this slave, dressed in fine livery, stockings, and buckled shoes, blowing season's greetings upon his horn to Boston's most prominent citizens, be the same man who had blasted the trumpet on the *Charles* as it sliced through the azure-blue waters of the Brazilian coast?

The final fate of fallen local hero Thomas Larrimore also remains to be discovered. Captain Cary, whose mission to London had ended so badly, had confided to the Board of Trade in March 1704/5 that Larrimore had been briefly spotted at the Exchange in London. This would have been the logical place to go for a captain in search of a ship, prowling where the moneyed men of commerce planned their voyages to the ends of the earth. However, Larrimore sidestepped the authorities and disappeared from view. Despite this escape, it would seem that his intentions to break the Queen's law remained a strong motivator. In November, 1706, Captain Jonathan Underdown, commander of Her Majesty's Newfoundland fleet and recently arrived at Plymouth from St. John's, wrote to Sir Charles Hedges: "I am also to acquaint you that I have on board as Prisoner one Thomas Larrimore who is a person suspected of very ill designs and Practices as may appear by the Inclos'd Coppy of his Examination . . . the Commis[ion] w. which he so Impudently personated of Capt. Larrimore is also inclos'd."

It is not certain that this man, caught with a forged captain's commission, is the same, but it is likely. Larrimore knew Nova Scotia: he had been marooned there by the navy after the fiasco of the Jamaica expedition. Returning to this somewhat lawless English outpost of a few hundred souls on the North Atlantic, perhaps he thought he could regain his fortune in the maritime world. Regrettably, Underdown's examination notes, which might have shed more light, are lost, and with them, so too the details of Captain Larrimore's last daring plan. He may have been tried and incarcerated in Plymouth, shipped off to the Caribbean, or eventually released. But at this juncture, as he sits miserable and damp, chained below decks in Plymouth Sound, his trail goes dead cold. However, a question remains. Upon reading the letter, did Sir Charles recall the name of Larrimore from the Quelch affair two years gone by, and if so, did he also remember Dudley's plea for clemency for a brave New Englander?

John Halsey, the third and final captain of the ill-fated brigantine *Charles*, also managed to embarrass his employers. In 1706, Halsey had steered the *Charles* to yet more prizes in the Atlantic. He took a French ship of 130 tons, put some of his crew on it, and ordered it to rendezvous at Fayal in the Azores where it could be officially condemned. It never turned up. Frustrated but unbowed, he took a Spanish warship, which he sent into Madiera for legal adjudication. Next, he fell into a furious engagement with a much larger forty-gun Spanish warship that he nearly managed to defeat but which broke away from him and ran. Pressing on to the Canaries, he captured and sank yet another Spanish vessel. By this time he had little to show for all his efforts and hanging over his head was the knowledge that his privateer's commission was soon to expire. Remembering the Byzantine machinations of the Massachusetts admiralty court and all that had happened to him before, he finally decided to eliminate the middlemen. Halsey turned pirate and led his crew to Madagascar where over the following months they fought several pitched battles in the Arabian Sea, taking several ships and some £50,000 in treasure.

The battered brigantine *Charles*, though repaired many times, finally met its end in a hurricane off India sometime in 1707. By then, Halsey had at his disposal a small pirate fleet and so had transferred his command to another ship, the *Neptune*. He met his own end a short time later, of fever, aged forty-six, in a pirate haven on Madagascar. Immortalized in a chapter of Captain Charles Johnson's *A General History of the Robberies and Murders of the Most Notorious Pyrates*, published in 1726, the author said of him: "He was brave in his person, courteous to all prisoners, lived beloved and died regretted by his own people."

With the second and final disappearance of the *Charles*, the Boston syndicate broke up as well. It must have taken months for the owners to have discovered the ship's fate; word passed from vessel to vessel across the globe until the tale was told at some tavern along Boston's seafront by some recently arrived captain in from the West Indies or Madeira. The Dudleys would have been quietly satisfied with the news but Colman and Hobby must have been mortified.

Benjamin Gallop and William Clarke fell out over business arrangements in April 1706. Gallop sued Clarke successfully for £32 in losses but Clarke immediately appealed the ruling.

John Colman, in spite of the whiff of scandal that surrounded his own business dealings, remained prominent in Boston's affairs and kept his position as royal receiver of customs (unfortunately this ended for him in 1708 with the death of Prince George). He also remained an enemy of the Dudleys for the rest of his life. A financial gadfly for many years, he was a major proponent of establishing a private bank in Massachusetts and wrote several tracts to build support for the scheme. His pamphleteering landed him in jail in 1720 for sedition, but he was immediately released upon providing bonds. The establishment of a private bank to help stabilize the colony's finances was the great issue in the province shortly after 1710 and the continuing currency crisis brought on vehement public debate for over twenty-five years. Colman's most vocal critic in this enterprise was, unsurprisingly, Paul Dudley. Colman finally got his wish in 1739, when his private bank was launched with the issue of 150,000 notes and the blessing of the General Assembly only to be shut down by the Parliament just months later. He died, no doubt irascible as ever, in 1753.

His brother-in-law, Charles Hobby, never gained the governorship. Indeed, the knighthood he received in 1705 may have inadvertently played a role in his declining fortunes for when he arrived in London to receive it, his backers were repelled by his louche and dissolute manner—an extraordinary situation given the bawdiness of London at that time. But more the reason was Joseph Dudley's concurrently rising personal capital in Whitehall. As Cotton Mather wrote to a confidante in 1706, the governor's career had become "wondrously revived" with the arrival in London of Portuguese gold, given over "with advantageous representations." So it was that Hobby's loss of his pirate treasure became Dudley's political gain, a turn of affairs that hastened his own political demise. Joseph Dudley's biographer, Everett Kimball, notes that when Hobby arrived back in Boston in 1708, "before the year was out he was won over to Dudley's party." This was an unexpected change of direction for a man who had sparred with the governor for years and who had written to the Board of Trade asking to be kept informed of Dudley's gossip against him. Had the governor won over Hobby by reminding him of his role in hiding Quelch's gold? Sir Charles died in London in 1715, broke and heavily in debt. His widow, Eliza, later petitioned the Massachusetts government for support.

Judge Samuel Sewall made a full recovery from his self-doubt, eventually becoming Chief Justice of the Superior Court in 1718, a post he held for ten years. He also continued to serve on the governor's council until 1725, at which time he declined reelection due to his advancing years. For most of his life he had championed causes that were wildly liberal in his time: improving the welfare of Native Americans and black slaves, narrowing the crimes liable to capital punishment, and fighting to limit the province's more outrageously harsh laws against treason. However his liberality ended when it came to those accused of piracy. During the second decade of the century he would sit in judgment on several more mariners once the Admiralty trials got into full swing. Yet, in the end, he is best remembered for his prosecution of the Salem witches, a legacy that must have always haunted him. His curious diary: at once touchingly honest and bland, sublime and mundane, he kept from 1674 until 1729 (the year before his death). It did not see the light of day until published 150 years later, an accurate, informative, if sometimes dull testament to life in early America.

Paul Dudley's professional life blossomed after his successful prosecution of John Quelch. A tireless champion of his father's administration and of the royal prerogative, he survived his father's eventual downfall and became a judge of the Superior Court in 1718, rising to Chief Justice in 1745. As imperious as his father, he could also at times be generous and hospitable, according to one biographer. Off the bench, he pursued a lifelong interest in New England's natural environment. This was more than dilettantism: He was one of only a handful of American-born men to be elected to the Royal Society in London and to be published in their renowned journal, *Transactions*. In his later years he apparently drifted away from Anglicanism, adopted Puritan dogma, and wrote a number of religious tracts. When he died in 1751, he left a bequest to Harvard College to provide an annual theological lecture, a tradition that continues to this day.

Governor Joseph Dudley leaves a more complex and nuanced record to posterity. In many ways, his roughshod victory over Quelch and the favor it brought him marked his zenith in government. By 1707, he was fighting for his political life. Accused of countenancing (and perhaps profiting from) illegal trade with the French in Quebec, Dudley found himself under attack in Boston and London. It is unlikely that he had a personal stake in such black marketeering but evidence exists that he knew of its existence and tolerated it to earn the goodwill of certain merchants in the province. With the governor off-balance and under investigation by an angry Massachusetts legislature, the implacable Mathers and their faction did their best to topple him.

They anonymously published a pamphlet in London entitled, "*A Memorial of the Present Deplorable State of New England*," a lengthy and vicious attack on the governor's administration that within months had made it back to Boston's streets. Two of its statements seem to reflect on the machinations that had swallowed up John Quelch.

"Whales are taken by Her Majesty's Subjects, he takes from them by Force, not giving them the Liberty of a Tryal at Common Law, but for his own Ends, decides the Matter in the Admiralty, where his Son Paul is the Queen's Attorney and Advocate thereby Encroaching the whole to themselves, a thing never heard of before."

While poaching whales may not be piracy, the implication of abuse of Admiralty law was clear. Even bolder was the accusation that, "There have been odd Collusions with the Pyrates of Quelch's Company ... That there was Extorted the Sum of about Thirty Pounds from some of the Crue, for Liberty to Walk at certain times in the Prison Yard; and this Liberty having been Allow'd for Two or Three Days unto them, they were again Confined to their former Wretched Circumstances."

After a drawn-out political battle and no little outpouring of libel and slander, Dudley's enemies could not manage to produce any real evidence to implicate him. The General Assembly voted to vindicate him of what they termed a "scandalous and wicked accusation." Dudley followed up his hard-fought victory at home with a defense of his record in London, writing to the Queen in great detail to refute the charges against him. The Board of Trade clearly recognized that there was political maliciousness afoot and eventually dismissed the charges as "frivolous." But his enemies again went on the offensive, lobbying for Sir Charles Hobby's candidature for the governorship. Ultimately unsuccessful, the attacks upon the governor had nevertheless taken their toll and the libelous pamphlets did nothing to improve his popularity at home. Dudley hung on to power until the death of Queen Anne in 1714. The new Hanoverian king, George I, had other men in mind for the administration of the province and Dudley's erstwhile allies at court had now faded from the scene. Dudley, once out of power, did not long outlast the monarch who had kept him in his job, dying in 1720 at the age of seventy-three.

Kimball, arguably Dudley's most sympathetic biographer, writes, "From 1682 to 1715 it is doubtful whether, outside of his own party and those who were bound to him by fear, interest, or gratitude, a single well-wisher could be found for him in all New England." Sincerely believing that Massachusetts's best interests (and his own) lay in closer union with England and royal control, he could never be loved by those in Boston who cherished the old colonial charter and who remained steeped in the belief that they had a God-given right to conduct their own affairs. In serving the crown so faithfully and for so long, Dudley had become the Englishman he always strived to be, tossing away the mantle of the native-born colonial. Whether the crown rewarded him sufficiently is something that Joseph Dudley himself may have questioned.

In June 1706, the Queen and her council had granted him the sum of only £200 for his trouble in bringing Quelch to justice and in rounding up the treasure. It was £20 less than he would have received had he stuck to his original request of a 5 percent fee due him as a judge of the admiralty court.

The bulk of Quelch's treasure, now transformed into shiny new coins under the watchful eyes of Sir Isaac Newton, was destined for an altogether different end, one far removed from the pine forests and rustic towns of New England.

Epilogue: "Extraordinaries"

On the afternoon of March 30, 1705/6, the Lord Treasurer of England, Sir Sidney Godolphin, a short, rotund, and long-faced Cornishman, sat in a high-backed chair at a dark oak table in the main receiving room of his London townhouse. Spread in front of him was a sea of parchment, papers, petitions, and a small mountain of oversized account books. Seated with him was his clerk, quill in hand and scribbling furiously as Godolphin dictated notes and orders. Godolphin, friend of the Marlboroughs (and now a father-in-law to the Duke's daughter Henrietta) was first counselor to the Queen and the man with his hands on the purse strings of the crown. And the crown, for better or worse, was still at war, a war that it was his chief responsibility to finance.

He had served the Stuart monarchs since he was a young man. As a Groom of the Bedchamber to Charles II, he had entered the ways of the royal court and all its intrigues. Charles had remarked of his service that he was "never in the way and never out of the way." That was a long time ago. Now one of the most powerful men in the kingdom, he was acknowledged as a financial wizard and, unusual in his time, scrupulously honest in his job.

With the Duke of Marlborough back on the continent leading the allied armies on spring campaign, just weeks from yet another major victory against the French at Ramillies, Godolphin was struggling to keep the forces fed and watered while at the same time keeping the allies from grumbling by ladling out generous subsidies of gold. Complicating matters even further for the Lord Treasurer was the fact that thousands of pounds in payments for expenditures were still wanting from the *previous* year.

Joining him in the room are two gentlemen with very different purposes. The first is James Brydges, Paymaster-General of Her Majesty's Forces Abroad. Brydges presents Godolphin with yet more petitions for payments: for wounded soldiers, for food, lodging, supplies, payroll, and even for payments to other crowned heads of the alliance to pay for *their* troops. The amounts are staggering. A bill for a two-month subsidy alone to the Duke of Savoy for nearly £30,000 is presented.

The second man, resplendent in velvet and lace, a large wig falling about his shoulders and chest, stands at the table and addresses Godolphin. He is Sir Theodore Janssen, founding member and key director of a still relatively new institution, the Bank of England. Janssen proposes to ease the burden on the crown by advancing money at a rate of "60 pence for a Crown of 82 sols of money in Piedmont." As the clerk dips his pen and again scratches away at the minutes of the meeting, Godolphin protests "that is very high." Janssen, knowing full well that the crown has little alternative, replies that he believes nobody can do it cheaper. Godolphin agrees to the terms and the Bank of England continues to build its profile as the biggest creditor to the throne.

But Mr. Brydges is not yet finished with his business. He mentions bills for £68,546 in "extraordinaries" not provided for in previous years. An exasperated Godolphin cannot pay it all. However, a recent windfall that has come his way will offset some of it. He orders that £5,466 be paid "whereof 3142*l* 2*s* 2*p* is to be out of money coined from gold dust brought from New England . . . " The money is specifically earmarked "to be applied for clearing the extraordinaries of the Saxe Gotha Troops . . ."

Quelch's gold, having made its way to England, was now about to embark on a further journey east, to the treasury of the King of Prussia, Frederick I. No mention was ever made of the original owners of the treasure and it is unlikely that even a passing thought was given to returning it to the Portuguese crown. Such ethics would have to wait for a different century. In 1706, the treasure of pirates reverted to the crown whose forces had recovered it, although victims could turn to the courts to obtain compensation. Few, however, could manage this in practice. Such high-handed action on the part of governments constituted a theft in its own right, even if it was an accepted convention of the times.

Indeed, it was the pirates themselves, through their rejection of the rules and their protodemocratic anarchy who challenged the established order and exposed the double standards of merchants and royal administrators. One accused pirate at his trial in South Carolina in 1718, when asked by the court why he and his men had resisted the government vessel sent out to capture them, mischievously replied, "We thought it had been a pirate." He was convicted and hanged.

The trial and condemnation of John Quelch and his crew remains an unrecognized watershed in the "Golden Age" of Atlantic piracy. It was the first English Admiralty trial against piracy outside England and in the words of New England historian Abner Goodell, "one of the clearest cases of judicial murder in our American annals." For the crown it became a judicial model to be emulated, a swift sword to combat piracy in its last and most violent stage from 1714–1726.

Royal governors, armed with their new commissions, followed Boston's lead and established their own pirate-prosecution factories along the eastern seaboard, through the Caribbean, and as far as the West African coast. With the end of Queen Anne's War in 1713, thousands of tars from the navy and from the privateer fleet that bolstered it, found themselves broke and on the docks, looking for work. Mariners' wages contracted to only half of what they had been back in 1707. Such dismal conditions dramatically boosted the fraternity of those "going on the account" and by 1720 some 2,000 men are believed to have been sailing under the Black Flag.

The fury with which the resulting storm struck the mercantile world took the authorities by surprise. Even the adoption of a policy of unconditional amnesty by the crown in 1717 and 1718 proved ineffectual in bringing back the hundreds of sailors to the "right" side of the law. Many would turn themselves in and clear their names only to disappear, steal another ship, and resume their careers. The authorities rapidly changed tack: they reinforced the existing legislation to try captured pirates, directed the navy to vigorous pursuit, and took public measures to isolate pirates by criminalizing any commerce with them (as Dudley had done in 1704).

It was a bloody decade. In what Marcus Rediker has termed a "dialectic of violence," mass pirate hangings in Boston, Newport, Charleston, and Jamaica precipitated a wave of revenge killings of merchant captains and officials across the maritime world. The same "brotherhood" that had prided itself in the 1690s as loyally English and intent only on foreign prey had become by 1720 a brutalized band that raided and killed Englishman and foreigner alike. Increasingly marginalized in port and at sea, it was a war they could never hope to win—or survive. Rediker has calculated that some 500 to 600 Anglo-American pirates were executed between 1716 and 1726.

If Boston's rough justice to Quelch can be considered the prelude to the final war against the Atlantic pirates, a test-case that set the standard for the next twenty years, it can also be considered a harbinger of an even more consequential event: American independence.

The Quelch affair and the ill will it engendered against the governor, echoed down through the years of the eighteenth century. Quelch's trial was seen locally as an application of crown justice, not local justice. In this way, Quelch, outlaw that he was, is viewed sympathetically as a local entrepreneur brought low by the conspiracy of Tory rulers. Boston became increasingly radical and hostile to royal administration; by the middle of the century it was the cradle to revolution. In the cries of "Liberty and Property!" shouted by the merchant-baiting mob during the riots against the Stamp Act in 1765 we also hear a faint echo of the rebellious pirates of the golden age.

In life, celebrity was short for John Quelch. In death, he has been denied a place in the pirate pantheon of popular imagination and legend. Those who came after him, their careers forged in the final spasm of violence: Calico Jack Rackham, Charles Vane, Stede Bonnet, Black Bart Roberts, and Blackbeard are remembered. He is not.

Today, on the Isles of Shoals the shouts of drunken fishermen, outcasts, and pirates are no longer heard. Star Island is private property, owned by a nonprofit corporation set up by the Unitarian Church in Boston and the venue for theological conferences and bird-watching during the summer months. Yet they still draw those seeking treasure. For over a hundred years, legends have persisted of pirate silver and gold hidden on Star, Appledore, Smuttynose, or Lunging. But in a twist of fate, these tales refer only to Blackbeard, even though there exists not a scrap of evidence that he ever set foot on these islands. Truth and folklore are often at odds. Those who search and prod among the outcrops of these windswept rocks in the Gulf of Maine have no idea that what they are actually searching for are a few fistful-sized lumps of gold dust, congealed solid inside a long-rotted canvas pouch after 300 years in the ground. The last of Quelch's gold.

Notes and Sources

PROLOGUE: SPLENDIDUM FURTUM

It is still not known with certainty exactly where John Quelch was apprehended by the Boston authorities. I have recreated his capture at the Noah's Ark on Ship Street (present-day North Street) a popular watering hole of mariners and ship captains at this time.

The Diary of Samuel Sewall (Massachusetts Historical Society, 1973), a primary source for much of the detail concerning the story of Quelch and his men, mentions that Paul Dudley apprehended one of the pirates in the town of Lynn the next day, but annoyingly, he does not name who it was. The possibility remains, however, that Quelch was taken into custody anywhere on the road between Boston and Marblehead.

The long history of piracy, stretching back to ancient times, is well documented. As a very young man, Julius Caesar was kidnapped for ransom by Aegean pirates near the coast of modern Turkey. When informed of the amount of ransom they would ask for of him, Caesar was indignant. It was far too low a price for a man of his standing. He demanded it be raised. Prior to his release, while laughing along with their jokes, he promised them that one day he would return and kill them all. His captors roared. A year later, proconsul Julius Caesar did exactly as he promised.

Piracy's cozy relationship with authority, which is the central theme of Quelch's story, probably reached its zenith in the late-sixteenth and early seventeenth centuries. A renewed surge in sponsored piracy occurred during the reign of Charles II before a change in institutions and foreign policy finally soured governments on the links at the beginning of the eighteenth century. See *Villains of all Nations* (Boston, MA, 2004) by one of the foremost writers on pirates Marcus Rediker as well as Robert C Ritchie in *Captain Kidd and the War against the Pirates* (Cambridge, MA, 1986). While European states had for decades been content to use pirates when it suited their purposes, after King William's War of 1688–1697, the rules had changed. As Ritchie points out, "The new states would be set on another course: they would prefer to exercise the state's growing monopoly of violence."

For a contemporary fictional account of piracy (based on fact) in this era, see Daniel Defoe's *The King of Pirates* (London, 2002).

CHAPTER ONE: ILL TIDINGS

There is no shortage of works on the early history of Massachusetts and New England in general. A highly readable account of King Philip's War is to be found in Russell Bourne's *The Red King's Rebellion* (New York, 1990). A more recent work on this near-forgotten conflagration examines the aftereffects on the American psyche and on how wars are remembered and reinterpreted. See *The Name of War* (New York, 1998) by Jill Lepore. For a fuller telling of the experience of the 1690s and King William and Queen Anne's wars, there is *The New England Knight* (Toronto, 1998) by Emerson W. Baker and John G. Reid and also *The Border Wars of New England* by Samuel Adams Drake (New York, 1910). The latter work, while highly detailed in chronology, has racist overtones and is simplistic in its analysis. With that caveat, it is still a highly informative work if read with caution.

The saga of Captain Baptiste is noteworthy in its own right, particularly as it sits at the heart of military diplomacy during the Nine Years' War in America. For a discussion of this episode and hostage negotiations between New France and Massachusetts, see *The Unredeemed Captive* by John Demos (New York, 1995).

The mindset of colonial New England, and the infamous witch hysteria, which remains a leitmotif, cannot be understood without an understanding of Puritanism and its proponents. See *The Puritan*

Experiment (Hanover, NH, 1995) by Francis J. Bremer and *The Life and Times of Cotton Mather* (New York, 1984) by Kenneth Silverman. For an exhaustively detailed view of what it was like living over 300 years ago in New England, still one of the best works available is George Francis Dow's *Every Day Life in the Massachusetts Bay Colony* (New York, 1988). Originally published in 1935 and illustrated, it covers every aspect of civilian life.

A definitive work on the Anglo-American maritime community at this time, as well as piracy and privateering in general, is Marcus Rediker's *Between the Devil and the Deep Blue Sea* (Cambridge, MA, 1987). For an extensive analysis of the strategy and challenges underpinning English and French naval operations in the Atlantic and Caribbean during Quelch's time, see N.A.M. Rodger's *The Command of the Sea* (London, 2004).

Information on the owners of the vessel *Charles* has been drawn from records of the Massachusetts Historical Society, and the documents of the Board of Trade at the National Archives of England, Wales, and the United Kingdom (Public Records Office) at Kew. Captain Plowman's letters were preserved by the owners and entered into evidence at Quelch's trial. They were published along with the trial transcript at Boston and London in 1704 and these were obtained from Harvard University Law School Library.

CHAPTER TWO: "IT WILL NOT DO WITH THESE PEOPLE..."

For a history of the founding and development of Marblehead, where Barnard's and Cotton's comments are taken from, see Samuel Roads Jr., *The History and Traditions of Marblehead* (Boston, 1880) and *Marblehead in 1700* by Sidney Perley (Phillips Library of the Essex Institute, Salem). For a much more scholarly approach, invaluable for economic details, see *Farmers and Fishermen* (Williamsburg, VA, 1994) by Daniel Vickers.

Captain Plowman's commission and general orders were entered into evidence at the Quelch trial. The original resides at the Massachusetts State Archives and is reproduced in the publicly printed broadside of 1704.

The story of Captain William Kidd is a familiar one: in myth. For the truth of his story read Robert C. Ritchie's exhaustively researched *Captain Kidd and the War against the Pirates* (Cambridge, MA, 1986) and also the no less thorough but more entertaining *The Pirate Hunter* (New York, 2002) by Richard Zacks.

For a rich account of the importance of London at the time, refer to *1700: Scenes from London Life* (London, 2000) by Maureen Waller.

Admiralty records referred to are to be found in the U.K. National Archives at Kew: Pitcairn-Jones's list of *Commissioned Sea Officers of the Royal Navy 1660–1718*, Bruno Papparlardo's recent index to *Royal Navy Lieutenants' Passing Certificates 1691–1902* (List and Index Society, 2001), and the original entry book of passing certificates for 1691–1703 found in ADM 107/1. ADM 10/10 is an alphabetical list of captains and flag officers and a chronological list of commanders with annotations is found in ADM 8/5 for 1696–1697. Commission and Warrant Books are in ADM/6-14; ADM 106/2908. John Quelch was not found in any of these sources.

For more information on the life of a mariner during this time, both of Rediker's above-mentioned works are invaluable. Rediker clearly details the formalities of signing-on a crew for merchant service and the types of problems this engendered.

CHAPTER THREE: A CHANGE OF PLANS

The roles of sailors Holding, Whiting, and Roach in the mutiny aboard the *Charles* were brought to light as part of the testimony of their comrades turned "Queen's Evidence." Even so, the general reluctance of those captured crew who underwent trial to take credit for the action is obvious in the court transcript. Holding, who was ultimately fingered as the key ringleader by witnesses, was never apprehended. Quelch's own role in the seizure of the vessel was never elaborated upon by the crew in testimony and he himself evaded the court's questioning, if the transcript is an accurate one.

For interesting elaboration of the "pirates' code" see Rediker, who places it in its sociological context and also Charles Johnson in *A General History of the Robberies and Murders of the Most Notorious Pirates* (London, 1998), originally published in 1724. Johnson, at one time believed to be the author Daniel Defoe, provides a complete set of pirate articles said to have been drawn up by the crew of Captain Roberts around 1720. There is considerable doubt now that Johnson was actually Defoe, for his detailed knowledge of seaman's terminology and navigation was probably beyond the reach of Defoe, quick study that he was.

Regarding Captain Plowman's fate, the Court of Admiralty transcript does not directly implicate Quelch in murder or manslaughter. What detail did come to light was only that supplied by the Queen's witnesses for the prosecution. These confessions, of course, cannot be taken at face value. Traditionally, legend says Captain Plowman was thrown over the side within sight of "Halfway Rock" several miles off Marblehead. It is generally believed that he died within forty-eight hours of the ship setting sail.

No plans or descriptions of the *Charles* survive. Her dimensions are approximated based on her tonnage of displacement, which is noted in period records, as is her rig. Details of her probable layout are based on similar vessels of the period and the advice of the U.S. Navy Historical Center in Washington, DC. Howard Chapelle's benchmark study, *The History of American Sailing Ships* (New York, 1935), contains a drawing and dimensions for a 1721 Royal Navy brigantine, HMS Swift. Displacing some ninety tons, she was probably very similar to the *Charles*. As for the *Charles* being a galley as well as a brigantine rig, Governor Dudley himself refers to this fact in his correspondence with the Board of Trade, see *Calendar of State Papers, America and the West Indies* [CO 1274] (July 25, 1705). For general information concerning ship design and rigging, see John Harland's *Seamanship in the Age of Sail* (London, 1984). Kidd's predicament regarding the *Adventure Galley* is covered at length by Ritchie and Zacks.

Both Ritchie and Zacks describe the perilous crossing of the Atlantic and Indian Oceans in their works. Johnson gives a graphic account of the suffering of Captain Roberts' pirate crew stranded for a week on their sloop in contrary winds and currents off the coast of Guinea. They eventually fashioned rafts out of deck planking and paddled back to the mainland to obtain fresh water.

Extensive work has been done on the socioeconomic conditions of average seamen in the Golden Age of piracy. Rediker's calculations put the average age of a merchant seaman at twenty-seven. Those turned pirate would have been of similar age or perhaps even a bit older. Barnaby Slush's plea for better treatment of sailors, *The Royal Navy: or a Sea Cook Turn'd Projector* (London, 1709) is a fascinating (but politically motivated) glimpse into the naval world of the age. For representations of period costume, one can begin with the Osprey series of books, particularly *Pirates: Terror on the High Seas* by Angus Konstam (London, 2001). David Cordingly's several works on piracy, particularly *Under the Black Flag* (New York, 1996), provide a wealth of period detail and social commentary.

CHAPTER FOUR: "SUCH DESPERATE MEN"

The most detailed descriptions of old Boston are collected in Victorian-era and early twentieth-century volumes. See *A Topographical and Historical Description of Boston* (Boston, MA, 1890) by Nathaniel Shurtleff for maps and contemporary documentation on the layout of the area as well as the changes that occurred between the 1670s and 1740s. The most detailed map of the period of this work is chiefly the John Bonner map of Boston published in 1722 (Massachusetts Historical Society collections). For a comprehensive, street-by-street travelogue of Boston in the early eighteenth century, Annie H. Thwing's *The Crooked and Narrow Streets of Boston* (Boston, MA, 1920) has yet to be surpassed in its level of detail.

The original of Governor Dudley's portrait is held by the Massachusetts Historical Society. Until this was recently moved, the governor stared down upon users of the card catalogue. There are copies in the State House in Boston and in Concord, New Hampshire. The most thorough work on Dudley probably remains Everett Kimball's *The Public Life of Joseph Dudley* (New York, 1911).

The letter from the owners to various governors in the West Indies concerning their suspicions of the fate of the *Charles*, as well as Governor Dudley's letter in support, were read aloud in court at the trial of Quelch and his men and were subsequently published in broadside form in Boston a few days after the trial was concluded. The texts contained here are from the broadside subsequently published in London in 1704: *The Arraignment, Tryal, and Condemnation of Capt. John Quelch.* My copy was obtained courtesy of the Harvard University Law School Library in Cambridge.

Regarding the route taken by the *Charles* to the South Atlantic, because the ship's log does not survive, it is informed conjecture by the author, based on common sailing practice of the time and advice taken from modern-day Atlantic sailors. The circuitous paths of the Trade Winds are used to this day and the Doldrums remain nearly as much of a hazard to competition yachtsmen today as they did to merchant seamen 300 years ago. The problems of eighteenth century navigation are handled engagingly by Dava Sobel in *Longitude* (New York, 1996).

Quelch's initial destination of Fernando de Noronha came to light in a brief mention during his subsequent trial. It was a well-known waypoint for voyages to the Brazilian coast and a convenient haven for replenishment with little danger of discovery. Today, the islands are still under the jurisdiction of Pernambuco state after having been a federal province under Brazilian military administration for many decades. The archipelago survives on eco-tourism and is a protected nature reserve for many species. The number of tourists allowed on the islands is strictly controlled by Pernambuco and it has already become a favorite location among international scuba divers. For descriptions of Noronha dating from the time of Quelch's stopover, see Woodes Rogers *A Cruising Voyage Round the World* (London, 1712) and Edward Cooke *A Voyage to the South Sea and round the World* (London, 1712).

The full particulars of the Methuen treaties, of which today only the continued British interest in the port wine trade remains extant, can be found in *Hertslet's Treaties and Conventions* (1893).

CHAPTER FIVE: "WE ARE FRENCHMEN"

For the colonial history of Brazil and life there in the seventeenth and early eighteenth centuries, one of the most detailed works is C.R. Boxer's *The Golden Age of Brazil* (Los Angeles, CA, 1964). Also of interest is *Portuguese Brazil: the King's Plantation* by James Lang (New York, 1979) and *Licentious Liberty in a Brazilian Gold-Mining Region* by Kathleen Higgins (University Park, PA, 1999). Good firsthand accounts of coastal Brazil about the time of Quelch's visit can be found in the journals of William Dampier as well as Rogers and Cooke (see above).

John Twist's role as translator for Quelch's voyage came to light during court testimony when one of the witnesses mentions that he did not survive the voyage. Details of Quelch's various captures come from the three principal witnesses at his trial. Whether by accident or design, the notes of the interrogations of the other prisoners, taken by Paul Dudley, Nathaniel Byfield, and Samuel Sewall, have not survived.

Both Rediker and Cordingly provide much analysis and detail concerning how pirates launched their attacks, how these were resisted (when they were resisted), and the myth that most pirates took great fortunes home with them. Further details of pirate operations can be read in the authoritative Johnson history (see above).

The association of John Quelch with a "skeleton flag" probably originated with the Floridian journalist and author Ralph D. Paine in his work *The Old Merchant Marine*, originally published in 1919 and now out of copyright and widely available on the Internet. Paine did not state the source for his description of the Quelch flag in this work but he had also written an earlier book on piracy, *The Book of Buried Treasure*, published in 1911. No mentions of any flag other than the English colors can be found in any of the primary sources relating to the case. As a result of Paine's error (or embellishment) in 1919, nylon reproductions of the "Quelch" pirate flag can be purchased today on the Internet and at maritime souvenir shops.

CHAPTER SIX: PATIENCE AND PLUNDER

Regarding the share system, specifically in relation to Captain Kidd's voyage, see Zacks as above. The calculations concerning the sharing out of the gold amongst Quelch's crew are based on the amount confiscated by Major Sewall on the Isles of Shoals. The value of a Troy ounce of gold in 1704 is based upon figures for the year 1699 obtained from The Bank of England's archives in *The Pound Sterling* by Sir Albert Feaveryear (Oxford, 1963). Calculating the purchasing power of sterling or colonial money and comparing it to prices today is a somewhat difficult exercise. I have used figures based on the research of Maureen Waller in *1700: Scenes from London Life* (London, 2000) as well as the Economic History Services Web site at http://www.EH.net.

The curious notation of dates at this time stems from the fact that England did not adopt the gregorian calendar until 1752. The legal or civil year in the Old Style began on March 25 and so dates were notated to take this into account.

CHAPTER SEVEN: "KILL HIM!"

The ship involved, nameless to history, was Quelch's ninth and last victim before the *Charles* returned to Massachusetts. Although much of Captain Bastian's actions before the incident are conjecture, they are based on the typical circumstances of Brazilian coastal craft of the age.

A benchmark work on Brazil at this time, C.R. Boxer's *The Golden Age of Brazil* contains good detail on the gold rush of the 1690s, social conditions, Spanish and Portuguese rivalry on the River Plate, and the economics of the coastal trade. Bastian's lading, port of destination, and crew details are from the Massachusetts Court of Admiralty records as published in broadside form at the time of the Quelch trial.

There is no exact date for the general adoption of the ship's wheel by European maritime nations. It is first mentioned in records around 1700. For details on vessels of the late seventeenth and early eighteenth centuries including steering and rigging, see Harland's *Seamanship in the Age of Sail*.

Crew members aboard the *Charles* said that the vessel only raised her colors at the very end of the chase, roughly one-half hour before capture. For background on naval hand-to-hand combat during the era, Johnson's work provides some hair-raising detail. However, for more detailed descriptions, then one should refer to various accounts from both the American Revolution and the Napoleonic Wars. These are still applicable to combat one hundred years previously as the weaponry had not changed appreciably. As literacy was better by the early nineteenth century, there are far more firsthand accounts that have been discovered.

For the finer points of fighting with broadsword or cutlass, the U.S. Navy manual from 1869 gives what is the definitive technique for self-defense, even though by this time hand-to-hand combat at sea with edged weapons was rare. *Principles of Squad Instruction for the Broadsword* (The Navy and Marine Living History Association, 1999) was written by A.J. Corbesier, a Frenchman who was swordmaster at the U.S. Naval Academy at Annapolis. Although not concerned with swordsmanship at sea, Donald MacBane's *The Expert Sword-Man's Companion* (Edinburgh, Scotland, 1728) is also an extremely useful primer for understanding swordplay on foot with heavy and light weapons. His autobiography that prefaces the edition is a first-rate first-hand account of combat and dueling during Quelch's time.

Concerning naval guns of the Marlburian era, see John Seller *The Sea Gunner: Shewing the Practical Part of Gunnery as it is Used at Sea* (London, 1691).

CHAPTER EIGHT: DIASPORA

Copies of *The Boston News-Letter* for the year 1704 were obtained from the Massachusetts Historical Society. For a background of John Campbell and newspaper publishing in Boston at the beginning of the eighteenth century, see David Sloan's "John Campbell and the Boston News-Letter" (*The Early America Review*, Winter-Spring 2005).

Sarah Kemble Knight's remarkable diary is an inadvertent sociological study on the class structure of colonial New England as well as a commentary on everyday life in her times. Her account of the journey by road from Boston to New York is one of the best sources available concerning travel and infrastructure in the early eighteenth century. Excerpts taken from *The Puritans: A Sourcebook of their Writing*, edited by Perry Miller and Thomas Johnson (New York, 1938).

The testimony concerning Quelch's alibi for where the treasure was obtained, is obviously biased but not necessarily untrue. The original interview notes of Dudley and Sewall regarding their interrogation of the captured pirates before trial have never been found. The sole source of the testimony available is the one published in *The Boston News-Letter* and approved (indeed, written by) Joseph and Paul Dudley. The original correspondence concerning the trial was lost at sea on its way to the Privy Council in London in October 1704. The Massachusetts State Archives have been unable to locate any copies that may have been retained by the governor and all that remains in the *Acts and Resolves* are receipts for expenditures relating to the capture and trial of the pirates.

Bearing in mind the thoroughness of Boston's authorities at this time, it is hard not to entertain the theory that much of the written evidence of Quelch's trial was intentionally disposed of to prevent further investigation by those who had an axe to grind against the Dudleys.

For an account of Captain Thomas Tew (and other New England pirates at this time including John Quelch) see *The Pirates of the New England Coast 1630–1730* by George Francis Dow and John Henry Edmonds (Dover Books, New York, 1996). Originally published by the Marine Research Society of Salem, Massachusetts, in

1923, this work remains a benchmark in colonial histories. More anodyne, but also containing a separate chapter on Quelch, is *Under the Black Flag* by Don Seitz (London, 1925)

CHAPTER NINE: THE DEVIL HIS DUE

As there are no records to his exact movements, the journey of John Quelch from Marblehead to Boston and back must unfortunately be the subject of conjecture. I have sought to place his travels in the context of what is known about his visit and in what would have constituted a logical time frame. The Quelch trial transcript makes it quite clear that he had delivered up the majority of the gold to the shipowners. It is also probable that he visited the shop of the silversmith John Noyes in the same trip. Quelch was apprehended within just days of these events. The illnesses that afflicted Quelch's crew were mentioned in various sources. These included the subsequent trial transcript and Samuel Sewall's diary. Those that were committed to the jail in Boston also inevitably became ill. The jailor and his men received compensation for clothing, feeding, and caring for the pirates—from the captured treasure.

For the description of Charlestown and of Boston in 1704, I am indebted to the help of Boston's town archaeologist, Ellen Berkland, who provided several excellent sources of information. These included reports commissioned by the Massachusetts Highway Department in 1992 and 2000, dealing with archaeological recovery efforts in the area. Thwing's *Narrow and Crooked Streets* again proved indispensable in providing street-by-street locations and descriptions. Also of help is Nathaniel Shurtleff, as above, and Edwin M Bacon's *Rambles Around Old Boston* (Boston, 1921). The extent of the influence of alcohol in colonial New England is widely discussed in *Drinking in America* by Mark London and James Kirby Martin (New York, 1982).

Regarding John Colman, most remaining sources deal with events later in his life during the currency debates that gripped Boston in the 1720s. The writings of his brother Benjamin, the pastor of Brattle Street Church and a trustee of Harvard, are better known to historians of New England. John Colman does, however, rate an entry in the *Dictionary of American Biography* (New York, 1937), which provides the major details of his life but strangely, no mention of the Quelch saga. Apart from his pamphleteering efforts in the 1720s (for which he was arraigned), his writings survive in the form of his letters to the Board of Trade in London, in which he complained bitterly of the behavior of the Dudleys.

The remarks of Dankers and Sluyter (who both happened to be Jesuit monks) and the observations of John Dunton, I have taken from *St. Botolph's Town* by Caroline Crawford (Boston, MA, 1908). For more on race relations in New England at this time, particularly the situation regarding African slaves, freemen, and Native Americans, see Twombly and Moore in "Black Puritan: The Negro in Seventeenth Century Massachusetts" (*William and Mary Quarterly*, April 1967).

Crime and punishment in Boston has been extensively chronicled. A good introduction to the subject during this period is Dow's *Everyday Life in the Massachusetts Bay Colony*. Waller's *1700: Scenes from London Life* is unsurpassed at providing details of crime and punishment as well as a myriad of other details in England. Much of this would also apply to life in Boston at the same time.

Boston's architectural development is extensively chronicled. I am indebted to Ellen Berkland, Town Archaeologist in Boston, for providing descriptions of residences at the turn of the eighteenth century, particularly a 1707 drawing by draughtsman Will Antram showing the frontal elevation of a house belonging to Governor Dudley that was home to the Society for the Propagation of the Gospel among the Indians in New England. The only remaining original domestic structure from this time is the Paul Revere House, built in 1680. It is typical of the style and construction that Quelch would have known. For more on local inns, taverns, and businesses at this time see Thwing's *Narrow and Crooked Streets*.

Of Quelch's meeting with John Colman, there is no surviving record. But Quelch did go to Boston and did hand over the owners' shares of the gold, as attested by Colman himself. Further, the details of Quelch's tale must have sufficiently alarmed Colman for him to personally make the trek back to Marblehead within a day or so of Quelch's visit to his house.

The work of John Noyes, the silversmith, can still be seen. His candlesticks and forks are on view at the Boston Museum of Fine Arts, while many of his carved headstones dot the old cemeteries in Sandwich and Barnstaple on Cape Cod. See Kathryn Buhler

American Silver 1655–1825 (Museum of Fine Arts, Boston). He testified as a witness at the trial of Quelch, explaining how Quelch entered his shop and melted down coins. That same year, he was selected to serve as a town constable but declined the position paying a fine in lieu of taking up the post.

CHAPTER TEN: "VIOLENTLY SUSPECTED"

Colman's deposition against John Quelch and his crew was published as an addendum to the trial transcripts. Those items found aboard the *Charles* were detailed during the opening of the trial, as recorded in the official transcript.

My source for the description and function of the Town House is *The Story of the Old Boston Town House* (Boston, MA, 1908) by Josiah Henry Benton. Biographical details on Paul Dudley are drawn from the *Dictionary of American Biography* and from Kimball's *The Public Life of Joseph Dudley.* Thomas Povey's small role in Boston's history is documented in the well-known *History of the Province of Massachusetts Bay* (Cambridge, MA, 1936) by Thomas Hutchinson and in the biased but exhaustively detailed *History of New England* (Boston, MA, 1875) by John Gorham Palfrey.

There are regrettably few surviving details of Boston's Old Stone Jail from this time. *Acts and Resolves of the Province of Massachusetts Bay* (Boston, MA, 1895), edited by Abner C. Goodell, notes various improvements over the years but no overall layout has come to light. The original jail was leveled in the mid-eighteenth century to make room for a larger more extensive prison and this, in turn, was leveled in the nineteenth century to make room for the Boston City courthouse. Zacks paints an extremely bleak picture of the jail during Kidd's incarceration in *The Pirate Hunter.* A list of those pirates captured in Boston during the first days of the pursuit were published in *The Boston News-Letter*, Number 6 (May 27, 1704) and further details are mentioned in the trial transcript.

Quelch's share of the gold must have been hidden where he lodged; it was not recovered until Governor Dudley returned to Boston later that week. Lieutenant-Governor Povey's proclamation against Quelch and his crew was published as a broadside (Massachusetts Historical Society, microfilm collection) and also in the same Number 6 edition of the *Boston News-Letter.*

Isaac Addison's role in government affairs in the province was subtle but very influential. He was Dudley's right-hand man and had served under several governors before him. At the time of the Quelch affair he was not only Secretary of the Council but also Chief Justice of the Superior Court of Massachusetts Bay, having filled in at the death of his predecessor, former acting-governor William Stoughton. Due to Addington's ill health, Samuel Sewall was serving as *acting* chief justice and hence became active in the prosecution of Quelch and his men.

CHAPTER ELEVEN: THE GOVERNOR TAKES CHARGE

Again, the diary of Samuel Sewall is invaluable for small details of daily life in the province. He recorded his surprise and dismay of being drafted as a constable to escort one of Quelch's crew back to Boston and over the following month made several entries concerning the capture and subsequent execution of the pirates. The story of his wife's dowry, probably apocryphal, is told in Crawford's *St. Boltoph's Town*. Its value was thought to be in the area of £3,000. Insights on Sewall himself can be found in *Samuel Sewall of Boston* (New York, 1964) by Ola Elizabeth Winslow. See also the more recent *Judge Sewall's Apology* (New York, 2005) by Richard Francis.

Paul and Joseph Dudley's pursuit of the crew of the *Charles* is discussed in considerable detail in Goodell's *Acts and Resolves* and this historian probably went to more pains than any previous or since to assemble the timeline of the Quelch case. I have obtained copies of both Povey and Dudley's proclamations from the Massachusetts Historical Society and Governor Cranston's from the Newport, R.I. Historical Society. For more on Rhode Island's involvement with piracy in the 1690s and beyond, including the exchange of correspondence between London and Cranston, see *Records of the Colony of Rhode Island 1703* (R.I. Historical Society) and Jane Fletcher Fiske's *Records of the General Court of Trials, Newport Court Book A* (Bedford, MA, 1998). For details on the Munday and Cutler trials, see *Colonial Records of R. I. vol III* (Providence, 1858). Also of interest is Alexander Hawes' *Off Soundings: Aspects of the Maritime History of Rhode Island* (Chevy Chase, MD, 1999). Dudley's complaint to the Board of Trade and Plantations survives in the *Calendar of State Papers, America and West Indies* (1703, p. 691). For a general background on the fiscal conditions of New England at this time, a good starting point is "Current Lawful Money of New England" (*American Historical Review* 24, October 1918) by Charles Andrews. The introduction of Massachusetts bill of credit is discussed by Alvin Rabushka in "Colonial Roots of American Taxation, 1607–1700" (*Policy Review* 114, August 2002) and "Representation without Taxation" (*Policy Review* 122, December 2003)

"Pine Tree" shillings minted in Boston remained in circulation for many decades. According to folklore, as recorded by Crawford in *St. Boltoph's Town:*

It is related that not long after the starting of the mint Charles II in great wrath questioned Sir Thomas Temple, the first agent officially despatched by the General Court to London, as to why this Colony presumed to invade His Majesty's rights by coining money. Virtually, Sir Thomas said: "The colonists have but little acquaintance with the law. They are simple folk, meaning no ill, and they thought it no crime to make money for their own use." Sir Thomas took a "pine-tree" shilling from his pocket.

"See, your Majesty, here is the coin."

On one side of the piece had been struck a tree, which, though there is no record of its identity at the time, has later been called a pine-tree. It may, however, have been any New England bush.

"What is that tree—what does it mean?" said King Charles, frowning.

"That, your Majesty," said Sir Thomas, "is a royal oak. Your colonists, not daring to put your Majesty's name on the coin, have struck thereon the emblem of the oak, which preserved your Majesty's life."

"They are a parcel of honest dogs," cried Charles, at once restored to good-humor.

Regarding the potential effects of a sudden infusion of hard currency into essentially a barter economy upheld by government-issued credit notes, I am indebted to Dr. Gustav Horn, economist and director of the Institute for Macroeconomics and Economic Research in Düsseldorf, Germany.

Governor Dudley's frustrations at obtaining a regular salary from the General Assembly is well documented by Kimball and also in Dudley's correspondence with the Board of Trade London.

For an overview of the Lords of Trade and Plantations, subsequently the Board of Trade, see Winifred Root, "The Lords of Trade and Plantations 1675–1696" (*American Historical Review*, October 1917) and I. K. Steele, *Politics of Colonial Policy: The Board of Trade in Colonial Administration 1696–1720* (Oxford, 1968). Also of interest is "William Blathwayt, Imperial Fixer: Muddling Through To Empire, 1699–1717" by Stephen Saunders Webb in *The William and Mary Quarterly* (July 1969).

CHAPTER TWELVE: TRAIL OF GOLD

John Marshall's diary (Massachusetts Historical Society, Ms. N-1626) provides an interesting glimpse into daily life and although he was predominantly concerned with Braintree events, he often noted what was happening in Boston, providing a good reflection of the importance of certain events as they occurred. He would later make note of the Quelch trial and subsequent executions.

Details concerning the prison at Boston from Council Records (State Archives Series GC3/327 Executive Records of the Governor's Council 1650–1977, volume 4, pp. 25–30) indicate that refurbishment was ordered in June 1704. For comparisons with the surviving jail at York, as well as penal procedures, I am indebted to information provided by the curator of the Old York Historical Society, Tom Johnson. Additionally, Zacks and Waller provide much period detail of what it was like to be incarcerated at this time in history.

Events of the week of June 7 are mainly from Council records and the Sewall diary, in particular, the commission's actions in Salem and Marblehead and the mustering of troops there. A full account of the expedition later appeared in *The Boston News-Letter*, Number 9.

Sources for the history and experiences of the New England militia include: "A New Look at Colonial Militia" in *The William and Mary Quarterly* (April 1963); *Colonial American Troops*, volumes 1–2,

Rene Chartrand (Oxford, 2002); *Arms and Armor in Colonial America,* Harold Peterson (New York, 1956); and in *The Border Wars of New England,* Samuel Drake.

Thomas Larrimore's life is worthy of further exploration in its own right, particularly his alienation from the authorities and his subsequent descent into piracy. Mentions of Larrimore appear in the *Calendar of State Papers, America and West Indies, Salem in the Eighteenth Century,* James Duncan Phillips (Salem, 1969); *History of Salem Massachusetts,* Sidney Perley (Salem, 1928); and *Privateer Ships and Sailors,* Howard Chapin (Toulon, France, 1926).

CHAPTER THIRTEEN: TO THE ISLES OF SHOALS

Stephen Sewall's adventure to the Isles is chronicled primarily by his brother Samuel in the *Diary* and in the *Boston News-Letter* (Number 9, June 12–19, 1704*),* the latter drawn from Major Sewall's presentation to the Governor and Council. There are considerable sources for the history and folklore of the Isles of Shoals. I have drawn primarily from *Ten Miles Out: Guidebook to the Isles of Shoals* (Portsmouth, NH, 1984) by Lyman Rutledge.

CHAPTER FOURTEEN: "PLAIN MATTERS OF FACT"

Since the trial transcript provides latitude and land references to where each of the pirate attacks occurred, and because the ship's log was destroyed or defaced before the return, it is safe to assume that the prosecution researched the locations in conjunction with testimony taken down in jail from the mariners.

The drama at the Isles of Shoals was given extensive coverage in *The Boston News-Letter,* Number 9, probably given to Postmaster Campbell by Samuel Sewall as it fits largely in detail with the latter's diary entries.

Some insight into the decision-making apparatus of the province can be discerned through reading the *Record Books of the Governor's Council.* The originals are held by the Massachusetts State Archives in Boston. The minutes during June and July record the problems due to overcrowding of the jail and also detail the recovery effort in regard to the treasure. For the architecture and floor plan of the Old Boston Town House, which was destroyed by fire

in 1711, I have used Josiah Henry Benton's *Story of the Old Boston Townhouse*.

The transcript of the trial presents its own problems as it is obviously a censored version of the actual event. Even the transcript contained in *Complete Collection of State Trials*, volume XIV (London, 1816) is virtually identical to the broadside published in Boston in 1704 that is held at the Massachusetts Historical Society. Aspects of the trial from the prosecution's point of view are analyzed in *The Forwardness of Her Majesty's Service: Paul Dudley's Prosecution of Pirate Captain John Quelch* by Stephen O'Neill (Massachusetts Legal History, volume 6, 2000, pp. 29–34).

CHAPTER FIFTEEN: "WHERE IS YOUR GOLD?"

The *Calendar of State Papers, Americas and West Indies, 1706* [CO 5/864 & CO 5/863] contains both the allegation and refutation concerning the illegal sale of the Brazilian slaves in Boston. In the end, Paul Dudley submitted a sales certificate completed at auction to prove his contention that the sale was honest and legal.

The governor's full account of the collection of the treasure, and the monies paid out of it, is contained in the U.K. National Archives, *Calendar of Treasury Books, April 1705 to September 1706*, volume XX, part II. *Treasury minutes, Treasury warrants, etc. 1705* (London: Her Majesty's Stationery Office, 1949). Through these detailed accounts it is possible to trace everyone involved with the trial and execution: even knowing where the governor and his fellow commissioners dined out for lunch.

CHAPTER SIXTEEN: THE LAST VOYAGE

Dudley's letters to the Board of Trade make clear his anxiety during the weeks surrounding the trial and execution. These are all reproduced in the *Calendar of State Papers, Americas and the West Indies* over 1705 and 1706.

Cotton Mather's sermon, published shortly after his public recital, *Faithful Warnings to Prevent Fearful Judgments* (Boston, MA, 1704) was obtained on microfiche at the Massachusetts Historical Society. Over the course of his ministry in Boston, Mather delivered other sermons to condemned pirates, all of which found their way into print. Such life and death events were unsurpassed for providing useful instruction to churchgoers and Mather was not one to waste such opportunities to save souls.

Dudley's letters to the Board of Trade in July 1704 outlined his logic in the selection of those who would actually face the hangman. Indeed, the only written record of this is in Dudley's reports to London. Undoubtedly, there must have been discussion among the trial commissioners and the council but if this took place, minutes were never recorded or have been subsequently lost.

Much has been written on the logistics of execution in this era. Zacks, Ritchie, and Waller all provide much detail concerning pirate executions in their respective works. Boston's previous celebrated pirate trial and execution, in 1690, is covered in Dow and Edmonds work (see above). In that case, Thomas Pound and Thomas Hawkins were convicted but reprieved. Hawkins almost missed his reprieve as he was already on the scaffold with the rope around his neck when the governor's order arrived releasing him.

Eyewitness accounts of the Quelch execution come from Sewall's diary entry and the broadside published just days later, penned by John Campbell. Council records for execution day are short, proving that business was curtailed for the event. Dudley's travails at the hands of the mob in 1689 are covered at length by Kimball. Dudley's period of confinement at his niece's house partially explains his depth of grief at her death in 1704 and might also have sparked memories of the terror of the Boston mob at a time when the town was particularly vulnerable to rioting.

Sewall's diary explains what happened to John Lambert's body, but not exactly how Quelch and the others were disposed of. My interpretation is based on the fact that no sources indicate that the corpses were gibbeted as in later cases. There remains the possibility that the bodies were buried at Boston Neck, just outside the gate, as this was also a traditional "unhallowed" burial place for Boston's murderers (and Quakers) since early times.

CHAPTER SEVENTEEN: DOUBTS AND RECRIMINATIONS

The North Shore ditty commemorating the pirate capture has been ascribed to various locals, including the Marblehead minister, Samuel Cheever. It is noted in *Salem in the Eighteenth Century* by James Duncan Phillips (Essex Institute, Salem, MA, 1969) and in Ralph D Paine's *The Ships and Sailors of Old Salem* (Boston, MA, 1923).

Governor Dudley's accounts of the gold and silver are exact but there will never be certainty as to whether sums were embezzled by Massachusetts's officials. They were signed for by Issac Addington, Paul Dudley, and Jeremiah Allen (for Treasurer James Taylor). Line items include: "Sarah Page ... a spoon" and a memo at the bottom of the tally says: "A Small quantity of Sugar, Guns, Sails, disposed of at a Publick Sale amounting to the Sum of one hundred Eighty three pounds Eight Shillings and Seven pence." Outgoings are recorded in an equally precise manner, including a deduction "To the Governor as Judge of the Court" for £220. Although Dudley wrote to William Blathwayt saying that he had not taken his cut, this was not amended in the paperwork, leaving it open to conjecture whether Dudley kept the £220 *and* the Queen's later reward of £200. Details of the gold, including its handover to the navy for transport to London, can be found in *Executive Records of the Council*, volume 4, at the Massachusetts State Archives.

The lengthy correspondence between Boston and London in regard to the trial, the treasure, the witnesses, Captain Cary's mission, and the subsequent accusations against the Dudleys, is found in several volumes within the Colonial Series at the U.K. National Archives [CO 5/863, 864; CO 5/911; CO 194/4] as well as in *Calendar of Treasury Books*, volume XX. Sewall's reply to William Ashurst is quoted in Goodell's *Acts and Resolves*. Further correspondence is transcribed and bound in *Acts of the Privy Council (Colonial) 1680–1720* and in the *Journal of the Commissioners for Trade and Plantations* at the U.K. National Archives Library.

Details of the *Charles* syndicate's attempts to move their operations to Rhode Island are also well documented in the U.K. National Archives [CO 5/1263], in John F. Jameson's *Privateering and Piracy in the Colonial Period* (New York, 1923) and in Howard Chapin's work mentioned above. Further mentions (including the context for Governor Cranston's actions) can be found in *Records of the Colony of Rhode Island and Providence Plantations*, bound volumes held at the Rhode Island Historical Society in Providence.

The "attack" on Governor Dudley in 1705 is described in detail in Sewall's diary and expanded upon in the editor's footnotes.

The work consulted is the M. Halsey Thomas edition (New York, 1973). Dudley's winter that year was a trying one. After the road altercation, he was involved in a near-fatal accident when his sleigh broke through the ice while crossing a river near Boston. He and the driver were thrown clear but both horses drowned.

CHAPTER EIGHTEEN: FLOTSAM

The involvement of Sir Isaac Newton with the Quelch treasure has not been previously noted in any mentions of the affair. Newton's letter concerning the gold is contained in the *Treasury Money Book* for 1706 [T 53/18] at the U.K. National Archives.

The fate of the six jailed mariners is mentioned in *Calendar of State Papers (Domestic) Queen Anne*, volume III, in an order dictated by Sir Charles Hedges on April 17, 1705: "The governor of New England is directed to pardon the fourteen young men found guilty of piracy on their entering the sea service." Dudley's later reply makes it clear that they were sent to the *Deptford* [CO 5/751]. This ship is mentioned in Chapin for taking part in naval operations off Nova Scotia.

Thomas Larrimore's escape and subsequent recapture can be pieced together from several sources, namely Captain Cary's petitions to the Board of Trade while he was in London [CO 5/863] and in Captain Underdown's report to Hedges from Portsmouth [CO 195/4]. It is somewhat ironic that Captain James Halsey is immortalized in Johnson's *A General History* while John Quelch is not. The chapter on Halsey appeared only in the second edition of the book in which Johnson rushed to add additional pirate stories. The edition used by the author is one edited by Arthur Hayward (London, 1926).

John Colman's later career is drawn largely from the *Dictionary of American Biography*. His pamphlets, *The Distressed State of the Town of Boston* and *The Distressed State of the Town of Boston Once More Considered* can be found in *Colonial Currency Reprints 1682–1751* (Boston, 1910–1911). Kimball's biography of Dudley and Silverman's on Cotton Mather provide useful insights into Colonel Charles Hobby's character. Silverman, in particular, provides interesting background to Mather's plot to replace Dudley with Hobby and how this went awry.

Little biographical work has been devoted to the Dudleys, father and son, despite their long career in law and government. Kimball's 1911 work on Joseph has yet to be challenged. My profile of Paul is drawn from the *Dictionary of American Biography*. Quotations from Mather's pamphlet, *A Memorial of the Present Deplorable State of New England* is from the 1707 Boston edition published by "S. Phillips" and held at the British Library. Queen Anne's order to pay Governor Dudley a reward of £200 has not before been revealed. It says: *At Windsor, Queen, Lord Treasurer, Chancellor* present "Mr. Blathwayt proposes that 200*l* may be given to the said Governor and 100*l* to the Deputy Governor there for service in seizing and prosecuting a notorious pirate and sending over his effects to England, to the value of above 3,000*l*—Granted." It can be found in the *Journal of Commissioners of Trade and Plantations* (June 10, 1706).

EPILOGUE: "EXTRAORDINARIES"

For aspects of Godolphin's public life, and his relationship with the Marlboroughs, see Ophelia Field's *The Favourite: Sarah, Duchess of Marlborough* (London, 2002) as well as *The Marlboroughs* by Christopher Hibbert (London, 2001). The exchange quoted is contained in the minutes of the meeting (*Calendar of Treasury Books,* April 1705 to September 1706, volume XX, part II).

The details concerning the crown's efforts to combat piracy from 1717 are found in *Acts of the Privy Council (Colonial)* at the U.K. National Archives. This contains a further proclamation for the suppression of piracy in 1718 that among other things authorized naval captains off the coast of Africa to apprehend, try, and execute pirates aboard ship under Admiralty law.

There are numerous sources that deal with the Golden Age of piracy in the Atlantic, its causes, and how it was dealt with by the authorities. The best of these remains the work of Rediker (see above).

For an entertaining article on the search for gold at the Isles of Shoals, see J. Dennis Robinson's piece "In search of Blackbeard's Treasure" at http://www.seacoastnh.com.

Index

About the Author

CLIFFORD BEAL, born in Providence, Rhode Island, is the former editor of the authoritative London-based international news magazine *Jane's Defence Weekly*. He attained a B.A. in History from the University of Vermont and an M.A. in International Relations from the University of Sussex in Brighton, England. He has worked as an international defense and security journalist for over 20 years and currently runs a consultancy group in London. In addition to writing for several *Jane's* titles, Beal has written for other periodicals, including *Military History Quarterly*, *The Sunday Times of London*, *Toronto Globe & Mail*, *Dublin Sunday Business Post*, *New Scientist*, *Frontiers*, *Focus*, and *The International Herald Tribune*. He is currently at work on a historical novel set in England and France in 1652. When not writing, he indulges in seventeenth- and eighteenth-century swordsmanship and motorcycling.